WRITING FOR NEWS MEDIA

Writing for News Media is a down-to-earth guide on how to write news stories for online, print and broadcast audiences. It celebrates the craft of storytelling, arguing for its continued importance in a modern newsroom. With dynamism and humour, Ian Pickering, a journalist with 30 years' experience, offers readers practical advice on being a news journalist, with step-by-step guidance on creating a great story and writing the perfect news copy.

Chapters include:

- extracts from published news articles to help illustrate the dos and don'ts of storytelling;
- the ten golden rules for structuring and putting together a successful news article, including 'Nail the intro', 'Let it flow' and 'Keep it simple';
- instruction on writing stories for different specialist subjects, including politics, court cases, economics, funnies and celebrity;
- help for readers on how to write for broadcast news;
- tips on how to write headlines, how to use pictures, how to make the most of quotations and how to avoid common style and grammar mistakes;
- glossaries covering a range of different aspects of news journalism, such as types of news story, online and data journalism, typesetting and broadcasting.

This is an instructive and insightful manual which champions brilliant storytelling and writing with flair. It introduces a set of key creative and analytical techniques that will help students of journalism and young professionals hone and refine their story-writing skills.

Ian Pickering has spent more than 30 years as a journalist, working on print and digital publications in regional and national news organisations. He has trained and mentored many young journalists . . . and is still learning himself.

'From raw trainees through to the most experienced journalists, this is an essential handbook for any writer. *Writing for News Media* has been created by someone who clearly loves words and knows the importance of using them correctly for effective storytelling.'

Dave Morgan, Head of Copy and Style, *The Sun*, UK

WRITING FOR NEWS MEDIA

The Storyteller's Craft

Ian Pickering

Routledge
Taylor & Francis Group

LONDON AND NEW YORK

First published 2018
by Routledge
2 Park Square, Milton Park, Abingdon, Oxon OX14 4RN

and by Routledge
711 Third Avenue, New York, NY 10017

Routledge is an imprint of the Taylor & Francis Group, an informa business

British Library Cataloguing-in-Publication Data
A catalogue record for this book is available from the British Library

Library of Congress Cataloging-in-Publication Data
A catalog record for this book has been requested

ISBN: 978-1-138-65584-3 (hbk)
ISBN: 978-1-138-65587-4 (pbk)
ISBN: 978-1-315-62226-2 (ebk)

Typeset in Bembo
by Apex CoVantage, LLC
Printed and bound by CPI Group (UK) Ltd, Croydon, CR0 4YY

CONTENTS

ILLUSTRATIONS

Figures

Table

PREFACE

Much has been written and said about the supposed decline of journalism in the digital age. Most of it – from claims of sloppiness to trivialisation to fake news – is dispiriting poppycock. Yes, some of the rules have been rewritten and traditional publishing models are under threat but we now have unlimited scope and unprecedented access to bigger and bigger audiences. The public's appetite for news is not diminished; it's ravenous. These are exciting times.

What may have faltered in the mad technological scramble of the past decade or so is an emphasis on storytelling. We have wandered into a dazzling world of special effects, where the visuals are sometimes stripping away the humanity and brilliant writing exists in pockets rather than as a norm.

But as *Star Wars* director George Lucas once observed: 'A special effect is a tool, a means of telling a story. A special effect without a story is a pretty boring thing.'

This book aims to redress that balance. It contains numerous examples of recent news writing; in some cases, their inclusion does not flatter. It is not meant to insult or excoriate any writer or publication, merely to illustrate. Today's journalists work under great pressure, often starved of resources and support and without sub-editors and others to polish and perfect. And so I am guilty of perpetuating a culture in journalism – that the 999 things someone does well are overlooked while the one thing that goes wrong is noticed and smugly commented upon. I apologise.

There are many people to thank for their help in preparing this book. For their insights and advice, I am grateful to Andy Hughes, Chris Stewart, Steph Scanwen, Lindsay Eastwood, Richard Horsman, Andrew Knight, Ian Jones, Nick Petche, Simon Garner, Martin Ashplant, Hugh Bateson, Andrew Miller, Bret Painter and Dave Monk. Enormous thanks also go to my brilliant proofreaders, Mark Dorman, James Cadman, Emma Clipp and John Corney. Also love and gratitude goes to my wife, Sally, for her forbearing, support and endless cups of tea.

INTRODUCTION

Ask a roomful of aspiring news journalists what they do for a living and there is rarely accord.

Most will offer a job title, such as reporter, aggregator, trainee, news writer, content provider, news specialist, even video news writer or data journalist. It might even come with a word in brackets afterwards.

They say they want to inform, to educate, to investigate, to aggregate, to sift, to decipher and explain, to curate, to publish.

The high-minded might aspire to be seekers of truth, to shed light on or to hold to account those in authority.

For others, it is the chance to be at the heart of current affairs, to travel or just to meet fascinating people. Others say it is writing about a hobby or passion, such as sport, fashion or theatre, and getting paid for it.

Almost all will say they love what they do: they get a buzz from being in a newsroom and the access they are given to an audience for their work.

They are all right.

You, the storyteller

Few, however, will get right to the heart of the matter. Their focus – the one that applies as much to the grizzliest of war correspondents in far-flung trouble spots as it does to the parish pump reporter rounding up the results from a village flower show – should be the same.

They are there to **tell stories**.

It doesn't matter how they do it. In the columns of a local newspaper or a celebrity gossip magazine, on a website dedicated to shove ha'penny or a TV broadcast seen by millions, they are all there to perform one function.

They are storytellers. Their mantra should be:

I am a storyteller

The long tradition of storytelling

News is a fast-paced, churning, uncertain business. Anyone who has worked in it will tell you that it is a unique environment and that those who populate it require a similarly unique – and often difficult to define – mindset.

It is special. It is often exciting. It is hard to believe that many other occupations routinely provide such variety, put you at the heart of important events and provide the opportunity to bring about change for the common good.

But amid the hurly-burly it can be forgotten that telling the news is no more than a tradition stretching back to the dawn of civilisation.

People love to receive news. It provides them with essential information, perhaps vital to their very survival. It fulfils their need to connect with others. It entertains.

Listeners and readers have received and devoured news in caves, over camp fires, in the village square or meeting halls, in coffee shops and drinking dens, in family homes and at work on factory floors or in canteens and offices. They devour it even as they move in cars, on trains, on buses and tubes and while they walk the streets.

It has been brought by travelling minstrels, town criers, proclamations carved in stone, notes painstakingly copied by hand on to parchment, via books, magazines, diaries and journals, letters, carrier pigeons or gossipy conversations across the garden fence, in newspapers pressed by the dozen in back rooms or churned by the millions on vast presses, over the radio, through TV, via Twitter feeds or email. Every means imaginable, save thought waves. And, doubtless, that will be here before we know it.

Today's news writers, aggregators and content providers are part of this long, and occasionally noble, tradition.

Yet imagine a travelling minstrel, armed with a lute and a head full of songs and tales, gathering a crowd of listeners in the town square. If he failed to engage and to entertain, then his audience was lost. His news would not travel.

And so it is for today's storytellers. Only the prize has changed – today we compete for readers, viewers, audiences, clicks and dwell time, not a few groats in a feathered hat.

More than information

In news, we are armed with information we feel it is important to put across. We are only effective at doing this when we project it in the most engaging way possible. Our stories must entertain.

Think of the most boring college or university lecture or public talk you have attended. The speaker might have fascinating information to impart, but the presentation and delivery sent you to the edge of insanity with boredom. If the speaker confuses with long-windedness, drowns with statistics or just talks like a robot, the audience is doomed.

So it is with news. If we write it, photograph it, film it, broadcast it or turn it into a table or a graphic we must make it accessible, coherent, logical, clear and, above all, engaging.

Too many journalists feel they can just put information before an audience and call it news. It is not enough to regurgitate a statement about an event, quote the source and add a comment culled from Twitter and then leave the reader to make up his or her mind about it.

Our audience has as much access to that information as we do. If they want to read the latest proclamations of a celebrity or politician, they can follow them on Twitter as easily as a journalist can. They can assimilate, aggregate and filter as we do.

There is too much information out there. The audience is drowning in the stuff.

Hence, journalists have an ever more important job to do. They need to make sense of the information, as well as clarify it, explain it and contextualise it.

The cleanest and easiest way is to make it a story – as dramatic, as engaging, as informative a story as possible.

We do not tip out the contents of a jigsaw puzzle box and expect our audience to complete the picture themselves. Few will have the inclination to do so and even fewer will have the time or the patience. We must pull together the pieces of the puzzle for them and present the picture already made up.

We must add value, providing clear-headedness in a confusing, sometimes scary, world overloaded with news providers. Our readers will thank us for it - and they will come back again.

Steal from fiction

News writers should steal shamelessly from storytelling techniques used by those in the entertainment industry. That doesn't, of course, mean abandoning the principles of sound reportage or creating a work of fiction but it does mean learning from those whose professional raison d'etre is story construction and presentation.

Great works of fiction are not put together by random forces of creativity but are considered and crafted carefully.

'Storytelling is work. Pleasurable work, usually, but it is work,' says American author Maggie Stiefvater.

The digital era

For news, the future – at least as far as anyone can predict – will be a predominately digital one. Newspapers will probably survive, much as music on vinyl persists in the age of downloads and streaming.

Digital has created many new realities for journalists.

For some, it has removed much of the elegance and craft that went with working in print. The charges are manifold. Sloppy writing, endless plagiarism, ugly layouts, intrusive ads and dubious clickbait lead to a Hadean pit of vacuity. It has all but destroyed witty and inventive headline writing. It is a race to the bottom.

Myriad inventive and dynamic ways have been found to deliver news in the digital world. Some are faddish; some will persist. For every BuzzFeed there lie the shattered hopes of a thousand dreamers who thought they had nailed the next big thing.

What sets apart those who succeed from those who do not is the quality of material which is put before the reader and the brilliance with which it is told, not the method or gizmo by which it is delivered.

'Content is king' is the now dog-eared mantra of the digital news publisher. In other words, there's no point in having the whizziest app, slickest site or technology to die for if we stuff it with garbage.

For journalists that should mean one thing: **brilliant stories**.

If we tell it through words, through graphics, through video, through animation, through aggregation – **brilliant stories**.

Exceptional writing

For those working with words – and they are the focus of this book and, research suggests, still the much preferred format of digital news readers – it is about exceptional writing to create that exceptional storytelling.

Furthermore, the digital audience is made up of hunter-gatherers who actively seek news. They are flitters, scavengers, promiscuous. They have so much to choose from, all for free, and are easily bored. They will love you briefly and leave you.

Their fickleness has become a news writer's enemy. It makes clarity and the quality of the storytelling more crucial than ever.

Badly structured stories, laboured or confusing sentences, waffle and inaccurate or imprecise detail will drive readers away. Beware, too, the charmless firing out of information in blunt, colourless bullet-point sentences more reminiscent of a PowerPoint presentation.

Never disappoint

Disappointment must be avoided. Time-starved readers, tempted by a great social headline or inviting link from a search engine, will arrive eager for information and entertainment. If they find something baffling, illogical or uninspiring, they will be frustrated.

They will not dwell. They will find better storytelling elsewhere.

Part of the new reality for many journalists is a paucity of resources. Often in regional publications, for example, underpaid reporters are expected to file copious written reports for online, then refile for print, compile video footage and keep an eye on social media output. And that's all before the 10am coffee break.

Many online newsrooms run on empty. Whatever job description they are given, writers are all too frequently reduced to desk-bound jacks of all trades.

Often they do it without senior support readily at hand. Usually they have to do it without another set of eyes going over their work. Quantity trumps quality.

It is yet another reason why the storytelling has to be spot on. And it has to be spot on at the first time of asking.

Words, words, words

Whatever the future holds, words remain the most powerful instrument journalists have. Yes, we will have audio, video, graphics, virtual reality and countless other as yet-to-be-imagined methods to tell stories.

But words evoke. They have beauty and potency in equal measure. They plant images which, because they are conjured from within us, are far more powerful than seeing a picture or watching a video clip.

Words are writers' building blocks. Without them, we are nothing.

If you do not love words, then put this book down, go away and train as an accountant.

Fashioning those words into news is not a science. Neither, though, is it an art where anything goes.

Great news writing embraces innate skills passed down since the dawn of man. It is a craft akin to building a bespoke piece of furniture and, in a flat-pack world, it must possess a human heart.

It is the craft of the storyteller.

Focus on the story – it is the most effective way of delivering the news
Focus on the telling – great writing will lift your material out of the ordinary
Love words – they are the tools of your trade, so work at using them skilfully

*Key*points

1

YOU, THE STORYGATHERER

Tenacity mixed with charm. Intelligence allied with common sense. Knowledge of current affairs plus a keen nose for a story. Organised. A great work ethic, can-do attitude and flexible mindset. Motivated, dynamic, self-starter, communicator and a team player. A willingness to learn.

These are the qualities you would hope to see in an aspiring news reporter.

They are all but guaranteed to be among the requirements listed in a recruitment ad for that elusive, underpaid first job.

And that's just for starters.

News reporters will also need a good interviewing technique, understanding of the law and public administration, computer and keyboard proficiency, command of social media and shorthand and excellent English.

And why not throw into the mix some knowledge of video editing, content management systems, a bit of Photoshop and perhaps familiarity with page or web design programs, too.

Sometimes it feels as if the demands are unrealistic. (Hint: they are.)

For this book, though, we shall take them as a given.

We are more concerned with the one quality the job ads often overlook . . . the ability to write a story.

The first step – **gathering the information** – will require all of the skills and attributes listed in those job ads.

Of course, there is no typical newsroom. All have different priorities, produce different publications, have different leaders and, as a result, have different working practices.

But whatever the environment you work in and however you gather your material, there are unstated qualities which will make all the difference when it comes to your one goal . . . compiling a brilliant story.

Empathy is all

The best reporters have this: They are people first and journalists second. Maybe it is the way they are wired, maybe it springs from something in their upbringing, perhaps it cannot be taught or learned.

But the ability to adjust their behaviour and attitude in whatever circumstances they face and according to whomever they may have to talk to sets some reporters apart from the rest.

As this job ad puts it:

> " Could you interview the Prime Minster one day and a WI committee president the next?
>
> *Western Gazette, January 2016* **"**

The best reporters form an instant connection with anyone and everyone. It makes them likeable and trustworthy. They are **social chameleons** who can switch seamlessly from the awkward formality of a council chamber or business gathering, to the earthiness of a sports locker room or factory canteen, to the exposed human-ity of the poor or distressed.

Best of all, they do it naturally without sounding forced (putting on a strange accent), unconvincing (throwing the odd 'mate' into the conversation to sound more down to earth), creepy (flirting or sycophantic) or patronising ('I can help you, if you tell me all about it.').

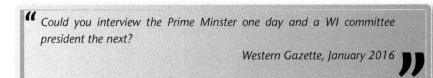

Put yourself **in the place of your subject**. Imagine what it would be like to be faced with the challenges and problems they face.

You might think it sensible to run from danger. So where did they find the courage to stay to tackle the fire or confront the thief? You might think it sensible not to drink too much or not to waste money on gambling. So what in their life caused them to become addicted? You might think it foolish to waste half your life campaigning on an issue when others would have let it go years ago. So why do they keep on going?

*For*example

Perhaps it is hard to sound interested when covering a story about replacement parts for a wind turbine or the intricacies of stamp collecting. But to the people you are interviewing, it is the most important thing in their lives.

The **people** who build the wind turbines and collect the stamps are what make the story. If they are single minded to the point of obsessive, it adds another layer. You need to get inside their world.

You will also have to climb into bed with those whose views, pet causes or personalities you find distasteful. Deal with them with grace, try to understand and to see their points of view. You can empathise without agreeing.

On the other hand, the encounter where you are charmed may mean you are also disarmed. It is just as much of a challenge to set aside feelings for those you find likeable as it is for those you do not.

Empathy should make you ask the right questions. That's half the job done.

Scepticism not cynicism

Scepticism is healthy; cynicism is not.

Good reporters should **question** what they are told. They should scratch beneath the surface. They should seek alternative points of view.

Everyone who talks to you has an **ulterior motive** for doing so. They want publicity. Some come seeking celebrity. Others have a cause to promote, a political message to impart, an image to protect or just a product to sell.

The sceptic will properly question them. The cynic will dismiss them as having nothing of value to say.

The sceptic might seek another opinion. The cynic will assume they are lying.

The sceptic will start from the healthy position that most people are trying to do and say the right thing most of the time. The cynic has a savage view of human nature.

Consider the infamous case of Chris Jefferies, who was arrested over the murder of landscape architect Joanna Yeates in Bristol in 2010. He was later cleared of any wrongdoing and a sex-obsessed neighbour was convicted of strangling her.

After Jefferies' arrest, the media piled in with a string of background pieces which all but convicted the former schoolmaster, based, seemingly, on the absurd prejudice that he had wild hair, spoke poshly and seemed a bit odd. News outlets ignored his legal representatives' requests to be careful. It was cynical and brutal.

After Jefferies was exonerated, he won an apology from the police and damages from eight newspapers. Two publications were fined for contempt.

It was a high price to pay for cynicism. Maybe what was required was more scepticism over why an innocent man was being put in the frame.

*For*example

Listen carefully

The **interview** still lies at the heart of the best newsgathering. Nothing is more complete than when people tell their stories in their own words. It outstrips any other source for its authenticity and its humanity.

There is an art to a news interview, an art which requires training and practice and, even in experienced hands, can still go horribly wrong.

More than anything, however, a successful interview depends on one thing. A reporter who **listens to the answers**. Actually listens. Not nodding when it seems appropriate while thinking of how to turn this into good copy or wondering what to have for dinner that night.

You are there to tease out information, preferably a first-hand and personal account of, or response to, an important event. If you listen, you start a conversation, which will be far more revealing.

In 2002 a disappointed Kelly Holmes walked off the track at the European athletics championships after being beaten into third place and was interviewed for the BBC by Sally Gunnell.

When Holmes, later to win two Olympic gold medals and become a Dame, said at least she was running clean, Gunnell wasn't paying attention, didn't ask her what she meant or who she was apparently accusing of taking drugs.

Instead, Gunnell, a world-beating hurdler but a novice journalist, crashed on with her irrelevant platitudes. She committed the first sin of interviewing – she didn't listen to the answer. Wiser journalistic heads outside the BBC were listening and piled in.

The lesson was crystal clear. If, like Gunnell, you don't listen, you will spectacularly run straight past the story of the day.

*For*example

Fifty shades of grey . . . and then some

You have an idea of the story you would like to write. Your editor may also have an idea of what story he or she would like you to write.

The pressure may be on gathering quotes and information that support your preconception of what the story is about.

There may be a tone of voice or a political viewpoint your publication adopts which your stories are expected to sustain.

You may have already cast your 'hero' and 'villain' of the piece.

The biggest fear is that you will hear something that means the story is not justified – worse still, that there is no 'story' and you are wasting your time when you are expected to produce something to write about.

But life isn't like that. There is **no black and white**, just countless shades of grey.

Suddenly, people you do not expect to come out well from your inquiries turn out to be those with the most clear-headed view.

Not all politicians are self-serving careerists; some do have high principles and want to give back to society. Few charities are paragons of virtue, while big corporations can be more than evil, money-making machines for their greedy masters. Private enterprise is rarely more efficient than bungling council or government officials. Schools and universities are run by people who are passionate about educating and helping young people. The health service is full of wonderfully caring people who want to make sick people better, rather than a bunch of clipboard-wielding, overpaid middle managers. There are probably some decent lawyers, estate agents and bankers out there, too.

Always start your information gathering with an **open mind**. You may well end up with nothing more than you were told to expect. However, you will often be surprised and rewarded when preconceptions are shattered.

And that is what makes a story truly fascinating.

Grab the moment

Going out to cover a story is what reporting is all about. Being there at the heart of important events, witnessing them unfold and hearing about them from those involved is what draws many people to a career in news.

Whether you are dashing to a crime scene or to a planned event, grab the moment and get the story covered in one hit. **Don't leave the scene without everything** you will need to write it.

Speak to **as many people as possible**. The lesser players may have an insight that the principal characters do not. It may even give you a unique way into the story that stands out from all the other coverage.

Once an event is over, don't rush away at the end. Take the chance to chat to the participants, such as the lawyers, the councillors, the speakers, the press officers, even the ushers and security guards. You will get your face known, build contacts and be surprised how many other angles and stories emerge.

Make sure you leave with all the details, such as dates, locations, ages, addresses, timelines, contact details and other functional information you may need. It will be

At court, a verdict is passed and the family of the victim is there to see it. Make sure you approach them as they leave the court. Respect their wishes if they wave you aside but it is more likely they will want to give their reaction. Either way, this is your chance. You may not be able to trace them later – they may live far away or abroad; they may have decided to take a holiday to get over what has happened. Furthermore, they may give you a reaction in the heat of the moment that they won't after a few hours of thinking about it.

You are covering a council meeting where a highly controversial planning decision is discussed. Opponents and supporters have gathered to hear the outcome. They will, doubtless, leave as soon as the councillors have voted. Don't hesitate. Speak to them as they leave and get the reactions there and then. Again, you may not be able to get a hold of them once the dust has settled.

*For*example

much harder to check it afterwards and especially frustrating when you realise the person who knows, and who you can no longer locate, was sitting in front of you a few hours earlier.

Catching people in the moment is always more fruitful. Away from the scene, they may have had time to reflect and become more guarded.

These occasions put the main players in front of you in one place at the same time. They are available for, and probably expect, media scrutiny. That is too good an opportunity to miss.

Meet your new BFF

It used to be us and them.

Journalists claimed to be serving their readers but liked to keep them at arm's length.

Their opinions were welcome as long as they were confined to the occasional vox pop and letters to the editor. They might even be useful when they phoned or emailed in with tips for stories – and as long as they didn't write in green ink.

Now **readers have influence**, through online comments, blogs, forums, email and social media, to offer instant feedback and first-hand accounts. As soon as a story breaks, they are able to contribute.

The **reader is very clever**. Far, far cleverer than anyone in a newsroom. Far cleverer than all the brains in the newsroom put together.

They're an extraordinary resource. They can provide insight, expert knowledge and analysis which can give fresh lines of inquiry en route to a new story no one has thought of before. A live blog, for example, comes alive through their input.

Better still, **engage with them before you write** anything – perhaps by throwing out questions to social media followers – and your story may be enriched beyond measure. They may even save you from embarrassment by **verifying questionable information**. With luck, they will become engaged as part of the storytelling process.

Don't be afraid of **feedback**. Be brave enough to ask your sources and your readers what they thought of your story. The response is unlikely to be glowing or damning but may spin off into new avenues of inquiry which generate a follow-up.

Of course, **not all comment is helpful**, accurate or verifiable. In 2013, for example, Reddit mistakenly claimed it had identified the Boston Marathon bombers from its social media sources. It was horribly wrong and was forced to apologise. In the meantime, several mainstream news organisations had leapt on its dangerous assumptions.

*For*example

There are plenty of **hoaxers** and disruptive smart-arses out there hoping to set you on a wild goose chase.

Furthermore, the input **will not be representative**. Those who offer information or comment are, by definition, the most engaged with matters of public interest but it doesn't mean they are closest to the story.

Some commentators refer to this as the 90–9–1 rule, which means 90 per cent of people won't post any comments, nine per cent will post infrequently and one per cent will account for the vast majority of the postings. Most readers still expect you to do the work for them and not the other way round.

But **apply sensible filters** and storytellers have an invaluable resource delivered to their desktop.

Think holistically

If you are a writer, it is easy to get lost in the pursuit of words.

But a website or a newspaper is **much more than words filling spaces**. The words may be pivotal but no one will read them if they stand in boring, black and white isolation.

As you gather your information, consider, too, how you might obtain pictures, the value video may bring or how to find the data for an engaging graphic. What about Q&As, social media reaction, statistics and all the other decorations readers love and that round out storytelling?

Indeed, before writing anything, **ask yourself if a story can be told without many words** at all. Maybe it lends itself to a pictorial approach, or it might work as a dazzling interactive graphic.

Weigh up, too, how you might break or promote the story. Decide how quickly it needs feeding out on social media and how much to reveal. If you work for an organisation which has an online and printed platform, evaluate how you might present it for each – it may be you need to prepare two versions, or you might reserve it exclusively for just one.

Remember your stories need to fit into a rounded, engaging product. The pursuit of material and ideas beyond words may add to your workload but to neglect it is to risk part of the story going untold.

Get out of the media bubble

Newsrooms have a rarefied atmosphere, full of **intelligent, well-read media people**. They tend to mix with similarly intelligent, well-read media people.

And they are rarely representative of the audience for which they write. For a trade, rather than a profession, there is a frightening bias towards the male, the white, the university educated and the middle class.

They can be obsessively urban in outlook; at a national level, they are absorbed by what happens in London and the south rather than what happens in the rest of the country.

And they often fall into the trap of applying that standard to everything they cover. The most limited see things only through the eyes of the aware.

The arrival of **web analytics** has shown us precisely what people like to read and how long they spend reading it. Yes, they can be serious and deeply engaged when the issue is close to home but they are rarely turned on by the high-brow, distant and deeply abstract.

When judging the merits of stories, journalists need to **apply the Pointless test**. The TV quiz, with its we-asked-100-people-to-name format questions, reveals all you need to know about what engages the British public. In one question only 69 per cent could name an Eton-educated British prime minister with the initials DC (when David Cameron was prime minister). Ask 100 journalists the question and 100 would have given the right answer.

*For*example

It's not about sinking to the lowest common denominator, it's about recognising **how far outside the norm we sit**. If you want a relevant opinion, don't ask the white, university-educated, middle-class male sitting next to you.

Don't follow the herd

In news, as in life, there is **safety in numbers**. If everyone else is doing this story and everyone is covering it in this manner by interviewing these people, then surely it can't be wrong. It will ensure you don't risk a ticking off (or worse) for missing something that everyone else has.

However, it may also mean you risk becoming predictable or colourless and in today's crowded media landscape you struggle to be heard above the noise.

You **cannot ignore the basics**. If the principal character in a story makes an announcement or does something newsworthy, you have to be there to report that.

Make sure you cover these basics and cover them completely but, if time and resources permit, have something extra to offer.

You will rarely have the luxury of hours to waste chasing dead ends, personal interests or wild speculation. However, perhaps you could seek out people to interview with different perspectives on a story. If you can't be first, the saying goes, **be freshest**.

Perhaps it means not waiting for hours with a press pack for something to happen or someone to say something when you could be busy **talking to other people**.

Perhaps it means **asking more questions**, picking at a detail or making an extra phone call or two when you could just rewrite a press release.

More often, however, it is about **thinking a little differently**. Narratives quickly become established in the media and varying from the consensus might be frowned upon.

These narratives often determine a villain to boo and a hero to cheer. Why not turn that on its head, starting perhaps with a different perspective . . . maybe the hero is more self-serving than it seems and the villain is misunderstood? A more sympathetic approach perhaps reveals angles others have missed.

> Try to look at a story sideways. A factory closes in your town, the management is apologetic but has a business to protect, the union is apoplectic with rage.
>
> So far, so predictable. But what about the woman who runs the tea shop where the factory workers get their sandwiches every day? What now for the glorious Art Deco factory building and its landmark chimney? Maybe there are people living nearby who will be glad the factory is closing, as it will end years of disturbance and pollution in their neighbourhood?
>
> ### *For*example

The herd will carry you on safely and securely but sometimes, like whales in a feeding frenzy, they end up stranded on the beach.

Master the internet . . . don't be a slave to it

No journalist can survive without the internet. It is information source, reference book and cuttings library all at the click of a mouse.

Social media brings us news, comments and even live footage from the farthest flung corners of the world. Mastery is a must.

But it is **only another tool**. Rather than the end, it is the means to getting a story.

The temptation in hard-pressed newsrooms is to scour for information online, rewrite what you find and hit publish. At the very least, you will be doing your job as a collector and sorter of information.

Yet that's the moment to ask some crucial questions . . . Am I reporting on the internet or telling a story? Is it believable or, in every sense of the word, real? Have I added anything to the information already available for all to see? **How can I enrich it** so I am more than a gatekeeper?

The answers lie with people and places you can't reach online.

Be positive

The best news for journalists is said to be bad news. Inevitably, your working life will be spent covering death and misfortune. Gloomy talk is always more dramatic than optimism.

But great – indeed, the best – stories can be **celebratory**. Learn to recognise and **salute achievement** with just as much vigour as you would expose failure, disaster and disappointment.

It may not mean much to you that a group of Brownies has collected a record haul of badges, that a rare species of bird has been saved, that a play has reached its 1,000th performance or that a council official has become an OBE.

But **it matters greatly to those involved**. It's your job to ask the right questions and make the storytelling come alive. And, be assured, the **story behind success is every bit as fascinating** as is the one behind failure and disaster.

Find the Brownie who has overcome severe disability to earn her badges, speak to the man who spent every day for a year watching over the nest, interview the official about the terminally ill nephew who inspired his charity work that earned an OBE. Salute their triumphs.

Grudging recognition is no recognition at all.

Always look for the human consequences

Stories are written for people. To understand them, they need to see people in them.

It means putting human beings, not organisations, ideas or numbers at the heart of your storytelling.

> **"** If you describe a landscape, or a cityscape, or a seascape, always be sure to put a human figure somewhere in the scene. Why? Because readers are human beings, mostly interested in human beings. People are humanists.
>
> Writer Kurt Vonnegut **"**

A campaigning charity issues a press release lamenting the crisis caused by the cut in housing benefits. It has a slew of statistics which prove there is a crisis. But so what? It would say that, wouldn't it.

There is worthy and mildly interesting information to be published here. It will fill a space but it won't spark debate or fizz across social media.

So, ask the charity to prove it, not with figures, but with people.

Ask the charity to introduce you to Mary, single mother of two, deserted by her husband, struggling to pay the bills and bring up her boys, one of whom has asthma, in her small but well-kept home, while juggling a job and care for her disabled father. Her benefit has been cut and it is close to pushing her over the edge.

You had a press release from which to fashion a report. Now, thanks to Mary, you have a story.

> **Your reporting skills are a critical part of the storytelling process –** how you learn the information dictates what you learn and, in turn, how you tell it
> **Be a human being first, a journalist second**
>
> *Key*points

Parts of a story

Add: Additional copy, filed separately but to be added to a story already written. Not to be confused with *ad*, which is short for advertisement

Blob par: Paragraph, usually at the end of a story, that begins with a blob or other cypher. It may be a linked but separate, a single sentence story, a link for further reading, a pointer to how a reader may respond, or a note for legal or other purposes

Bullet points: Series of blob pars used in text to set out a list

Byline: Used to identify the writer. **Picture bylines**, more often seen on features than in news, contain a head and shoulders picture or drawing of the writer

Caption: Line of text which appears under a picture, explaining what is happening in the picture or identifying who is in it

Credit: Name appearing alongside a picture caption to identify the photographer, or at the end of a story to identify the writer

Cross-ref: A line at the end of the story directing readers to an associated story.

Graphic: A diagram or illustration, such as an annotated graph, chart or map, explaining part of a story. Interactive graphics allow online readers to adjust them by inputting data or applying filters

Headline: Or **head**. Summary of the story in a few words in large type, usually at the top of the story

Intro: Short for **introduction**. The first sentence of your story. Also the **nose**. In the US it is called the **lead** or **lede**

Kicker: A two- or three-word phrase, followed by a colon, to start a story, caption or headline. In a story, the kicker may be just a place and/or a date. In a headline it might be a marker such as the name of an event or running story, e.g. *Election 2015:*, *Wimbledon:* or *7/7 attacks:*. On lighter material, it might be a pun or exclamation

Para: A paragraph but sometimes just a **par**. Americans refer to it as a **graf**. In news writing each paragraph is usually one sentence – ideally, no more than 25 words in print and even shorter online or in broadcasting

Pay-off: The last line, particularly on a lighter story. A final comment, quote or detail which rounds off the story neatly

Pic: Picture. Sometimes a **shot, image** or **snap**. A **filer, file pic, library pic** or **stock shot** is a picture used previously and archived rather than a current one. A **handout, collect** or **pick-up** is one given out to news organisations, usually from a press office or maybe a photo released by relatives. A **lift** or **steal** is one taken from a website or other published source. A **mug, mugshot, head shot** or **head and shoulders** is a photograph just showing someone's face. A **grab, video grab** or **pull** is a still taken from video

Quote: Words spoken by a character in a story, attributed and used with speech marks. A **break-out quote** or **pull quote** is a particularly pithy quote set using larger type in a story for emphasis or to break up chunks of text

Standfirst: Introductory sentence or two summarising the background and teeing up a longer piece. Usually includes writer's name. Occasionally a **blurb** or **sell**

Strap: Introductory line of headline above the main headline

Sub deck: Secondary headline with further detail but in smaller type than the main headline

Sub–head: A one- or two-word phrase across a column of text to break up chunks of copy when it is also known as a **crosshead**. Confusingly, is often used instead of **sub deck**

Suspended intro: Also called a **dropped** or **delayed intro** and more common on lighter stories. Creates a softer approach to writing, where the news line is introduced a paragraph or two into the story

A few online extras

Alt text: Descriptive text that appears over an item, such as a picture, when hovering a cursor over it. Crucial to include to help SEO, but also to help partially sighted use a website

Categories: Assigning a category to a story ensures it appears under the right menu

Comments section: The space for reader feedback at the end of the story, sometimes referred to as **below the line**

Channel: A section of a website on a particular theme, such as news, sport, videos or weird

Embed: A picture, video, tweet or other social media post lifted, with permission, on to your site

Hyperlink: An embedded link online which, when clicked, sends the reader to another web page

Menus: The headings, usually across the top of the website, for dividing up content

Navigation: How a reader is directed through a website, using links and menus

Post: Another word for a story (and the act of publishing it online)

SEO: Search engine optimisation. The dark art of making sure that a story can be found by search engines and, hopefully, helps it to appear high up in a **SERP** (search engine results page)

Sidebar: The space down the side of a web page. It contains summaries and links to other stories

Summary: A paragraph at the top of the story or on the front page, er, summarising the story

Tags: Keywords or phrases which appear at the end of copy to help readers browse stories by topic, place or personality

Theme: The general appearance of a website. Can be created by web designers or, with popular publishing systems such as WordPress, bought off the shelf

Web analytics: A crucial tool for assessing how well stories are being read. There are many different types of software used for the process but they all show how many people are visiting a site or page, how they arrive at a story, how long they spend reading it and where they click next. Editors can then decide which stories should get greatest prominence or which need amending to get more views

Newsroom Lingo

Angle: The approach a writer takes to a story. Usually, it will form the intro. Also referred to as the **line, the take, the peg, the hook** or **the way in**

Attribution: Identifying the source of information or quote

Catchline: A word used to name a story (or a picture). Avoid using **embargo, kill, spike** or **add** as catchlines, as they can be confused with other instructions. Sometimes referred to as a **slug**

Contacts: Your personal sources who bring you stories or tip-offs. Should be more than someone you follow on Twitter

Copy: Another word for a story or stories. **Hard copy** is a print-out

Cuts: Archive of previously published stories. From the days when clippings of stories were filed for future reference. Nowadays it will be an electronic database or part of your content management system. Also known as **clips, cuttings** or **library**

Deadline: The time by which a reporter must have completed a story. Also the time when editing must be completed to get a story published

Death knock: Visiting the family or friends of someone who has died. Dreadful and rewarding in equal measure

Doorstepping: Hanging around outside someone's home or news waiting for them to appear so you can question them. Dreadful and essential in equal measure

Embargo: A stipulation on the earliest time or date when a news item can be published or broadcast. It is a point of principle not to break an embargo and to do so risks losing a contact. Sometimes reporters are invited to a **lock-in** or **lock-up** to view embargoed material, such as a major government report, on the proviso they will not publish any of it before an agreed time

Flatplan: The proposed layout of sections and pages in a newspaper, with places earmarked for adverts and stories. Usually prepared on screen, although many editors like to have a print-out to scribble on. Occasionally called the **book**, although that is also the name for a complete set of proofs folded together to make a **dummy copy** of the next issue

House style: News organisation's guidelines for how words, pictures and other elements are used to ensure consistencies and set the tone for a publication. Should be written out in a **style guide**

Imprint: Panel containing the name and address of the publisher. In a newspaper, it will contain the name and address of a printer; online it might state who has designed the web page

Lift: To take a story or quote from another publication and use it in or as the basis for your own story. It is good practice to offer some attribution or hyperlink to the source material

Literal: Spelling or typing mistake. Also called a **typo**

Masthead: Name and title on the front page or home page of a publication

More follows: Written at the end of copy to signify that there is more to come. Can be shortened to **mf**

Must: Copy that must appear, usually an apology or correction or something demanded by an editor

News agency: Agencies supply material on spec or to order to news publishers who then adapt it to their own needs. In Britain, the Press Association is the dominant supplier. Associated Press, Reuters and AFP are also widely used. There are many other agencies, some are part of groups covering large tranches of the country, while others are one-person operations with specialities or patches of their own. **Freelances** also supply material on an ad hoc basis

Newslist: A daily list, prepared by the news editor, of items for possible publication

Off-diary: Stories that come in ad hoc and are not planned. Usually the best kind

Off the record: Information you can publish but without attributing it to the source. Some sources mistakenly believe this phrase means the information is not going to be published, so care is needed to establish exactly what they intend

Padding: Adding extra material, often irrelevant, inconsequential or repetitive, to a story just to make it longer

Patch: Area covered by a reporter. Also **beat**

Proof: Print-out of a completed page for reading and checking

Puff: Story which shamelessly promotes the person, organisation or event it is about. Also used for graphics, headlines and promotional material on the front page to get readers to pick up, buy or turn inside a newspaper. They are also called **blurbs**

Re-jig: A rewrite. Sometimes a **dress** if new detail needs working in

Slow-burner: Story with a quiet or seemingly insignificant beginning which eventually erupts into something more dramatic, maybe days or weeks later

Snap: Very early summary by news agency warning of an important story which is breaking

Sources: People, organisations or other publications which give us information for stories

Spike: To scrap a story, usually because it is dated, too weak or cannot be substantiated. Also **kill**

User-generated content: Material, from comments or letters, to pictures to videos, provided by readers

Wires: The feed of stories, features and images supplied by agencies

Types of story

Advertorial: Advertisement in the form of an editorial piece, which should be labelled as an advert, as it will have been paid for

Anchor: Story which appears across most or all of the bottom of a newspaper page. Also **basement**

Backgrounder: Longer piece, often written in a feature rather than hard news style. As the name suggests, it sets out the background to a story

Box out: Standalone piece of copy, which sits alongside the main story. It may be a background piece or a linked story with a different angle. Also known as a **box, fact box, panel, break-out** or **sidebar**

Breaking news: Story which has just happened. Details may be scarce to begin with and frequent updates are needed

Colour piece: Background piece, usually softer in tone and without a hard news intro, which focuses on details that set the scene for the reader. In political journalism it can be satirical in tone and is called a **sketch**

Feature: Longer item not necessarily connected to hard news or immediate events. In general, it will examine an issue, situation or personality in greater depth, often with multiple interviews. A **news feature** may examine the background to a current story in great complexity, although it may appear some time after the event which prompted it. Other features cover subjects as diverse as the arts, lifestyle, cooking and fashion

First person piece: A personal account of a news event, written by a reporter who is on the scene and may be involved or particularly moved by it

Follow-up: Story based on new information about something which has already been published

Funny: Light-hearted story, often just a single paragraph long

Gallery: A collection of pictures online. May stand on its own or as part of coverage of a bigger story and usually requires few words other than explanatory captions. Often presented as a **slideshow,** so readers click or scroll through

Holding piece: An early take on a story, sometimes written in advance or before an event has reached its conclusion or before the full details are known. The **holding line** will be an early, often straightforward, approach likely to be replaced by something more exciting later

Key points box: Break-out outlining important facts from a story in blob par form. Also known as an **at-a-glance** box

Lead: Main story on a page. Another word for **splash**

Listicle: News content presented as a numbered list online

Live blog: Rolling 'as it happens' coverage of an event online, with updates from reporters at the scene, wire reports, social media, picture desk and graphics

Native content: An advert online, presented in the same style as other stories or videos on the site. Should be labelled clearly as sponsored content

Nib: News in brief, a short story, perhaps just a single paragraph long. Also called a **filler, brief, quick** or a **short**

Obituary: A tribute appraising the life and achievements of a person who has died recently. Also called an **obit**

Opinion piece: Usually written by a by-lined writer, it can appear as commentary alongside a major story or within the opinion pages, known as **op-ed** in the US. Also an **editorial, leader, thinkpiece** or simply **comment piece**

Picture spread: A showpiece page or spread of pages in a paper with striking images, often used with few words

Poster: A striking newspaper front page dominated by a single image with few words

Prepiece: Story written ahead of a news event to tee up that something significant is going to happen. Also an **advance**

Profile: Piece about the life and times of a personality in a story

Q&A: Question and answer piece, where the writer poses a question the reader may ask and provides the answer

Quote box: Series of individual quotes about a story, maybe set as a series of blob pars

Rehash: Rewrite of news stories published elsewhere without any significant original research. A **cuts job** is a story compiled from old stories or other source material. Although necessary sometimes for backgrounders or listicles, it looks lazy if presented as a breaking news story

Review: Comment piece offering a critical assessment of concerts, plays, films, TV programmes, books, restaurants, art shows and any other form of entertainment

Round-up: Story that links two or more events with a common theme, such as weather, road accidents, election or sports results

Running story: Story which unfolds over time. Some complex running stories take weeks, months or even years to unravel

Running turn: A story which continues from one page of a newspaper, usually the front or the back, to another inside. The turn is usually made mid-paragraph and marked by a phrase such as *turn to page xx* and above the continuation inside by a phrase such as *from page xx*. Sometimes called a **flying turn**

Splash: The main story on the front page of a newspaper or, less commonly, website. Sports desks sometimes refer to a splash, although it usually appears on the back page

Spread: Facing pages in a newspaper of pieces linked to a single story or topic. Also called a **double-page spread**

Stat box: Break-out on a story highlighting a significant figure or figures from the story

Timeline: Chronological list of the events leading up to a news story or setting out a programme of what will happen next

Top: Story which appears across most or all of the top of a newspaper page. Also called a **hamper**, although they are designed slightly differently

Vox pop: Series of short interviews with 'ordinary' people on the street or at an event as a crude gauge of public opinion. Nowadays, more commonly achieved by combing social media such as Twitter

Wing: Story which appears down a single column of a newspaper page

Wrap: Story which pulls together all the major strands of a complex story in one central piece

Write-off: Short, self-contained front- or back-page version of a newspaper story, which is run in full inside. Summaries on the home page of a website might also fit this description

2

WHAT IS NEWS?

Before putting finger to keyboard, it's worth asking: What is news?

Let's start with the prosaic answer:

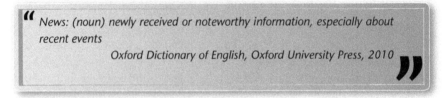

> **❝** News: (noun) newly received or noteworthy information, especially about recent events
>
> Oxford Dictionary of English, Oxford University Press, 2010 **❞**

Many great minds have tried to put a bit of flesh on that bone. These and their variants have become newsroom standards:

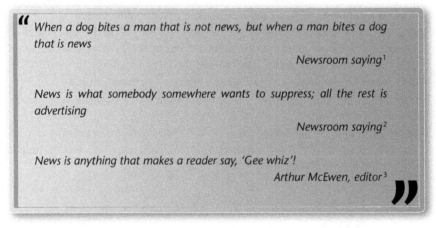

> **❝** When a dog bites a man that is not news, but when a man bites a dog that is news
>
> Newsroom saying[1]
>
> News is what somebody somewhere wants to suppress; all the rest is advertising
>
> Newsroom saying[2]
>
> News is anything that makes a reader say, 'Gee whiz'!
>
> Arthur McEwen, editor[3] **❞**

And these are wise words on what makes for well-written, effective news:

> **❝** Good stories flow like honey but bad stories stick in the craw. What is a bad story? It's a story that cannot be absorbed in the first time of reading. It's a story that leaves questions unanswered
>
> Arthur Christiansen, editor[4]
>
> Hard news really is hard. It sticks not in the craw but in the mind. It has an almost physical effect, causing fear, interest, laughter or shock
>
> Andrew Marr, editor and broadcaster[5] **❞**

In some cases they are decades old but they should still underpin every word you write.

Better still, observe this mantra:

> **❝** It's all storytelling, you know. That's what journalism is all about.
>
> US TV journalist Tom Brokaw[6] **❞**

Content – a new definition

In the digital era, the definition of news has widened.

Today there are billions of potential publishers who need nothing more than a social media account, a mobile phone and the luck to be in the right place at the right time to set words, pictures, audio clips and video before the world.

And anyone with a phone can read it, for free, the instant it is sent.

So, news rapidly loses its new-ness. Disaster strikes, violence erupts or a major public figure dies and the announcement creates a sound wave which washes around the planet in seconds.

Where have publishers turned? They are redefining news as *content*.

Most news sites will include traditional stories covering familiar topics from crime to the arts. Text and picture formats still predominate.

However, many stories which have been bread and butter for newspapers over the decades often attract little interest online.

So, we have a new wave of material – sometimes trivial, gossipy and humorous or with an offbeat spin on a serious subject but ideally suited to time-starved, gadget-hugging millennials. Often collated from social media, it is intended as a conversation starter and is a more than happy bed partner to entertainment.

> **❝** However it comes to pass, the 'news story' is every day becoming more like a dynamic, living conversation than a series of discrete, disjointed, atomized points of view[7]
>
> Maria Bustillos, US journalist **❞**

It arrived with a host of buzzwords . . . snackable, clickable, mobile-friendly, viral and so on. Pioneered by the likes of BuzzFeed, it has been aped by most mainstream publishers scrambling to connect with a digital generation.

It irks some of the old school, who prefer some gravitas to their reporting and believe it to be divested of some of the traditional skills of newsgathering.

Online news can be a numbers game, where the target is to publish plenty and publish it quickly, even if quality can suffer.

A third of those working online voiced concerns in a *Press Gazette* survey in 2015. Or as one respondent put it when asked about the downsides of the job: 'Quality of journalism, need for vitality making us collate crap from the internet instead of doing real research.'

Old news values are sometimes swept aside. What, after all, is the story behind a video of a cat chasing a spider? It's amusing and mildly diverting for those who like cats – but is it news?

The simple answer is that if it brings readers, who enjoy it and engage, then yes. Maybe a few will even say 'Gee whiz!'

What it means for news writers

The notion of news writers as information gatherers and disseminators is withering. Instead, the focus is on collation and curation of what others are saying.

To create content involves far less interviewing, by phone or person, to collect information. It means scouring social media and other news channels to generate ideas. Often it is not about breaking news but reflecting upon it and reacting to it. It is vacuuming up the comment and chatter that surrounds it.

Structure, style and use of language are much looser. It needs to be enriched by embedding tweets, Facebook and Instagram posts, images, videos and graphics, with boxes and break-out quotes also keeping it lively.

Formality is often abandoned. The fourth wall – that invisible divide between writer and audience – has gone, a shock for generations of writers told never to use the word 'you' in copy for fear of being patronising. Comment is encouraged, another shock to the old-fashioned journalistic notion of neutrality.

It should be a chance to shine, to write with humour and flair, freed of some of the traditional constraints. But this conversational style is hard to pull off, as it is critical to strike the right balance between the informal and the informative.

At its worst, it becomes juvenile and sketchy, trying too hard to be youthful in tone or in vogue rather than clever and witty. Being informal does not mean forgetting basics such as sentence construction and spelling. It's still a piece of writing that needs to have authority and to be understood by all.

Worst of all, it falls apart when the writer forgets the principle which has driven news since the dawn of civilisation. It is still storytelling.

As *Guardian* editor-in-chief Katharine Viner observed in 2013:

> **"** It makes me think of this line from The Cluetrain Manifesto, one of the most influential business texts of the internet age, back in 2000: "What if the real attraction of the internet is not its cutting-edge bells and whistles, its jazzy interface, or any of the advanced technology that underlies its pipes and wires? What if, instead, the attraction is an atavistic throwback to the prehistoric human fascination with telling tales?"[8] **"**

In other words, we should never forget:

> **"** Platforms – they come and go, but storytelling is forever.
> YouTube pioneer Michelle Phan[9] **"**

Welcome to the news party

The world of news is like a party. A giant, noisy one with myriad confusing, overlapping voices. Everyone is invited; no one wants to pay to get in.

Google and Facebook loom at the door like bouncers who grant entrance but only on their terms and only after confiscating wallets on the way in.

Newspapers are like those older guests who seem a little out of step with the modern world and who have retreated to proclaim from the kitchen. They can be wise and authoritative but their stories can lack freshness.

They started their retreat from the middle of the action when someone switched on the radio and then the TV to try to drown them out and left them blaring from the corner of the room 24 hours a day, seven days a week.

The competition for guests' attention is intense. There are many other proclaimers – news sites, apps, agglomerators, all wearing different clothing but not unlike the newspapers of old. Some have been spawned by businesses such as tech companies, often with little history of news publishing, few journalistic credentials and even fewer journalists.

Next to them, adding to the din, stand the new types of preachers – the bloggers, the vloggers, the specialists, the viralists and others with innovative ways of saying things.

With them are the social media types who seem hip and gain a lot of attention, especially among the younger guests. Some of these have become new messiahs, with millions of people hanging on every one of their 140-odd characters.

Imagine what it is like for the guest just arriving. The noise from the party is deafening, overwhelming and confusing. There is so much information out there.

You have amazing stories to tell but will anyone hear them? How do you, the news writer, make yourself stand out from the cacophony? You want to be the voice they trust, the one that entertains, the one to whom the partygoers will turn when they need clarity.

Of course, you could hope to be heard because you have the slickest and flashiest presentation or the technical wizardry that makes your voice carry further or arrive fastest. Maybe your publisher has the cachet or gravitas that makes it likely to be listened to.

You can aim to be the edgiest, quirkiest, funniest or even just the loudest – but that may not appeal to everyone.

There is only one sure-fire technique for ensuring that readers pick you out above all the others vying for their attention and make them want to hear you again and again – and that is to be a more accomplished storyteller than anyone else.

The bad party guest

You're invited to the news party. So, it's worth remembering what makes for a bad party guest:

Turns up late: If you miss a deadline, you're out of the game; if someone else is there before you with the story you are also playing catch up

Has nothing interesting to say: Who's going to listen if you turn up with dull material?

Long-winded: If your stories go on too long, then your listeners will lose interest

Monotonous tone of voice: If you tell a story with uninteresting words or without colour, such as quotes or clever detail, your listeners will find someone who entertains them more

Exaggerates: You will quickly be found out and, once you promise more than you can deliver, you have damaged your reputation

Repeats himself: Rehashing the same old story doesn't win new listeners and quickly bores those you do have

Too loud: Empty vessels, as they say, make the most noise. People quickly learn to distinguish between someone who proclaims often and loudly and those who have something pertinent to say and do so with quiet authority

Doesn't bring a bottle: It's not all take. Want to win over an audience? Then you need to play by the rules

Dominates the conversation: It's not just you who has something to say. If you don't learn to listen to and engage with your audience, they will soon switch and find someone who does

Misjudges the audience: Your laddish mates might like sexual or bad-taste jokes but it won't wash if the guests are civic dignitaries. Likewise, highbrow humour is great in sophisticated company but wasted on the gang from the rugby club

Stays in the kitchen: You can't be shy; you've got to be sociable. Be aware of the benefits of mixing, talking to everyone you can, sharing your company around

Goes off on one: If you're going to climb on to a soap box, you risk becoming a bore. Expect a backlash, too

Gets drunk: Incoherence and loss of sound judgment are a disaster. This guest rarely gets invited again

Digital publishing has **changed news**

Digital publishing has **reset all the rules**

Except one. **Great storytelling** is the key to being heard in today's crowded, noisy media world

*Key*points

Notes

1 Attributed to US journalist John B Bogart (Oxford Dictionary of Quotations, Oxford University Press, 1981), but also to US journalist Charles Dana and Alfred Harmsworth, later Lord Northcliffe.

2 Often attributed to Harmsworth but also to, among others, Randolph Hearst and George Orwell.

3 Widely attributed to Arthur McEwen, a Scottish-born editor who worked for US newspaper baron Hearst, and can be found quoted in, among others, History of the American Press: A Book of Readings (University of Minnesota, 1954), The Broadcast Journalism Handbook (Routledge, 2007) and Journalism Principles and Practice (SAGE, 2015).

4 Quoted in My Trade: A Short History of British Journalism by Andrew Marr (Pan, 2005).

5 My Trade: A Short History of British Journalism by Andrew Marr.

6 Dictionary of Quotations in Communications (Greenwood Publishing, 1997) plus multiple online sources.

7 News as a dynamic, living conversation, Nieman Lab, December 2013.

8 The rise of the reader: journalism in the age of the open web, AN Smith lecture in Melbourne, October 2013.

9 Michelle Phan Is Ready to Reach Beyond YouTube With Her New Icon Network, AdWeek April 2015.

3
TOOLS OF THE TRADE

The first step for any news writer is to master your ABBC.

is for
accuracy

A news writer has **nowhere to hide** if a story is not accurate. An error **damages the writer's credibility**, **hurts the reputation** of his or her organisation and, at worst, can have **costly implications**.

It should be a matter of routine and **personal pride** to make sure details are correct, inconsistencies are eradicated, names are spelt correctly, quotes are precise and figures add up.

In an age when so much information, including vast digital cuttings libraries, is available at the click of the mouse, there is **no excuse** for having failed to make as many checks as possible.

If information is impossible to verify or if it is a contestable opinion, it must be **attributed**. If there are differing viewpoints or allegations to be challenged, then balance, even-handedness and the right of reply become essential components of accuracy.

Any statement can be open to **legal challenge** – even an incorrect age or a seemingly harmless aside. You must be confident that before you hit publish that you can defend what you have written.

These are **red lines**, the very basics of good reportage. You cannot build credible news stories without observing them strictly.

Accuracy v truth

For all that, accuracy is not a clear-cut concept.

Critically, we must **separate accuracy from truth**. In news, truth does not exist. High-minded proclamations about journalists being the seekers of truth are based on unachievable fantasy.

In every story there are countless versions of the truth. Each is an interpretation of events, all equally fair and reasonable. As a storyteller you have a choice – to pick the one you judge to be the most believable or to share as many versions as you can even-handedly. Either way, truth is diluted by your decision.

Consider the press release:

> A quarter of married men admit they have cheated on their wives, some with as many as six other women, a survey has found. However, their wives are far more faithful, with only one in ten confessing that they have strayed.

So which is the more truthful headline?

> *Married cheats have up to six lovers*
> *A quarter of married men cheat*
> *Most married men stay faithful while wives rarely stray*
> *Marriage holds firm in age of easy sex*
> *Only a quarter of married men cheat? Really?*

How would it affect your thinking if the story is put out by a website which promotes illicit liaisons? Or a condom manufacturer or a Catholic pro-family campaign group? Maybe it's from a prominent university? Or based on information from a government statistics department, involving tens of thousands of respondents?

All the headlines are accurate. None of them is truthful.

Truth is corrupted by your perceptions, your world view, your choice of words and, equally, the perceptions and prejudices of your readers.

What really matters in your storytelling is **honesty** and **integrity**. They are the pillars of accuracy.

You must believe what you have written to be **precise**, **fair** and **justifiable** and have done everything in your power to make sure they are.

If you report something has happened, you must be able to **point to enough sources** – literally so online, by hyperlinking – to be satisfied that your interpretation, your story, is accurate.

is for
brevity

In an oft-quoted yet curiously wordy essay, George Orwell promoted five rules to succinct writing. They are best summarised as: *avoid using clichés, use short words not long ones, cut out unnecessary words, use the active voice not the passive* and *avoid jargon*.

All of this, unquestionably, remains as valid today as it did back in 1946, long before the arrival of the internet made it an imperative.

Readers have notoriously **short attention spans**. They are itching to turn to or click on the next page. A punchy and engaging style is imperative to keep them rattling through the story.

They will not linger if they stumble over **long words** or **incomprehensible jargon** or get tangled up in **complex sentences** with several names, subjects and clauses. News writers should use familiar one- or two-syllable words and keep each sentence to the straightforward **subject-verb-object** style.

In print, writing succinctly has the advantage of preserving precious space. Online there is limitless space but is there anything to be gained in making readers slog through 350 words when the same information can be imparted in 220?

Brevity, moreover, is key to all the fundamentals of news storytelling. Stripped-back sentences are always **clearer in meaning**; they are direct, bold and precise. They **avoid ambiguity** and that is halfway to ensuring accuracy.

Elegance counts, too

Interestingly, Orwell threw in a sixth rule, a get-out-of-jail-free card, allowing writers to break the other five if it prevented saying anything 'outright barbarous'.

It was a wise move. Brevity in news writing can drive us towards a language of staccato grunts. Sparseness should not mean inelegance.

There are reckoned to be more than 200,000 words in the OED and many experts believe English is the most diverse language on the planet. When a storyteller has such a rich dialect to choose from, it's a waste not to use as much of it as possible.

It helps us to draw subtle distinctions. A house, for example, can be a home but a home need not be a house.

Consider how many different words there are to describe someone running. Someone who darts runs in a different style from someone who sprints, jogs or flees.

Orwell was canny enough to let us keep such nuance. It helps us create the image we want to implant in our readers' minds.

is also for
boldness

These are challenging times for the news writer. Our news party is getting busier and louder and it is getting harder and harder to be heard above the din.

Of course, you need eye-catching material – that is down to your skills as a story spotter and gatherer.

But if you have good stories, you have to **sell them hard**. Vague, flaccid and guarded words will not win readers. They don't want to struggle through turgid, badly structured, laborious prose covered in caveats and maybes. If you, the writer, don't believe in the story, then it is doomed before it starts.

Boldness means **assertiveness**; it does not mean wild exaggeration or replacing information with opinion. It is certainly not a passport to writing something legally or ethically dubious.

Our story stands and falls by its accuracy. So be sure of the details but deliver them with panache, using sparky, colourful language.

You want your readers to be engaged, to take something from your story. Nothing is more disheartening than an empty comments box, a lack of retweeting or no debate in the letters' column.

Don't be outrageous just for the sake of it but aim to **provoke and challenge**. Readers may wish only to disagree or nitpick but at least they are talking to you.

Boldness means **precision**. Don't just say something is large or long-winded, make sure you define how big it is and how long it has taken.

Where possible, state things outright rather than attribute them. Show conviction and **take ownership of the story, don't nervously deflect it to others**, such as the officials you quote. Don't hide behind the excuse that you are just the messenger.

If accounts of events differ, be honest. Make a virtue of the conflict by highlighting the disparity.

Use your **narrative skills** rather than telling a story through a succession of clumsy or broken quotes from others. Take a line and stick with it; don't let yourself be diverted into side issues.

Be different

In trying to engage readers, especially through social media, challenge convention. Predictable copy tends to result in a 'so what' or 'they-would-say-that-wouldn't-they' response. Remember, you are trying to start a conversation.

Which is a more enticing approach? *Environmental group demands more money for green issues . . .* or *Saving a few polar bears. Is it really worth £500billion?*

Increasingly, boldness is about **personality**. Individual writers are connecting more directly to their readers, usually through social media. It is harder for storytellers to walk away from responsibility for their words, so they might as well offer a little more of themselves. As long as you are being fair and honest, no one can take issue with that.

is for
clarity

News writers are in the **information business**. If your storytelling is messy or muddled and fails to get the crucial information across, then you have tripped at the first hurdle.

The reader will give up if anything is difficult to understand, long-winded or ambiguous and will head off to another site or turn the page.

Clarity starts with an **uncluttered, focused mind**. Before typing a word, go through the source material, absorb it, lean back for a second and reflect on it. Ask what is the most dramatic, significant and freshest detail.

It may not be in the first line of the press release or on the first page of your notebook. But once you have settled on it, once you have spotted the story you want to tell, then **grab it, run with it and don't look back**.

In a complex narrative, one with many different characters, locations, twists and turns, this approach is imperative. **You cannot present every facet** of a story, so settle on one – the reader will thank you for keeping it simple.

Polish it

Take as much time as deadlines allow to **hone your story**. Brevity and boldness forged into a short, sharp, punchy and direct style will take you much of the way towards clarity.

After finishing a first draft, step away, have a short break from the screen and then return. This will help you step into the shoes of the reader as if you are seeing it for the first time.

Suddenly, it will be manifest if it's not clear. You will see if it grabs and holds, if the copy flows, if sentences can be read in one breath. Glaring omissions, inconsistencies and any weaknesses in the structure will become obvious. You will see if important details have been included too low and if there are those which are unnecessarily prominent.

The final question you need to answer is this: **have I left any questions unanswered**? If there are, try again. You have not achieved clarity.

The writer's toolbox

If you were a carpenter you would not go to work without a saw, a chisel and a spirit level. If you were an accountant, you would be stuffed without a calculator, a guide to tax laws and a copy of Excel. If you were a priest, you would always carry a Bible.

As a storyteller you should not leave home without these:

- **A large dictionary**: The bigger and heavier the better. Whichever is preferred, make sure everyone in the newsroom uses the same one to guarantee consistency. If you are using the internet to check spellings, make sure everyone uses the same site
- **A grammar and English usage guide**: Again, ensure everyone in the team is using the same point of reference. Take it to bed at night to bone up on the difference between a gerund and a gerbil. At least it will ensure a good night's sleep
- **House style guide**: You will be loved by your colleagues and editors if you always follow the preferred approach to writing numbers, when to use capital letters and where to stick a hyphen
- **Technological nous:** Keep your computer skills up to date. You will struggle to survive without being proficient at deep searching the internet or having competence with social media
- **Common sense:** By far, the most important tool of all. Keep it honed by reading, watching, listening and, most importantly, never ceasing to love learning. Never leave home without it
- **The right attitude:** You must love telling people's stories. That requires a questioning mind but, most importantly, an open one. If you want to impress in a newsroom, always be prepared to make one more check, take responsibility for your mistakes and learn from them. Only watch the clock to make sure you are meeting deadlines
- **A sense of humour:** The best newsrooms are fun places to be, despite the long, anti-social hours involved and grim subjects you can have to deal with. The best stories are produced by lively, energetic newsrooms

- **A ladder. . . :** Not to reach high places or change to a light bulb but to understand the overarching importance of people. To explain . . .

. . . let's break out the chocolate digestives

It's easy to imagine a chocolate digestive. We can remember eating one, dunking it in our tea, the sensations that eating it gave us.

It gets a little harder if it is just described as a biscuit. There are countless varieties. And we rapidly lose sight of our humble digestive if we see it as confectionery, a dry good, a foodstuff or a consumable. Finally, it's just another product.

With each progression, we are trudging up the ladder of abstraction.

Popularised in the 1940s by linguist Samuel 'S I' Hayakawa, this literary concept has been adapted in countless ways to help writers, speakers, managers and many others to think about the way they work.

In news, we never want to leave the bottom rung. The higher we get, the further we get away from the tangible and the closer to the theoretical and esoteric.

Your audience needs to see and read things to which they can relate, things they might encounter in everyday life, understand and care about. It gives them a connection to your story.

In broadcasting, it is crucial. You can't film images of concepts.

Say hello to Sarah, 38, an office manager, intelligent, hard-working, happily married with two children, running club stalwart, great cook, who travels home on the train.

To her colleagues at work, she is Sarah – warm, helpful, diligent and reliable Sarah.

To her immediate boss, who speaks to her infrequently, she is a team member.

To the boss's boss she is an employee; on the next floor is HR, where she is just a human resource; to the payroll department she is number 47QR12; to the managing director she is just part of the workforce.

On her train journey home she is a passenger, perhaps a customer or a season ticket-holder, then a member of the travelling public.

Of course, she could be defined as a mother or a wife, simply a woman, a Briton, a human being, a living entity and so on.

With each step up we strip Sarah of her identity, become more and more conceptual and less interesting.

Conceptual is where those we seek to challenge like to keep it. Distant and impersonal enables the powerful to remain unaccountable.

If the managing director decides to make Sarah and 100 other workers redundant, it is easier if Sarah is a concept. Sacking them becomes a realignment of human resources, a workforce reduction, a deleting of a number on a payroll, an accounting adjustment.

*For*example

> For Sarah, facing an uncertain future while the MD collects a fat annual bonus, getting fired is a very real and painful experience.
> Which is the story? A human resource realignment? Or Sarah?
>
> *For*example

It is a constant battle. Humanising is seen by the high-minded as trivialising but the trivial is usually what lies at the heart of good storytelling.

Social media has confirmed this. It is the details of life – the minutiae and the moments – which often catch the public imagination. An act of kindness, an amusing put-down in a note left on a car windscreen – they become talking points because we can understand them.

Here, big issues are boiled down to the issues that trouble us in our daily lives. Consider Britain voting for Brexit – a hugely significant moment in the nation's history, a geopolitical shift following intense theoretical debate about concepts such as sovereignty, freedom of movement and trading partnerships.

But for many in your audience, the immediate questions are very personal. Will I lose my job? Will it reduce my tax bill? Will I still be able to go on holiday in Europe? How will it affect my holiday money exchange rate? Will my Latvian nanny have to go home? Will we still be allowed to enter the Eurovision Song Contest?

> The issue of mass migration deeply troubled Europe's leaders and provoked much news coverage in 2015. Figures were bandied about – hundreds of thousands of migrants were making perilous journeys to get to Europe. Fascinating though some of the hand-wringing was, the public viewed this from a distance, disconnected and struggling to understand why this vast surge of humanity was heading our way.
>
> Then, in September 2015, the story changed. Photos of a Syrian child, Alan Kurdi, a three-year-old boy who had drowned off the coast of Turkey, were published. The images of his tiny body lying face down on a beach moved the world.
>
> There was a noticeable shift in public attitude. Suddenly we were not faced with hordes of nameless migrants. Here was the heart-breaking reality of children, families, people, all with personalities and stories of struggle and hurt to tell.
>
> Alan was at the bottom of the ladder of abstraction and the tragedy that befell him, one helpless little boy trapped in circumstances way beyond his comprehension, made the world shudder. The effect may not have endured but at least the world noticed.
>
> *For*example

Of course, broad issues are important but a worthy yet laboured discussion about health spending policy rarely makes for compelling copy. A discussion about why a nurse could not find a clean IV drip for her intensive care patients would. And focusing on this kind of specific will shed far more light on the issues surrounding health spending than any number of quotes from well-meaning suits.

The powerful's desire to keep things conceptual – as high up the ladder as possible – results in contortions of the language which it is our duty to disentangle. Jargon, business speak and political doublespeak are a constant threat to great storytelling.

It is easier to hide behind the phrases of generality. When, in October 2015, coalition forces bombed a Medecins sans Frontieres hospital in Kunduz, Afghanistan, killing more than 40 people, they dismissed the incident under the unfeeling and conceptual phrase 'collateral damage'.

Collateral damage was the smouldering ruin of a vital medical facility, the six intensive care patients burning alive in their beds, a wounded doctor who died on an office table as his colleagues battled to save him.

Not all situations are as visceral, or the use of stultifying language so blatant. But it is there every day, waving at us from the top of the ladder. Learn to identify it, translate it and seek the real that lurks beneath it.

The conceptual is prevalent in stories about politics, health, education and social affairs and other matters of public policy. Sometimes, generalities are all we are offered to write about in dry-as-dust research and reports. If so, take another look – always try to pull your story towards the bottom of the ladder.

It does not mean dumbing down. In what way is it dumb to make something accessible to readers and viewers? That is our job: to tell it simply, to tell it well, to make it real.

Getting started

Go naked: Try to write your story entirely from memory. Close your notebook, think and then write. You won't at this point use any quotes nor precise statistics. It clears your mind, stripping it back to what you have heard, read and learned.

It will help you see the story before you see the journalistic process. You will tell the story as yours, taking ownership of it

You will write faster and it will flow better, as you will not be wrestling with how to fit the story to the notes you have made and the quotes you have recorded.

Once the first draft is completed, read it through. Now, and only now, use your notes to add the details, the statistics and the quotes while checking for omissions, spellings, ages, dates and so on.

Start in the middle: Struggling to come up with an intro? Can't quite decide what really lies at the heart of a story? And is the deadline pressing?

Don't always try to write the intro first. It is too important. It needs time to ferment.

Instead, organise your thoughts and start by writing a simple chronology. This will place events in logical order in your mind, starting at the beginning and finishing at the end. It will declutter your mind, especially if you are dealing with a complex story with lots of build-up, background and side angles.

Now you will see very clearly where you need to break into the sequence of events to generate your intro and first few pars. It will be much nearer the end than the beginning.

Move these paragraphs up to the top of the story and polish them.

Don't delay: Try to write your story straight away. Apart from the obvious danger that you might forget something otherwise, hesitation risks losing the momentum your storygathering should create.

Even if you have a looser deadline, it is good practice to get your notes transcribed immediately, even if you don't need to create a fully rounded story until later.

Go for a pee: You've written what you undoubtedly think is a masterpiece. It isn't. So, walk away. Go to the toilet, or the coffee area or smoking room (other less life-threatening activities are available). Go and chat to someone else in the office about the boss's terrible new haircut or the office Lothario.

Return to your desk and read your work. That masterpiece? It'll look less William Shakespeare, more William McGonagall now. You will see the sentences which don't flow, the unnecessary words, the glaring omissions and the spelling mistakes which somehow you read over while you were first typing.

If you have time, redraft it. If you have to press publish but are still not happy, read it on screen or on the dummy page as it will appear to the reader and offer to redraft it again for an update or later edition.

One last read: Always give a story a final read before you press the publish button. It's especially important if you have given it a substantial rewrite between first and second drafts. That is when most howlers creep in, often as a result of some clumsy cutting and pasting or misuse of the delete key.

Always check the published version: When you read the published version, compare it with your version. Has it been subbed between leaving your screen and being presented to readers? If so, don't be afraid to ask why.

Don't take umbrage because your masterpiece has been changed; instead, accept that the intention was to improve it and that it probably has been. Learn from it and try to emulate the thought process that lay behind it.

In the future it will help you produce work that needs little or no improvement before being published. Everyone in your team will love you then.

Does length matter?

At some point in their careers, every news writer will ask one impossible question about a story: 'How long should it be?'

It will usually be greeted with a reply from the newsdesk along the lines of: 'How much is it (insert expletive) worth?'

Ask 100 writers in a room about a story and you will get 100 different answers.

If you ask a sub-editor (if you can find one any more), they will always want more, because it is easier to cut a story to fill a space than it is to add extra material.

Ask a showbiz reporter about a picture of a personality walking down the street in a snazzy pair of trousers and they will wring 300 words out of something which amounts to no more than 'attractive person wears interesting trousers'. Ask a political comment writer about the same picture and they will say 'give me a caption'.

In newspapers, the ideal length is enough to fill the space available. But that means nothing because the space available may well change if the design of a page is altered.

Space is limitless online. Yet, readers are less willing to plough through hundreds of words, especially on a small, awkward phone screen. They'd prefer a short, snappy version with a video clip.

If you work for an agency, then overwriting may be necessary, as your job is to provide the information for others to adapt rather than to edit out details which may be crucial to some and worthless to others.

Strangely, the newsdesk answer (without the expletive) is probably the closest you will get.

Ask yourself how interesting is this story? Am I so involved in it that I have lost sight of how much my readers will care? How much detail is necessary to leave no questions unanswered? What must I include to cover the factual basics – addresses, ages and the like – as well as any legal niceties? How much fits the style and approach of your publication? This will be what it is worth – probably a lot fewer words than you first thought.

As soon as you start repeating yourself, stretching out information, padding with irrelevant side issues or screeds of quotes, it's time to stop typing.

*For*example

Learn your ABBC – we will see in Chapter 5 how all stories are built on it
Keep it tight – only keep writing if you are adding layers to your storytelling
Stay at the bottom of the ladder of abstraction – the higher you climb, the less interesting your story will be

*Key*points

4

BORROWING FROM BOND

Let's pretend to be James Bond.

It'll be fun. And 007 is the key to great writing.

The super spy has featured in more than five decades of wildly popular films, hauling in billions of pounds for their creators.

Whether you are a fan or not, Bond's sustained popularity shows one thing above all: that his creators know a thing or two about storytelling.

A Bond film begins with a bang. We are dropped into the heart of the action – an exotic location, a fight or gun battle and a spectacular chase, usually ending with our hero walking away unscathed, brushing dust off his suit as he delivers a witty one-liner.

It's five to ten minutes of breathless action. No delay, no explanation, no excessive characters, not a frame wasted.

The story doesn't begin at the beginning but at a point of high drama. It's an uncluttered hook to pull us into the world of 007.

And at the end of it, our senses have been assailed. We need a breather.

In Bond films, the breather – the theme tune, with its extended title sequence, usually featuring unclothed women dancing – has become an event in itself.

And then, we reopen with a quieter scene – often, Bond arriving at M's office to be dressed down or briefed before being sent on his latest mission.

Now, the rest of the story can unfold in a measured chronology. The plot unravels, with time to explore all the twists and turns, character development, exotic locations and action sequences. It is like peeling layers of an onion and will return, in its own time, to explaining the relevance of the opening sequence.

A structure to follow

It's not just Bond films. This approach is seen in countless successful movies. They have openings that tell you just enough to set up the narrative to follow. They observe the mantra:

Tell
don't explain

After that sequence, they give you a breather. Watch how many times an action-packed, cliff-hanging first few minutes is followed by a switch from ear-splitting noise and high-octane effects to a scene of serenity. A character asleep in bed before an alarm clock goes off is a particular favourite.

Of course, not all films open with eye-catching explosions, square-jawed action heroes and car chases.

But, even if it is subtle or character-led, they have to begin with something that sets its protagonist in an unusual or challenging situation, that intrigues and leaves explaining to do.

Remember these principles. As we will see in the next chapter, this is how we tell news stories, too.

Ideas you can steal

News and fiction writing are kissing cousins. We don't want them to marry because that will screw up the gene pool – but an examination of their DNA reveals the similarities.

So, what makes an outstanding film (or book, or play)?

It needs a **plot**, preferably one full of **surprises** and properly **paced**, told with **style,** in a **distinct tone of voice** and with a **strong beginning**, a **firm middle** that doesn't sag and a **great ending**.

There should be a **sense of peril**; it should be **immersive** with a sense of **escapism**, yet retaining **believability**. A great film **illuminates** and **informs**, too.

We can throw into the mix **settings**, layers of **detail** and **colour**, sharp **dialogue and humour**. **Bonus features, availability** and **affordability** all count, too.

But, above all, a film needs a **point** or **theme, contemporary relevance, originality, conflict** and great **characters**.

All of these factors are essential in news storytelling, too.

Plot v story

Just as in films and other fiction, the **plot is not the heart of a news story**.

Think of it instead as a sequence of events which build up to and include a news event.

While the two go hand in hand and dramatic twists make for great copy, the plot is a device to carry **contemporary relevance** – in other words, to reveal what matters to the reader.

Hence:

> London has been named the fifth most expensive city in the world in which to live

. . . is undoubtedly an important plot development. But the **story** is:

> London is becoming more and more expensive to live in as record property prices pushed it up to fifth in a league of world cities

Contemporary relevance means focusing on how the plot most affects the greatest number of your audience. It is, for example, the difference between *Banks are raising interest charges on overdrafts as they struggle to restore their profits* and *Customers will be hit with an extra £10 a month in interest payments as banks look to return to profit*

Originality means trying to tell the latest, previously unheard developments. It is a trump card – always present the freshest developments first, even if it at the expense of a seemingly more dramatic element which has already been widely covered.

Characters in news are real people, crucial in shifting stories away from the abstract. They should **evoke empathy**, making the reader ask, 'How would I act or feel in their position?'

Look for conflict

All news stories need conflict. Conflict is the exceptional which disrupts the routine of ordinary life. By creating the extraordinary, conflict becomes noteworthy. It becomes news.

Conflict injects dramatic tension or sense of peril. It immerses readers in the story because they ask themselves, 'What would I do?' and 'How would I feel?' in these situations.

Readers need and want this kind of attachment. They want to be involved, not only for entertainment but also so they feel inclined to take part. They want to comment, to demonstrate support or opposition, to discuss what they have just read or heard. They want things to talk about.

Without conflict there is no story. In news writing, it takes many forms.

Physical: War, acts of violence, crimes
Ideological: Differences on political, social, scientific, religious, artistic or other issues
Situational: When circumstances conspire to put people in peril, create difficulties or opportunities

Internal: The personal battles our subjects face, either by choice or accident. Also the discomfort, tensions or disapproval we might create in readers

Personal: Rivalries arising from clashes of personality or difference of opinion

Well-being: Our struggle with fitness, disease, ageing and threats to our personal security

Change: Progress v conservation

Environmental: Pitting man against natural forces

Remember, too, that conflict is a positive force – it is a source of rivalries and debate which can lead to great creativity, inventiveness and achievement.

A world without conflict would undoubtedly be a peaceful place. It would be a much duller one, too.

As storytellers we must embrace it.

Identify the elements

Before writing a news story, think about the information you have.

Try to define each element. Is it part of the plot or the setting? Is it an interesting but secondary piece of colour? Is it a surprise to the reader? Is it going to make them laugh? Crucially, is it original – that is, information which the audience has not heard before?

After assessing each piece of information, you can figure out where it belongs in the structure of a story. This is imperative for making a coherent whole from the events in front of you.

The most common error is to put background, context or older information too high, cramming in unnecessary detail and, especially where a story has many facets, confusing a reader or losing focus by going down a side angle or backtracking.

All are products of writers feeling they need to explain, rather than tell. As a result, the story will become ponderous or even stop all together as you disrupt the natural progression to fill in what most readers already know. (See *Tell now, explain later,* Chapter 7)

In film, this is known as an **idiot lecture** – where one character reveals unseen backstory to another in an obvious, wordy and unbelievable way on the pretext of helping the audience understand. It's a sin in film-making – and so it should be in news writing.

It shows a lack of trust in the audience. They are smart; they understand more than you realise and, if they want to fill in the gaps or seek nuance and context, they will read on.

The makers of James Bond films understand and trust their audience. They know viewers will recognise the character, sense he is in peril or needs to chase down a villain and can be trusted to stay with the story to have it explained later.

You have the same licence to tell.

Great fiction – films, books, plays, even poems and songs – are founded on **great storytelling**

Watch (or read) and **learn how structure and technique is used** to enhance storytelling

Steal shamelessly

*Key*points

5

BUILDING A STORY

Imagine. You have spotted flames sweeping through the college canteen. You burst into the classroom next door. There is no time to waste or lives could be lost. What will you shout? *Fire! There's a fire in the school.*

Or, you are racing to the station to meet the woman of your dreams before her train departs for a distant city and she disappears from your life. You get there with seconds to spare but only have time to say one thing. All that matters is that you tell her *I love you; don't leave me.*

Or, you are being chased into your village by a pack of hungry, man-eating wolves. What will you shout to the other villagers? *Run! The wolves are coming.*

When you have something urgent to tell, you do not delay. There is no time to explain, you just need to say what is happening as quickly as possible.

What you say in these circumstances is instinctive. It is also the first step in writing a news story.

The most interesting, significant and important information forms the essence of the first paragraph, or introduction. A news story doesn't begin at the beginning.

In our previous examples:

> *Hundreds of students were led to safety as flames . . .*
> *A couple married today after a last-minute dash to the station . . .*
> *Villagers fled for their lives . . .*

Many journalism teachers and newsroom sages use scenarios such as these to get writers thinking about how to start their stories.

But they only get you as far as the first sentence. We must carry on the analogy to get a better understanding of how to tell news stories.

Let's go to a party

So, imagine your friend – let's call her Alice – is getting ready to go to a party. She has a lengthy journey on the No. 43 bus to get there.

Are you sitting comfortably?

Alice's flatmate, Steve, is invited too. But he says he is feeling unwell and chooses not to join her, although she suspects it is because he would rather stay at home and watch football on TV.

It takes Alice longer than usual to get ready because she can't decide what to wear. When she finds the right item, she realises it has a dirty mark on it and has to change into something else. It's hard to choose because it is starting to rain.

So far, so ordinary . . .

On her bus journey, Alice starts chatting to two amateur rugby players who are on their way to training. They are flirty and she is sure one of them is about to ask for her phone number but the bus, driver takes a corner too fast and distracts him by sending his kit bag flying.

When she gets off the bus, Alice has a little way to walk from the stop to the party. Fortunately, it has stopped raining. She walks along the high street, stopping to glance in the window of her favourite clothes shop, which has a sale on, and she spots an item she has long had her eye on but that is now half price.

She glances at her watch. It's 7.30pm on a Friday.

Bored yet? A lot of scene-setting but not much else . . .

As she rounds the corner, a ginger-haired man in a green T-shirt is running towards her and bumps into her. He barely stops to mumble an apology and say something about being in a rush. She notices his badly discoloured teeth.

In the next street, she spots a crowd forming. As she gets nearer, she sees they are standing outside a house looking up at the first-floor window. Among them, she notices the two rugby players she was talking to earlier. Someone is shouting, 'Fetch a ladder, fetch a ladder.'

Looking up, Alice can see flames licking around one of the upstairs windows. Smoke is billowing from another. In a third upstairs room, she can make out a couple, a man and a woman, with a baby. They are desperately trying to force open the window.

Suddenly, there is a flash and the flames light up the room where the family is trapped.

Ah, now this is a bit more dramatic . . .

A moment later, there is a loud crash and a chair comes flying through the window from the inside, showering those below with glass. The father is seen kicking away the remaining glass from the frame so they can escape.

The sound of approaching sirens grows louder but the flames and smoke are beginning to engulf the room. There is no time to waste. The man ushers his wife forward. She hands him the infant.

She hesitates as she eases herself through the window frame. 'Jump, jump,' the crowd is calling.

The woman, who is in her late 20s, leans forward and leaps the 15ft from the first floor to the ground and lands awkwardly in her front garden. She crumples on landing and clutches her ankle.

. . . now we are into the pivotal events

Inside her husband is coughing and spluttering through the smoke. 'You can't jump with the baby. Throw the baby, throw the baby,' the onlookers call up to him. 'We'll catch her, we'll catch her,' they assure him. Alice recognises someone else in the crowd – he was one of the finalists in The Apprentice.

The father kisses the baby's forehead and leaning as far out as he can, he gently throws the baby down.

It seems to last an age, the moment frozen in time as Alice watches the child leave its father's grasp and drop through the air. The baby's body spins as it falls towards the waiting arms of the people below.

The infant is caught safely by one of the rugby players, who cradles her closely. She coughs and then cries gently.

But there is still more to come . . .

The onlookers clap as the rugby player takes her to the mother, who is sitting, still in pain from her injured leg on the ground.

'It's a bloody miracle you caught her,' says his pal as he slaps him on the back. 'Last week, you dropped about six high balls, if I remember rightly.'

Upstairs, there is a bang – the fire has taken hold. There is no sign of the father; he has disappeared from view.

By now, the fire crews have arrived and one of the firefighters in breathing apparatus goes up a ladder and climbs through the window.

Moments later, he reappears at the window, with the father over his shoulder. A second firefighter joins him and they manoeuvre the limp body of the father through the window and down to the ground, where he is given oxygen.

And breathe . . . events now start to wind down

More emergency services arrive and move the crowd back. The family is taken away in ambulances; the father looks in a bad way and the mother has her leg in a splint. The fire crews are bringing the flames under control.

Alice asks a policeman what is going on. He says the family seems to have been the victims of an arson attack and they are asking if anyone has seen a ginger-haired man in a green T-shirt in the area.

She gives the police her details and decides to head on to the party, as it is now nearly 8pm and there is nothing more to be done other than gawp.

Now, time to tell her friends

When she arrives, the house is already full of party guests. The room is noisy, the music is loud and the guests are in party mode, chatting in small groups, distracted by conversation and food and drink.

But Alice has something she's bursting to tell them.

How will she do it so they understand the dramatic nature of the events she has witnessed?

First, she has to get their attention and hook them in. She will tell them the most extraordinary thing she saw.

She might well say something like:

> *Guys, I've just seen a baby's life being saved when it was thrown out of the window of a burning flat and it was caught by a passer-by.*

It's much more of an attention-grabber than if she started at the beginning with her flatmate umming and aahing about whether to come and her choosing a dress.

She doesn't bore them with details about whether it was raining, or what time it was or which bus she caught. She won't tell them about a side issue, such as the bargain in the shop window, the ginger-haired man or the Apprentice finalist.

In news terms, she has just written her first paragraph – her intro.

She takes them to the heart of the drama. The party guests will probably be looking at her, open-mouthed.

They are starting to picture the scene; they have picked up the keywords about a fire and a baby being tossed to safety. They are ready to hear more and they are beginning to formulate questions Alice needs to answer urgently.

What she says next is crucial to keeping their attention. Again, for good story-tellers like Alice, the next few sentences will come naturally.

She continues:

> *The baby was in a house with its mum and dad; there were flames all around them and they couldn't get out until the dad smashed the window.*
>
> *The mum jumped and landed OK but the dad only had time to throw the baby and it was caught by a bloke, a rugby player, in the crowd below.*
>
> *But the flames and smoke got so bad the dad couldn't get out and he had to be pulled out by firemen but didn't look in such a good way.*
>
> *And you know what, the bloke they think started the fire, well, I think I bumped into him as he was running away. I wish I'd realised and done something to stop him.*

Still, the listeners are in the heart of the drama. Still, she does not bog down the story with unnecessary or insignificant details. There is one focus throughout, with the minimum number of characters introduced.

She has reached a point where she needs a breather, a chance to gather her thoughts before continuing.

Equally, her listeners have absorbed a lot of information very quickly. They will have gained an impression of what is going on – they want a breather, too.

It could be one of Alice's friends has to dash off. Alice reminds him that his friend is a firefighter and that he could fill in the rest of the details.

Meanwhile, the others will have many questions; they will want to know more about what happened, who was involved, how it happened, why it happened, when it happened, where it happened. They will want to hear details, colour, explanations, other accounts and viewpoints until they are satisfied they have the full picture.

And so Alice is invited to go on? How to explain it coherently and satisfy unanswered questions.

At this point, she will take them through the events again, this time starting at the beginning of the evening to make sure she does not leave out anything crucial.

Thus, she might go on:

> *Well, I wasn't meant to be on my own but Steve said he wasn't coming because he felt ill.*
> *Anyway, it didn't matter because I met these two rugby players on the bus . . .*

And so on, in chronological order.

She might still choose to edit out some details – Steve's supposed illness, what the weather was like and the bargain in the shop window might only be for those listeners who are really sitting comfortably.

Leading the listeners through the events in a logical order, she now adds layers of detail. Some of those details can now be explored because they no longer distract from the central drama. Hence, she will say more about her encounter with the ginger-haired man, mention the Apprentice contestant, perhaps repeat what the rugby player said to his friend.

She will build up sequentially to the central drama of the baby being thrown to safety, move past it again and leave her listeners with what happens next:

> *Well, I hope the father is OK. I gave police my details and they said they'd be round to interview me properly tomorrow.*

Alice may even comment that there are bound to be more details online, on social media or in the papers.

At this point, her listeners should be sated. It's probably time to stop for fear she will be repeating herself. A good storyteller knows never to overstay one's welcome.

The way she relates this story sounds completely natural. It suits the listener's ability to absorb information.

And, without realising it, she has just told a perfectly constructed news story.

Building a perfect pyramid

You can't build a house without foundations and walls.

A news story is no different. It needs a structure on which to hang the decorations of plot, characters and conflict.

All the hard work in getting the information, checking the facts and winkling out the killer quotes is wasted if you fail to deliver them in a coherent order.

To achieve this, generations of news writers have been told to think of a story as an **inverted pyramid** (see figure 5.1), with the most interesting stuff at the top, tapering to the least significant point at the bottom.

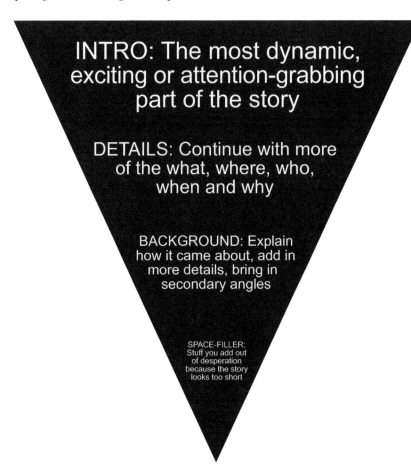

FIGURE 5.1   Inverted pyramid model

Some believe the inverted pyramid was devised to save money in the days when correspondents sent their stories by telegram. As publishers were charged by the word, writers were encouraged to put the crucial material as high as possible.

It also evolved during the days of hot metal printing when trimming copy to fit was a technical challenge. It allowed a story to be cut from the bottom up without fear that the most important information would be lost.

Yet even in the digital era, most news stories are still published in a traditional headline, picture, text format. The familiar and trusted pyramid approach is commonly used.

Nonetheless, the original model needs refining. It is too vague and doesn't fully reflect the way we naturally tell stories. It needs updating for the digital age, too.

Let us begin by turning the concept on its head (see figure 5.2).

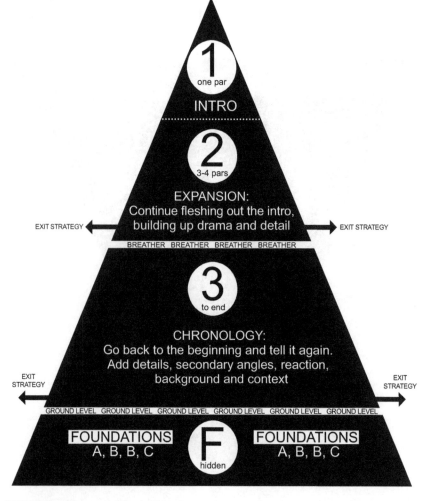

FIGURE 5.2 The pyramid reinvented

There is no logical reason to invert the pyramid. The image of a story tottering on a single point, the flimsiest of foundations, seems wrong. A story should feel solid, with a firm journalistic base and an understanding of the principles of writing to prop it up.

Furthermore, should the intro, the beacon that lures readers, not be the sharpest point, the pinnacle, the most visible, even to those looking from afar? Hence, it sits atop our re-imagined pyramid.

Turned the correct way up, the pyramid looks strong and trustworthy. Now we add details to make it more precisely built – a higher standard of craftsmanship, if you like.

The sections explained . . . the intro

There are now three clear sections to the pyramid story, an **intro**, an **expansion** and the **chronology**. Hidden from the reader below ground level are our ABBC, the **foundations** of great journalism and great storytelling.

The intro is the baited hook with which you hope to catch the reader.

It's crucial, like a James Bond movie, to dive straight into the action. No waffle, no build-up, no explanation. Bang, and you're in.

After the intro is a thin dotted line. It's drawn thus to suggest **permeability**. The intro **must flow sweetly** into the second par, carrying the reader through uninterrupted. Don't put a blockage here, don't make them stop and think by jumping from one subject to the next. They have stepped on to that tightrope and, if you jolt them, they will be lost.

. . . the expansion

The second section – the **expansion** – does what it says on the tin.

Take the story you have suggested with your intro and flesh it out it in three or four paragraphs. Focus only on the freshest, most dramatic information and, critically, don't get sidetracked.

This is where many storytellers go wrong. After writing a killer intro, they lose confidence and feel the need to stop to explain, repeating history, background and context, before continuing with the story. In their heads, readers are screaming: *Get on with it.*

Readers do understand and poor storytellers underestimate them at their peril.

Indeed, it's intriguing to leave things unsaid at this point. If you give it all away and cram in information to answer all the readers' questions in the first four paragraphs, then why would they carry on? In a film or a novel, the twists do not come in the first few scenes or pages.

Of course, the intro and expansion must contain enough context to be broadly comprehensible. But that's all – otherwise, keep it clear of clutter or nuance.

If our mantra is *I am a storyteller*, then, here, we add a second line:

The intro and expansion should stand as a story in its own right, containing the key elements of drama – conflict, plot and character – but stripped of distracting detail and background.

. . . the breather

Remember how at our imaginary party our storyteller, Alice, and her listeners take a **breather** to absorb what has been said so far.

On our pyramid, this is the thick white line between sections two and three.

The breather slows the story down, allowing readers to gather their thoughts before, intrigued and engaged, they go back to the beginning and carry on.

By accident or design, many websites and other digital platforms are set up with a physical breather in place, as they habitually introduce a picture, graphic element or break-out text at around this point.

The theory goes that online readers cannot absorb more than a few paragraphs at a time and need a visual break. It is also a tactic to keep them scrolling down the page to increase dwell time. But it can serve writers well in forcing them into an intro-expansion mindset.

. . . the chronology

Section three is a **chronology**. The story needs to be rebooted – this time at the beginning, rather than in the thick of the action. It is our quiet scene – the reset after 007 has walked unharmed from the opening pyrotechnics.

Set out the events logically and, as the name suggests, in the order in which they happened.

Begin with a little scene-setting or a paragraph or two of history. Then amplify events, add contradictory versions of them, caveat and nuance, bring in new characters or explore those the reader has already met, and give reaction and more context.

For this section, we live by this mantra:

You will, of course, perhaps only after a paragraph or two, return to the point where you began your intro and expansion. Here, don't repeat but expand again, adding any layers of detail you left out from the first two sections.

Finally, you may progress beyond the events covered in the intro/expansion to the **aftermath** and **reaction** and into the future with a sense of **what will happen next**. This tees up any follow-up story.

. . . the exit points

The pyramid has **exit points** built in at two places – before the breather and at the end of the chronology. They are there because you want the reader to leave in an orderly fashion and you need to offer somewhere for them to go.

Even with the most brilliant writing, many readers will have had enough after a few paragraphs – getting them to the breather is an achievement. Perhaps they don't have time to go any further; perhaps they just wanted the essentials of a story in which they were never going to have more than a passing interest; perhaps the story headed in a direction they had not expected.

Remember Alice's party friend who had to dash off? Alice instinctively gave him an exit point, reminding him he could get details from his firefighter friend. At the end, she commented that there would be more details in newspapers or online – another exit strategy.

An exit strategy can take many forms. Sometimes, they lie out of the control of the writer and are determined by the layout of a newspaper page or the design of a website.

Sometimes an exit strategy is no more than a **visual break** or **embellishment**, with the hope that the reader will return to the main story afterwards. It might include a picture, gallery, video or graphic, a break-out quote or sub-head, a stat box or break-out panel.

But if they are to leave the story entirely, then offer them a chance to share or like via social media, a chance to comment or offer other feedback, cross references or hyperlinks to earlier stories or other background material or a call to action, such as advice on how to help or even how to donate money.

. . . the foundations

Last but definitely not least, the pyramid has **foundations**. You can't build a house on sand. Similarly, you need firm footings for a story.

The foundations are the skills and techniques you have – our **ABBC of accuracy, brevity, boldness and clarity**, as well as the basics of good reportage. The more a storyteller masters – from the grand literary flourishes to the basics of grammar – the greater the resilience of those foundations.

The versatile pyramid

Although it was conceived a long time ago, our pyramid remains an elegant way to construct a story on any platform.

It suits readers who want to skim an intro or who only want three or four paragraphs. But it also gives us the best shot of keeping them until the end.

It works for any type of story – from sports to features – on any subject in any tone of voice and at any pace. It lifts the dull and untangles the complex.

The pyramid is not the only approach to news writing but it stands as the default. Its detractors complain, with some justification, that it is overfamiliar, tends to the formulaic and harks back to an era of news writers acting as all-knowing oracles, preaching to, rather than engaging with, their readers.

But news is still overwhelmingly consumed this way. Master it. It is the walking before a storyteller can run.

Using timelines

Draw a straight line down a piece of paper. It may be the best device yet for helping you structure a story correctly.

If we were to write the chronology of events in a news story down the page it will follow a pattern something like figure 5.5 on page 60.

The version on page 56 (figure 5.6) explains how it might work for our story about the baby rescued from the fire.

The biggest circles show us immediately where the focus of our story lies. They are the most dramatic moments, which become our intro and expansion. Because the fire is a sudden, one-off event, there is minimal history and scene-setting.

A timeline is particularly useful with a complicated story. It clears the clutter from the heart of the story so you don't get sidetracked by background, secondary angles and unimportant detail.

Use it if you adopt the tactic of writing the chronology first and then the intro and expansion last. It will give inspiration and create order from chaos.

The pyramid in practice

This has all been highly theoretical. Let's go back to the party.

How would the pyramid work in telling the story of the baby thrown from the burning house?

As we have seen, it is innate. Our version of the pyramid, with its natural flow, intro/expansion/chronology format, breathers and even exit strategies **is exactly how Alice told the story**.

Let's assume you are at the party and have heard Alice's account of what she saw. You realise it would make a great news story, so you make some calls to the police, fire service, hospital and others to confirm the details.

You learn, among other things, that the husband is Joseph Tupper, 29; his wife is Mary Tupper, 28; their child is Daisy, who is six months old. They live at 4 Arcadia Avenue, Burbton. The husband is critically ill in Royal Burbton Hospital with life-threatening injuries; his wife and baby were treated for smoke inhalation but have been discharged.

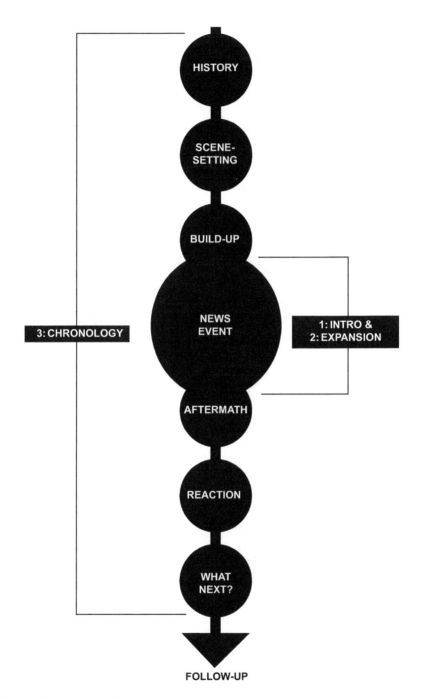

FIGURE 5.3   The news timeline

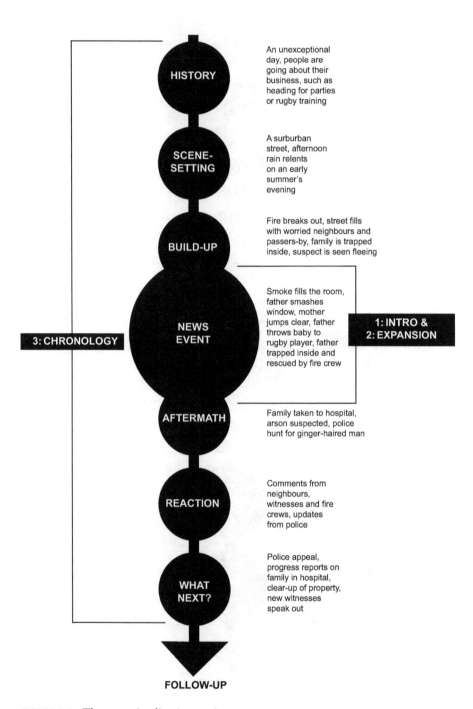

FIGURE 5.4 The news timeline in practice

Also, we will assume that you are writing for publication immediately after the event and it is the 'first break' – the first telling – of the story.

Write an intro

We need an intro. That means diving straight into the heart of the action. This takes us to the moment the fire was at its peak.

It is a multifaceted story with intriguing details and several angles. As with so much in journalism, the intro is a matter of personal judgment which will be affected by factors such as when we are writing and for what kind of publication.

In our theoretical setting, we should focus on the two key moments – the rescue of the baby and the father being seriously injured. The fate of either alone would make an acceptable intro but it is possible to capture both.

> *A baby was thrown to safety from the window of a blazing house during an arson attack which left her father clinging to life.*

You should not cram in too much information here. An intro is a taster which will leave an impression – and no more – with the reader. Readers will pick up the words *baby, saved, thrown, blazing house, father, clinging to life*.

Build the expansion

We now cross our permeable line:

> *Six-month-old Daisy Tupper landed in the arms of an onlooker 15ft below moments before the room was engulfed in flames.*

Here we have expanded the story from the intro, adding a layer of new information. Importantly, the subject (baby Daisy) remains the same and we are avoiding information overload.

We continue by switching subjects subtly from the baby to the father:

> *Her father, Joseph, who smashed the window to allow his wife, Mary, to leap clear before throwing the baby into the crowd, was trapped inside.*
>
> *He was pulled unconscious from the burning room by firefighters and taken to hospital where he was in a critical condition.*
>
> *Police said the blaze was started deliberately and are hunting a ginger-haired suspect seen fleeing the scene.*

These four paragraphs have all focused sharply on those critical moments. The final paragraph rounds off and takes us a little into what might be regarded as the aftermath (police investigation) on our timeline.

We have given enough information but not everything. It is told simply and focuses on the pivotal events without introducing too many characters at once or cluttering with background information.

While the reader assimilates this, we take our breather before heading back to the beginning for our chronology.

Now the chronology . . .

So where does the news story 'begin'?

As we have observed in our timeline, there is not much by way of history or background. However, there is a little scene-setting worth doing. It's a quiet paragraph after the breather.

> *The fire broke out early yesterday evening in a two-storey, terraced house on a suburban street in Burbton, London.*

And we continue logically:

> *It was started when the arsonist used a lit rag to ignite petrol which had been poured through the letterbox.*
>
> *The flames took hold quickly, trapping Mr Tupper, 29, and his 28-year-old wife in a bedroom where they were putting baby Daisy to bed.*
>
> *As smoke poured from the property, neighbours and passers-by gathered underneath the bedroom window where they could see the family struggling to escape.*

Now we are back at the heart of the action:

> *Unable to free the window, Mr Tupper hurled a piece of furniture to smash the glass.*
>
> *His wife, a solicitor's clerk, leapt to safety but injured her ankle as she landed awkwardly, witnesses said.*
>
> *As the flames grew fiercer, engineer Mr Tupper was forced to drop the baby from the window into the crowd.*

Here we expand again, adding colour to this crucial moment:

> *'Time seemed to stand still,'* said witness Alice Winterbottom. *'The baby was in the air for ages, it seemed. When she was caught safely everyone cheered.*
>
> *'The lad who caught her was a rugby player who told me he was on the way to practice. His mate was ribbing him because apparently he's normally rubbish and doesn't catch anything.'*
>
> But the cheers quickly died away as the bedroom was engulfed in flames and Mr Tupper disappeared from view.
>
> A firefighter wearing breathing apparatus climbed a ladder to get in the bedroom and brought him out a few moments later.
>
> Among those watching was the Tuppers' neighbour and former Apprentice contestant, James Chancer. The 28-year-old tweeted: *'Horrid scenes in my street, baby saved but dad looks in a bad way. Fingers crossed for him.'*

We are moving through our timeline and on to our aftermath:

> Mr Tupper was taken to Royal Burbton Hospital with life-threatening injuries and was said to be in a critical condition.
>
> His wife and baby Daisy were treated for smoke inhalation but have been discharged.
>
> Fire crews spent two hours putting out the blaze. *'The house is badly damaged throughout and is no longer habitable,'* said a Burbton fire service spokesman.
>
> Meanwhile, police have issued a description of their suspect – he is 6ft, pasty faced with pockmarked skin, bad teeth and spiky ginger hair.
>
> He was wearing a green sweater, grey jogging pants and has several facial piercings and a distinctive tattoo of a skull and crossbones on his hand.
>
> Det Insp Graham Plodd, of Burbton CID, said: *'We believe this fire was started deliberately by someone who poured an accelerant through the door.*
>
> *'It has had devastating consequences for the family involved and we need to catch the perpetrator quickly.'*
>
> Miss Winterbottom, a 26-year-old financial analyst, said she might have seen the man running away. *'He bumped into me. I'm sure it was him. I wish I'd realised and done something to stop him.'*

Planning an exit

There is plenty of scope to add extra detail, depending on space and how deeply your publication would want to cover the incident. You might present extra information as separate pieces, such as more witness quotes or perhaps a break-out on the family. There are countless possibilities and all might provide either a visual break or an exit strategy.

For our exercise it is time to leave. A standard round-off might be:

> *Police are appealing for witnesses. Anyone who can help is asked to call 0800 111 111.*

Other exit strategies online might be links to background pieces, video, a gallery of images, a 'come on' line asking for readers to comment, or asking if they witnessed the events.

Compare this final written version with the imagined telling at the party. There is no difference between the structure of the two.

Go to lots of parties. Listen to how people tell stories. You are, after all, only researching the best way to write the news.

The pyramid in elements

We have already identified story elements from film and fiction and how they chime with news storytelling. We can use them to construct our pyramid differently (see figure 5.5).

At the top, we create an intro out of the theme (the nutshell of the story), relevance (significance to our readers) and originality (the new bit of news).

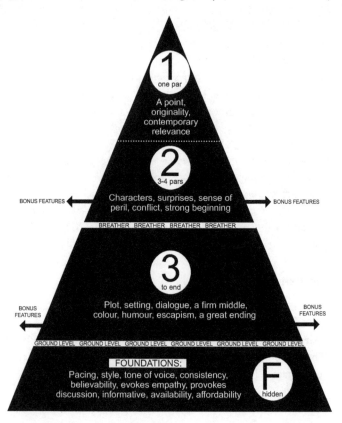

FIGURE 5.5 The pyramid model in elements

Character, conflict, twists and surprises feature strongly, too.

These are what really make a film stand out from others. It's the same with a news story.

Everything below the breather is explanation of what is going on.

Interestingly, this is where the plot belongs. It's critical to distinguish it from the story.

If we wanted to tell the story of Star Wars, we would say it's the age-old conflict between good and evil, a reworking of ancient mythologies set in space. It's about (spoiler alert!) fathers, sons and a struggle for identity and redemption. We wouldn't regurgitate the plot.

When you are writing a story, look at your notes or source material. Identify these elements, be they theme, peril, character, setting, colour, dialogue and so on.

They are pieces of our story puzzle. Use this template to slot them where they belong and you are on track to building a perfect pyramid.

The pyramid as questions

Another long-standing approach to news writing has involved the six Ws. The **what**, the **who**, the **where**, the **when**, the **why** and the **how**.

Jungle Book author Rudyard Kipling called them his 'six honest serving men' who taught him everything he knew.

Any story you write must answer them. It also gives us another way to look at our storytelling pyramid (see figure 5.6 on page 62).

The **what** is king. News is about events, the moment, the drama. If nothing happens, there is no story. It may be a one-off event (a crime, an accident, a natural disaster) or more low key (a statement or speech, findings of a report or research revealed), or even a new twist to an old story.

In our fire story, the family's plight, trapped in a blazing home, is an example. The when, where, why and how are very much secondary to the storytelling process.

Prominent, too, is the **who**. In any story, characters are essential to humanise it.

The **who** may even be more important that the **what**. Think, for example, of celebrity news, where the personality drives the story; the what happens would not be noteworthy if it happened to someone unknown.

Consider these examples from the same November 2015 edition of *The Sun*:

Strictly star Aliona Vilani shows why she's the bookies favourite on this year's show – and quite a few other people's favourite, too

(What: Woman poses in skimpy outfit)

Kate Moss is pictured for the first time with new love Count Nikolai von Bismarck – 13 years her junior

(What: Couple stand in street)

Prince Charles greets Rugby World Cup winner Dan Carter with a "manshake" yesterday

(What: Two blokes meet, awkwardly)

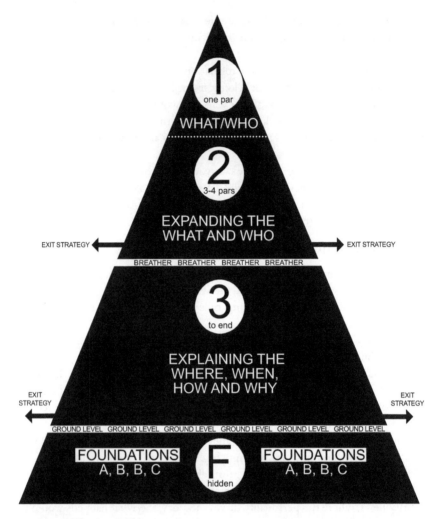

FIGURE 5.6 The pyramid by questions

The other four Ws complete a story but would ordinarily be confined to the section beyond the breather.

However, it's too restrictive to pigeonhole them in this way:

When: Coincidence or prescience increases the value of when in a story. For example, a minor cycling accident might normally be all but ignored, unless it happened at a time when cycling safety was under scrutiny.

We try to make news as current as possible. Stories online and in broadcast can lend themselves to the present tense to give them a sense of immediacy. Daily newspapers will use the phrase *last night* or *yesterday* to make them sound current.

Surprisingly, this intro from the same issue of *The Sun*, while reporting a legitimate update, uses the phrase *last month*, which makes it feel dated.

> *The cyber attack on TalkTalk last month was much smaller than feared, it emerged yesterday*

Where: Location climbs in importance if we are trying to impress on an audience that a story is local to them. The *Buchan Observer* took it to extremes, raising a few chuckles with this story about Donald Trump, who owns a golf course on its patch:

> *Aberdeenshire business owner wins presidential election*
>
> *November 2016*

Where becomes important if events happen in exotic or unexpected locations. Think of stories such as the Meredith Kercher murder or the Madeleine McCann or Ben Needham disappearances, where the settings add an extra dimension.

On world news it is usual to identify the location of the story earlier, even as high as the intro.

Sometimes the place can become the story. For example, *Britain has the highest teenage pregnancy rate in the world*, or *Stoke has the fewest people earning over £20,000 a year in Staffordshire.*

In *Blackpool hits rock bottom*, a story about the decline of Blackpool in the November 2015 issue of *The Sun* – the town is the central character, replacing the who and the what.

How and **why** are part of the explaining process and, if we follow our *Tell now, explain later* mantra, are secondary.

In follow-ups and reaction stories, we look to emphasise these recent events (the **what**).

> *Council leader Hugo Bookend was deposed when rivals in his own party formed a secret pact with the opposition, a leaked report shows.*
>
> *Captain Brian Glossop has blamed his side's slump in form on injuries to the side's star players.*

Slow news

It is worth noting, too, how explaining news is now thought as important as reporting it. Social media means that the **what** – an act of violence, a famous person dying, a major announcement and so on – breaks instantly. It leaves readers turning to news writers for the **how** and the **why**. In January 2017, BBC director-general Lord Hall pitched for more so-called 'slow news' when he added: 'I want us to do much more to help our audiences understand what's happening in the world today.'

The **how** and **why** may yet have their day.

The seventh W

For news writing we should consider another W – the **now.**

News is what is happening now, not what happened last year, a week ago or even last night. On running or updated stories this should be the focus of our intro and expansion, maybe at the expense of the more obviously dramatic event – the who did what – which has been reported on previously.

It is the cornerstone of our **tell now, explain later** mantra, which we explore in detail in Chapter 7.

Alternative story structures

The pyramid will never let you down when it comes to news storytelling.

It's clear, it's to the point and it delivers immediately what the reader wants. It works for any story in any style on any subject on any platform. Master it and you have a method to sustain you for life.

But it is not the only way.

Digital publishing, in particular, offers exciting and innovative variations.

For an online audience, the first question a news storyteller might ask is whether they need to write anything at all. Could the story be told using images, video, animation or by exploiting the internet's inherent interactivity?

However, if we decide words are needed, it is then worth asking, can we write it differently?

Atomise it

Big chunks of text look boring. Grey words upon grey words look and feel serious. They are hard work, something you need to study rather than something to entertain and inform.

In print, long, dense pieces may be salvaged by superb design and elegant use of pictures; online, text needs to be broken up.

Why not go further and smash it into pieces?

Much as a trendy chef will take the pastry, the filling and the gravy and break them up on a plate to create a deconstructed pie, the story becomes a deconstructed pyramid.

It gives readers a browsing experience rather than a fixed journey through a story, offering them digestible chunks.

It might look something like this:

FIGURE 5.7   The online news story deconstructed

Start with writing a short newsy piece – an intro with three or four paragraphs of expansion. Then, the story takes a breather.

This might be marked out by an element such as a break-out quote, a video, or a stat box.

After the breather, the story runs on, but broken down, and each section marked with sub-heads.

The precise make-up of the chunks on the page will vary from story to story but might include a timeline, analysis, key points, links, galleries, locator maps, graphics and charts, lists or best-ofs, profiles, statistics, quotes or social media reaction.

The variations are endless but each element should seek to answer one of the six W questions a reader may have.

In some cases, these elements may be substantial enough to warrant publication on a separate page, so only require a link from the main story.

It is not appropriate for every story. Sometimes a simple telling is enough. Sometimes just a few chunks are needed but not all.

Creating a fixed pattern also presents the danger of filling boxes for the sake of it. For example, a simple celebrity story might benefit from a short profile or a timeline but a complex graphic or an analysis is unlikely to add much. A scientific story is fertile ground for explainers and graphics but profiles and maps are less significant.

Examples of atomised stories could be found on the now-defunct Yahoo News Digest App, while the BBC news website often breaks down bigger stories this way. US news website Heavy, which atomises its material under a *Five Fast Facts You Need to Know . . .* channel, exploits a similar technique in everything from celebrity profiles to mass murders.

Questions and answers

Readers arriving on a news story online often come looking for answers to questions. They may even have input a question into a search engine.

Why not tell them the story in a similar question and answer style? It has a pleasing fit with the way readers use the internet – they come seeking answers to sate their curiosity.

We are returning to the six Ws – *what has happened? who was involved? where and when did it happen? how and why did it happen?*. We might also throw in, *will it happen again?, what will happen next?* and *how can I help?*

Again, this approach breaks down the text and makes it appear a little less daunting on the screen or page.

It is most frequently used as a backgrounder – part of the explaining process – rather than as a way to break news. It requires a few sentences to introduce the subject and then answers the readers' questions.

It is a style, in common with others, that TheSun.co.uk has adopted:

> *Red Shoe Diary: What was the Norma Dale 'red shoe murder', when did it happen and why was no one caught?*
>
> *October 2016*

After a couple of introductory paragraphs the story then unfolds logically through the questions:

> *Who was Norma Dale and when was she murdered? What happened to Norma Dale? Why was no-one caught for murdering Norma Dale? Why have police re-opened the Norma Dale case?*

Commentary

Sometimes the storyteller has to take a back seat to let events unfold at their own pace and in the words of those taking part.

This approach lends itself best to lighter material – what we have defined as news content.

Typically, it is seen on a social media–led story where the writer acts as a collator and narrator, interjecting only to offer context, background details and, perhaps, a knowing comment of their own.

It has more in common with TV or radio reporting, where the aim is to guide the audience by the hand, only pointing out what they cannot see or hear for themselves.

Structure is looser, without a hard news intro and travelling in a straight timeline and finishing at the end. Characters are introduced and the scene is set before reaching the heart of the action. The style is conversational.

Viral content pioneer BuzzFeed often takes this direct *in the beginning* approach with many of its stories:

> *Mark Rittman is a data specialist from Brighton, the south of England.*
> *Yesterday morning he tried to make a cup of tea with his Wi-Fi enabled kettle.*
>
> *BuzzFeed, October 2016*

In March 2016, a story about Harry Potter author J K Rowling making a surprise visit to Orkney library for a book club meeting was widely covered.

The BBC – and many others – covered it in traditional fashion with an intro:

> *One of the world's most successful authors dropped into Orkney Library for a surprise visit.*

However, tech site Mashable went for a commentary approach, setting it up with a walk through the social media sparring between the Orkney library and its neighbour in Shetland.

> *Libraries may have a reputation for being a quiet, well-mannered bunch, but the ones in Scotland don't mind a bit of banter on social media.*

The story unwinds slowly from here before, more than halfway through, the main character, J K Rowling, is finally introduced with the line:

> *And someone entirely unexpected responded.*

With this style, it's key not to overwrite. You are no more than the chairman of the discussion and you might need only to contribute an opening sentence or two and a few lines of explanation.

If you were using a tweet or Facebook post, for example, there is no need to repeat what is said in the posts if you are embedding them anyway. The writer only needs to introduce them.

Also, beware making the reader wait too long for the twist. Any preamble needs to be tightly written and to use only what is strictly needed to set the scene. It is pushed to the limit in Mashable's J K Rowling story, where it took five paragraphs and seven social media embeds to get to the point.

Most of all, stories only work in this style if the reveal is worth it. If you promise the reader something extraordinary or unbelievable, then it had better be. A disappointed reader will not return.

Freeform

Is it time to rip up the rule book?

Should we give up trying to apply order and structure to our storytelling? Should we present news events in whatever fashion takes our fancy as long as it works for the reader?

Traditional storytelling techniques are routinely challenged in other forms of writing, in film, in poetry and in song. Why not in journalism, too?

Visit news websites – especially those outside the mainstream – and you will find plenty of stories which lack structure. It is probably as much by accident, through a lack of training, discipline and writing skill, as it is by design. Many are a struggle but a few sparkle.

If you choose to go this way, you might pull it off. There is little harm in trying to be different. Writers should challenge convention.

But if you abandon established structures, you will need to be a supremely confident and talented writer. You have no formula or technique to fall back on and you can end up with a sprawling, illogical mess, which the reader will reject.

Don't excuse opaqueness as a style of writing. It's just bad writing. In news, if your meaning is not clear, your vocabulary limited, your spelling flawed or your sentences too long and convoluted, you are wasting your time.

Our ABBC – accuracy, brevity, boldness and clarity – remains paramount. Master these basics and get to grips with traditional approaches before trying to pull off any structural heists. You can't run before you can walk.

Let's have a conversation

In the theatrical or movie world it is known as the fourth wall – the invisible barrier between actors and their audience. Breaking it is considered a risk in case it shatters the pretence.

For years newspapers adopted the same stance. The pretence was that journalists were all-knowing, neutral superbeings, pronouncing to readers what they thought they needed to know.

Digital news has bashed the fourth wall down. First, there were reader comments and feedback. Then social media cleared away the few remaining bricks, leaving news storytellers and their readers in one giant, noisy open space.

Not only has it generated alternative story structures, but it has also spawned a conversational style of writing which defies many journalistic conventions.

This looser approach might seem to have lifted some of the constraints from the news writer. It is a precarious style to perfect – you need to have the discipline and authority born of **sound reporting skills** but use language which is more open and inclusive.

Remember, too, it's still an **exercise in storytelling**. You can even build a pyramid. Observe our rules for party guests – for example, you can throw in wry observations but if you start pontificating, readers will find you a pompous bore.

Pick the subject wisely. The conversational style is best suited to lighter, weird or celebrity stories. Ideally, it will be a slice of real life or a talking point, such as #TheDress, which was little more than a prolonged debate about the colours in a striped dress.

Imagine telling a story as if you were gossiping with friends or relating an anecdote at a party. **Precision, clarity and flow remain paramount**, so don't waffle or go off on a tangent.

Your **audience is likely to be younger** than a print or general online audience. You can use colloquialisms, social media speak, slang, profanity even. Fractional sentences and conversational additions, such as *well*, *really* and *actually* can add emphasis you wouldn't use in formal copy.

Don't overdo it, however, as you put clarity at risk for coolness. Worse still, you will sound like you're, yeah, about 12, literally.

Frat boy humour is appreciated by few others than frat boys. Crudity and profanity have long since ceased to shock or offend, show a lack of imagination on the part of the writer and quickly become tiresome.

There is a **knowingness** about the best conversational writing. Find phrases that are the equivalent of a raised eyebrow or a wink. Make it feel as if you and the reader are on the same wavelength, co-conspirators in a whispered exchange that can be read by millions.

> *The singer looked as though she turned up for a fancy dress party when she stepped out in a glittering emerald two-piece suit, which she teamed with monochrome platforms. It's quite possible she had a row with her hairdresser too before setting off for the Brits too.*
>
> *Mirror Online, February 2016*

It's not just about reporting that singer Jess Glynne wore a green suit and had frizzy hair – the picture makes this obvious. However, the knack is to say out loud only what the reader is thinking.

While you are trying to sound conversational, **good English still counts**. Give the rules of grammar a thorough pasting but only if the meaning remains crystal clear. Usually, though, you will find the two are rarely compatible.

When you've finished, re-read your story closely. A conversational style **does not mean writing as we speak**. Brevity remains a virtue, so knock out waffly phrases and jargon and rewrite any overlong and clumsy sentences:

> *During the broadcast, several viewers spotted the former 'Strictly Come Dancing' contestant – who also gave a solo performance during the concert – seemingly giggling in the crowd at the Royal Albert Hall, as she sang along to one of the night's hymns, while glancing at Rod Stewart, who she was standing next to.*
>
> *Huffington Post, November 2015*

Look at each sentence and ask yourself the fundamental question: **Does it make sense?** It's a common fault to write something which is sort of comprehensible . . .

> *Cue the screams from Spanish fans who had turned out to see the star turning to horror as J-Law's huge team of burly security rushed to save her fall (and blushes).*
>
> *Huffington Post, November 2015*

. . . but, when you examine it closely, isn't.

Spelling and typing mistakes will make readers groan.

> *He was referencing a Guardian interview with Ian McKellan, where the actor says making a reference to there not being an openly gay Best Actor.*
>
> *BuzzFeed, March 2016*
>
> *Within seconds the cyst pops and gruesome yellow puss comes pouring out.*
>
> *Mirror Online, Feb 2016*
>
> *For spendthrift travellers getting priority boarding can come with a hefty price tag, but it buys you the piece of mind that you will be on first.*
>
> *indy100, September 2017*

No one likes a boring party guest who waffles on or labours through a long-winded joke, so keep it **succinct and well focused**. Get to the point, then walk away, offering the reader an exit strategy, especially the chance to share, like or comment.

Cheerful, chatty material rarely goes hand in hand with extensive research; it is far more likely to be a rehash of material gleaned from social media, other news outlets or news wires. Be open and honest about this: **link to your sources and attribute appropriately**.

> Be careful if you are **poking fun at a public figure**. Don't go in with a sledgehammer; use a scalpel. Allow subjects to hoist themselves on their own petard and let the social media wags and other commentators bring them down. You need only to tee it up and add a witty pay-off. Remember, too, that a relaxed approach does not remove any legal dangers and that you still need balance and to offer the subject a right of reply.
>
> *Style*point

Hard news requires an all-guns blazing intro. In conversation, that will probably feel like coming on too strong but you must **make a good first impression**.

Your intro has to be eye-catching and, unlike this, easily understood:

> *It was no surprise not everyone was too happy when Facebook brought out the 'Reactions' option after many users begged for a dislike button.*
>
> *Metro.co.uk, March 2016*

Instead, imagine you are trying to chat with someone at a party. It'd be a bit odd to open with a hard news-style dramatic pronouncement – better to try a conversational gambit, setting up the moment when you might say, *Well* . . . :

> *As anyone who has ever tried to write a large body of words will know, writer's block is a very real thing.*
>
> *Well now an app has been created which aims to solve this by quite literally terrifying you into writing, non-stop.*
>
> *Huffington Post, March 2016*

End with a **good pay-off** – tactics might include closing the loop with a reference to the opening paragraphs, a wry observation or a let's-see-what-happens-next line.

The *Huffington Post* app story, highlighted earlier, rounds off nicely with an exit strategy to boot:

> *The app is completely free and if you're brave enough you can try it out here. Good luck!*

A story must have a tight, solid structure – if it lacks discipline and meanders, it will be dull and difficult to follow

Perfect the pyramid – it's your default method because it is natural and versatile

Explore innovative approaches – think before you write, especially online, if there is a different way of tackling a story

But remember the foundations – our ABBC remains critical; however, you decide to structure of your story

*Key*points

6

THE FIRST GOLDEN RULE

Accuracy is all

Haven't we already covered this? Yes, but accuracy is so important, we need to say it twice.

You must not get things wrong.

To repeat: You must not get things wrong. Never, never, ever. Period.

Accuracy in news writing is **rarely about the big things**. If you report an aircraft has crashed, there will be witness reports, photographs and video evidence to show you it has crashed. It's difficult to dispute.

Plenty try but it's also hard for a reader to sustain an objection over the tone or angle of a story. That is, after all, you exercising your judgment as a storyteller.

In July 2016, Conservative leadership candidate Andrea Leadsom accused *The Times* of gutter journalism for publishing her remarks about having children. Her complaint was a wail of despair over the negative reaction she had received. When *The Times* made the transcript of the interview available, there was little she could do but back off and apologise – within days she had withdrawn from the contest. If *The Times* had got Mrs Leadsom's age wrong and misspelt the names of her children, that might have cast a doubt on the veracity of the piece. Fortunately, it didn't.

*For*example

Accuracy is about the details, the tangible things which readers get most het up about. And rightly so. If the little things are wrong, what about the bigger ones?

Yes, we can see the aircraft crashed but you spelt the name of the airline wrong when it was written along the side of plane, the number of injured was incorrect and the airport where it happened is not *near the capital*, it's 90 miles away.

Why it goes wrong

Everyone makes mistakes. Mea culpa. Over the years, I've made countless errors. I have excuses for each and every one. Not one of them is acceptable.

> *The Labour leader said he had taken soundings from lawyers and he expected to be on the ballot paper automatically after Anna Eagle mounted a challenge for the top job.*
>
> *July 2016 (it's Angela, you idiot)*

Never defend the indefensible. It's wrong. It's your fault. The only proper response is to admit you are wrong, apologise, don't offer excuses and learn to be more careful. Don't say this:

- I assumed . . .
- He (pointing at colleague) said it was right
- It was on Twitter
- I heard it on the TV
- I checked it on this great website, www.spoofsrus.com
- Hey, I'm an English graduate, not an expert in astrophysics
- It was only three pars and didn't seem that important
- It was in the press release
- It wasn't in the press release
- It wasn't exactly clear in the press release and I didn't really understand it
- It was spelt like that in the photographer's caption

The real reasons are:

- You didn't ask
- You didn't ask enough questions
- You didn't ask enough people
- You didn't become an expert on your story
- You didn't use a dictionary, cuttings library or style guide
- You relied on the internet and social media
- You relied on your spellchecker

- You trusted what was published elsewhere
- You don't love words enough
- You rushed it
- You didn't read it through

The consequences

Errors come at a price. It is never worth paying.

A mistake can cost lots of **cash**. It can lead to a legal dispute, which, even if it doesn't end up in court or before a regulator, tends to make lawyers rich and the rest of us poor.

A complaint takes **time and effort** to resolve. At best, it might require a smoothing-over process with sources who may never get back on board but should that fail, it could mean an embarrassing **correction or apology** being run.

Perhaps worse is the damage done to **credibility**. Readers are astute and they will lose faith in error-strewn publications. They will be quick to point out mistakes, opening writers to ridicule in the comments section or letters page. It always ends with your publication looking stupid.

Errors are **damaging to you**. If you are seen as sloppy, your work will always be challenged and you won't be trusted with the most interesting stories. Make repeated errors and you will find yourself out of a job.

News is a team game and mistakes **bring down morale**. You are all trying to produce quality content, often with limited resources, against the pressure of deadlines. Don't let the side down.

How to avoid errors

You can never make enough checks or speak to enough people. Try to clear up any doubts and plug any gaps. It may mean more than a quick social media flick or an internet search. Some information needs verifying with a phone call or even a visit. It may be fruitless but not trying is a bigger failure.

Use all the **tools at your disposal** – dictionaries, cuttings libraries, web searches and so on. However, the most important is your **common sense**. If something is nagging at you, telling you it feels wrong, it probably is. Observe the rules that the easiest information to obtain is usually of the least value and that if something is too good to be true, it probably is.

Use the **experience of those around you**. They should be willing to help you as, ultimately, it makes it easier for everyone if you get it right first time.

Don't rush. Deadlines and the pressure to churn out stories can be overwhelming but it is better to be thorough and reliable than speedy yet sloppy.

If you can't fill an information gap, **never guess.** Even an educated one is still a guess and, in news, two and two doesn't always make four. If in doubt, leave it out.

There will be occasions when you cannot find the information you need and a burning question remains unanswered. Here, **honesty is a good policy.** The reader will spot the same holes in your story, so admit there is a gap by using phrases such as *it is not known what happened to* or *it was not clear.*

Accuracy rests on the other three pillars of our **ABBC.** Be brave, bold and clear in what you are saying and you will, at a stroke, sidestep most of the traps you can fall into. In news, **ambiguity is an inaccuracy.**

For instance, this sentence:

> *The pilot of the plane captured the video of Storm Eileen as it crossed the Indian Ocean at 300km an hour*

. . . could mean the storm or the plane was moving at 300km an hour

Finally, **polish your storytelling and writing techniques**. If your story is badly constructed and ill-focused, your sentences mangled and fail to flow, you will leave questions unanswered and your work will be open to misinterpretation. You also risk having errors edited in by colleagues.

The importance of attribution

Attribute anything which is a claim or an opinion.

Apply a simple test – can this information be reasonably disputed? If so, then you need to make it clear that the comment belongs to a speaker in your story.

Be particularly rigorous in court reporting, where it is essential to make it clear that unproven allegations are just that and to attribute them to those speaking in court.

However, as we shall see in *Take ownership* in Chapter 7, there is a balance to be struck. Attribution can impede storytelling.

The right of reply

This is a **fundamental principle** of good journalism. You cannot write a story, no matter how convincing, compelling and damning, without exploring every side to it. It presumes guilt. It's unfair. It's lazy and sloppy.

It might mean the odd uncomfortable conversation, it might mean throwing accusations at people, it might mean confrontation, but you have to do it.

It can be frustrating when you are asking for a response and you cannot get one, or the response is slow in coming.

It may feel like going through the motions or paying lip service to the notion of impartiality but it's worth listening to the response you are given. Sometimes the reply casts a story in a new light or undermines it altogether.

Obey the law

Our stories must be legally sound. The implications of publishing material which is offensive, dishonest, intrusive or damaging to society are enormous.

The financial penalties and lawyers' fees are enough to bring down a business. Just ask the publishers of gossip website Gawker.

Media law is a **complex and fascinating subject**. It is far from clear-cut; the margins are frequently fine and much disputed.

The landscape is ever-changing, leaving that which may have been fine to publish a few years ago no longer safe from legal action.

The internet, notoriously difficult to police, is outrunning laws and protections designed in the days of the printed word.

This book cannot cover the myriad legal intricacies which govern a news writer's life. There are excellent standard texts on the subject which any serious news writer must study. The best guides, rather than demonstrating the limits and restrictions we operate under, will show writers the surprising amount of freedom they have.

Defamation

Libel laws, most recently reformed in the UK in 2013, are there to protect those we write about from damage to their reputations – and their bank balances – from false statements published about them. Libel laws strive to balance that need with our right to freedom of speech.

The range of legal protections is reassuringly broad, not least the defence of **honest opinion**, which gives us the right to express our honestly held thoughts with a degree of impunity. We are also granted rights – known in law as **privilege** – to write about what is said in parliament, courts and public meetings.

However, the best defence against defamation is simple – make sure your story is **accurate**. It must be good reportage and cast-iron. Make as many checks as possible and keep complete notes and other records for future reference.

Don't jump to conclusions. Just because a politician has been seen receiving a brown envelope in an underground car park doesn't necessarily mean he is accepting a bribe.

Also, there is **no defence** if you report a defamatory statement someone else is making. The statement is still false and you are repeating it by republishing it. You can't point the finger and plead 'don't shoot the messenger' – it won't save you.

Contempt of court

News writers covering crime and the courts are haunted by the risk of contempt. Too many publications have pushed too far and found themselves in deep trouble.

Although it is a complex area, where accepted practice sometimes seems more important than the letter of the law, it is founded on a simple, utterly fair and very British principle – that defendants are **innocent until proven guilty**.

Don't publish anything that **implies someone is guilty** before a case goes to trial. Even if the police are loudly insisting they've got their man (or woman), it is not prudent to publish anything which can influence a jury.

Judges have always been very itchy about this and recent attorneys-general seem worryingly **eager to prosecute**.

Copyright

This is an area of increasing concern for news writers in the digital age, where the law is struggling to keep pace with technological changes.

The principle of copyright is simple – it aims to **protect writers**, photographers, artists and others from those who would steal their work and pass it off as their own.

Online it is easy to **cut and paste material**, especially pictures, from websites and social media and use it in your own publication. You mustn't do it.

Wherever it is published, the copyright rests with the person who took the picture or video, created the graphic or wrote the words.

The cast-iron defence against any copyright claim – and a wince-inducing bill – is to **ask permission** before using someone else's work. An even better one is to **generate your own material** and use that instead.

Data protection

Any information which is collected on a computer is data which comes under legislation designed to protect people's rights to privacy.

For news writers it is starting to have considerable implications.

First, it means you have to take care how you handle the **personal information** you collect on people. It means not passing it to others, storing it securely and not hanging on to it too long.

Second, you **should not obtain data on people by illicit means**, such as hacking into a computer system or blagging to get officials to reveal it.

Third, it is, often wrongly, thrown around by those in authority as a reason not to release information. To defeat the '**computer says no**' jobsworths, you need to understand the frequent flaws in their arguments.

Privacy

The rich and famous, in particular, are prepared to use legal means, such as injunctions, to protect their privacy, even though social media and internet gossip often make a mockery of their efforts.

At its heart lies the common sense principle that people, whether famous or not, have a **reasonable expectation of privacy**.

The law, in exceptional circumstances where the public interest overrides the right to a private life, will allow us to breach that ethic but the underlying message is clear: Respect their space.

Editor's code

The editor's code – most publishers subscribe to the one used by **IPSO** – is a sensible set of guidelines about how to conduct yourself as a journalist.

It's neither long nor complicated and most of it is plain **common sense**, promoting openness, fairness and sensitivity in your dealings with others. Don't steal information or harass people, respect privacy and don't intrude on grief – they all speak for themselves.

The first item in the code covers **accuracy**. Again, if you get it right and write with clarity, there is little chance you will be subject to a complaint.

Children

Children are a special case – they are, in most circumstances, **off limits** for journalists.

You cannot force children into the public eye, even those who may have committed serious crimes. The law grants them protection in every walk of life and media attention is no different. In court reporting, for example, there are blanket rights to anonymity.

At other times, your only protection if you want to interview or feature a child is to **get express permission** from a parent.

The public interest

This phrase is often bandied around by journalists looking for a defence for their less commendable actions and it is even **enshrined in some laws**. But don't take it literally.

The public interest is **not anything the public is interested in** – it has to be more worthy than that. Hence, the public may be interested in a story about a celebrity's new baby but it does not mean you have any legal cover if you are challenged over privacy or data protection breaches.

Similarly, its cousin – **in the public domain** – is not always a guarantee of legal safety. Just because people are gossiping about it, especially on social media, doesn't mean the information is safe.

Freedom of information

Britain has long had **an aversion to openness** – in contrast to other countries where rights were enshrined in law, information was passed out as favours to those who asked nicely.

The arrival of the **Freedom of Information Act** in 2000 gave everyone rights to obtain information from most public organisations. It's simple to make a request, it's normally free of charge and a response is required within a reasonable time.

There are caveats, restrictions and hooks officials can wriggle off and you won't get personal details. But if an organisation refuses to budge, there is even a **right of appeal**.

However, before rushing to exercise your legal rights and filling in the paper-work, there is still a lot to be said for just **asking nicely first**.

Don't be afraid

The law sounds like an intimidating enemy and it is possible to fall foul of it through an innocent mistake or the dishonesty of others.

But if you behave with decency towards others, are fair and honest in your judgments and are accurate in your storytelling, it is highly unlikely you will run into difficulties. Most disputes will still be settled with diplomacy and a friendly phone call.

Indeed, the law is your friend. It is there to protect you – your right to access news, your right to free speech and your right to challenge authority. Go use it.

Verification

With so much news content being culled from social media, accuracy is being replaced – or at least complemented – by a new watchword: **verification**.

Given the obvious pitfalls, it is surprising how often even well-resourced publishers whose reputations are built on their dependability have apparently failed to make even the most basic checks on dubious material.

Sometimes it is mischief-making:

> *'Phuc Dat Bich': man says he created name hoax to fool media and Facebook.*
> *The Guardian, November 2016*

At other times it is clever viral marketing. This was swallowed by plenty of reputable news publishers:

> *Scorned husband gives ex half of everything he owns – literally.*
> *Mashable, June 2015*

Sometimes it is an old story resurfacing, either by accident or design . . .

> *Weather girl boobs story provides cheap online hits for tabloids FIVE YEARS after the event.*
> *Press Gazette, March 2016*

... or through clumsiness, such as ten-year-old photos of a football homecoming parade being widely used to illustrate a story about Labour leader Jeremy Corbyn's rally:

> *There's something very wrong with these photos of Jeremy Corbyn's rally*
>
> *indy100. August 2016*

Under-pressure journalists in newsrooms around the world act like magpies, picking up this kind of material and recirculating it.

They can attempt to cover themselves by sprinkling the story with phrases such as *reportedly* or *the video appears to show.*

But these are soon lost in the frenzy of clicks and shares that follow, so that fakes, hoaxes and misdirection travel around the world, quickly moving from dubious to authoritative.

> In wartime it can be difficult to tell the propaganda from the fakes. The story of a boy hero saving a little girl in the Syrian conflict was given front page coverage in the New York Post. The *Huffington Post* wrote of the *shaky amateur video* and said *citizen journalists have pinpointed that the video was taken in the city of Yabroud near the Syrian-Lebanese border around March 2014.* Then the hoax was revealed:
>
> > *Norwegian filmmakers apologized on Tuesday for planting fake video of the war in Syria on YouTube last week.*
> >
> > *New York Times, November 2014*
>
> ### *For*example

By far your best defences are **common sense** and **scepticism**. If something doesn't look right, it probably isn't. If it looks too good to be true, it probably is.

If your suspicions are raised about any piece of content, it's a fundamental of journalism to **check it**.

The best method is to **speak to the originator**. A few intelligent – if tactful – questions will soon show if the material has been faked, recycled or erroneous. As soon as you start to drill down into detail, the answers will become vaguer and vaguer and the warning signs should light up.

Build your **digital contacts** with as much diligence as you do your real-world ones. This will ensure you have both trustworthy sources of information in the first place and, when something needs checking, experts on hand to verify it.

If you don't have a network established in the field of expertise or in the part of the world you need, then **throw it out to the crowd** – social media followers, readers and others – and ask them before you publish. It's surprising how often readers can turn into your best friends this way.

Verification involves **authenticating the source** as much as the information. The picture or video is staring you in the face but who has posted it and their motives for doing so may be far less certain.

You can carry out plenty of checks from the comfort of your desk. A **fake or unreliable Twitter or Facebook account** can be easy to spot – has it just been set up, does it have a proper profile pic, does it have genuine followers, is it verified with a blue tick and so on.

This should have been an easy spot:

> *Independent and Huffington Post fall for 'parody' Le Pen tweet praising Theresa May speech.*
>
> Press Gazette, October 2016

With so much of our lives lived online today, you can also **cross-check** an account against other social networks and other digital fingerprints, such as domain ownership checks. **Geolocation checks** can reveal whether your source is even in the same country as the event he or she claims to have witnessed.

For pictures and videos, there are countless tools for verification. Think a picture is old or recycled? Then run it through a free facility such as TinEye, or perform a reverse image check on Google Images to see whether it has been used before and where or when.

Photo files contain a digital fingerprint called **EXIF** data which may even reveal when, where and by whom it was taken.

The image or video may well contain **valuable clues** to the authenticity of material.

Look closely. Study the clothing worn, the haircuts, the badges on police uniforms and so on. Does anything look out of place?

Distinctive buildings, signs on street corners or over shops, billboards and registration plates on cars all could be tell-tale clues to authenticity. Use landmarks to check the location against images on mapping sites.

If it's said to be a picture taken at midday but shows long shadows, then there is something fishy. If it's sunny in the picture, you can check the date on weather-watching sites to see what the conditions were like in the area.

Online content is designed to be shared readily. The constant recycling from one account or platform to another can make it hard to trace the origin of material. It might just be that you need to settle in and go through the laborious process of clicking back through the trail, a trail which may have no beginning and may just send you into a frustrating dead end. It is the digital equivalent of knocking on every door in the street while hoping the person you really need isn't away for the weekend.

Verification can have the feel of **anti-journalism** – hunting for clues which knock down a story you desperately want to tell, rather than building up the pool of information so you can tell it properly. It starts from the disappointing standpoint that nothing and no one is to be trusted – even the well intentioned with an important message to spread. And it's not foolproof; you will never prove beyond all reasonable doubt the authenticity of the material you use.

But credibility is at stake. It might slow you down when you are itching to publish and have a great angle no one else is following. In this fevered environment, however, those who hesitate may not be lost – they may just have spared themselves from looking like complete fools.

Fake news

By the end of 2016, the issue of so-called fake news was on everyone's lips, not least those of then US president-elect Donald Trump.

Made-up stories are hardly new online – or, indeed, before the internet – but they have fresh impetus because they are readily spread through social media.

For Trump and others it became a handy epithet with which to beat the media. Anything which a politician or other public figure dislikes can be labelled as fake.

If you are following this chapter's guidance on **accuracy and verification**, there is no reason why your stories will ever run into this problem.

A bigger danger lies in falling for one of the fake stories and recycling it or putting it in your social media feed. There are countless examples of established news organisations biting on fake news because they **failed to make enough checks** in their haste to catch the wave.

Common sense is your best defence against fakery. Ask if the story is too good to be true. Does it look professional, well written and with a picture that you can verify? Is it from a reputable site? If not, an unusual web address or country of origin are giveaways. Make domain checks to see how long the site has been running, who set it up and where it was set up. Check the rest of the content of the site to see how believable it is. Finally, see if anyone else has recycled the story.

Fake news is designed to go viral to generate advertising income – so it is far more likely to be on **topics which pick up on readers' interests or fears** – divisive politicians, global celebrities such as Justin Bieber or Beyonce, an improbable but unstoppable health scare, the end of the world, the rise of Islamic State and so on. When you see such outrageous-but-just-about-believable material trending, the alarm bells should be ringing.

Always read it through

You think your finished story is ready for publication.

Resist the temptation to send it on its way. Read it through. Not just once but three times.

The first read

Read it for sense: You are looking for the big issues, such as angle, structure, flow. If you have to stop to re-read anything to understand it, then it is flawed.

Is all the information there? Have you left any questions unanswered? Check for the six Ws: who, what, when, where, how and why. Check for any obvious gaps, such as what was the sentence of the court? Which award was won? How many goals were scored?

Does it ring legal alarm bells? Is there anything that gives pause for thought? Is there a claim in the intro which is not substantiated within the story? Is it sufficiently fair and balanced? If so, it is worth taking advice.

Headline: Does the headline accurately reflect the story? Usually the headline goes too far, so amend if it is not justified by the story. On the other hand, a weak headline undersells a story, so beef it up.

System basics: Make sure your story is complete by ticking all the boxes in your CMS. Have you moved it to the right folder? Have you written clear, meaningful captions? A summary? Are the pictures, graphics, video and social media content embedded properly? Have you put in as many tags and hyperlinks as possible?

The second read

Are the details present, correct and consistent? Are all the people properly identified with occupations, ages, addresses, titles? Are they spelt correctly on every use? Are all proper nouns, such as the names of companies, organisations and products, spelt correctly?

Is it in house style? You have a style chosen to fit your audience, so make sure you're sticking to it. If you don't, someone else will have to correct it.

Does it add up? Check the maths to make sure that the sums make sense. Check conversions, totals, percentages, proportions.

Check spelling and grammar: Every CMS comes with an in-built spellchecker to flag up dubious words, so there is no excuse for letting mistakes through. Use the agreed office dictionary if you are still unsure. Get on top of grammar so you learn to spot any errors. If you know you have a weak spot in these areas, bone up so silly errors don't let your story down.

The final read

This is especially important if you have gone for a major rewrite in which you chop paragraphs around. Typos often creep in at this stage rather than in the first draft.

Preferably, make this final read after taking a few minutes away from your screen so you come back and look at it through fresh eyes. Try to read it as the reader will see it, either in a web page preview mode or as a printed page proof.

Accuracy is god – worship it

Learn from mistakes – don't defend them

All errors are costly – but **legal ones can be fatal**

Using social media means you have to **verify the source, as well as the material**

Check, check, check – and **read through, read through, read through**

*Key*points

7

THE OTHER GOLDEN RULES

Know your
audience

It's time to get intimate with your readers. They are, after all, your raison d'être.

The stories that you choose to cover, how you approach that story, the details you include and those you leave out should all be based on judgments about who is going to be reading them.

It is the nature of news that not all stories appeal to all people equally. As a result, publications look for a niche in which they develop an audience.

You will quickly need to grasp an idea of your typical reader so you can fashion stories that fit that niche.

How readers differ . . . by platform

Online news readers are traditionally regarded as information-hunting, time-starved, disloyal beasts who come to you because they have been steered your way, usually by a search engine or social media.

They want stories in a hurry. They are not relaxed; they're reading on awkward, uncomfortable screens, so they probably don't want lengthy pieces. You can't delay, you need to deliver hard news clearly and punchily in short, crisp sentences, straight to the heart of the drama, without fuss or nuance.

Words may not be enough. Online news readers want enriched content with pictures, videos, graphics, audio, social media streams and all the bells and whistles that online publishing offers.

And it all needs to be up there as quickly as possible, no matter what the time of day or night.

With such a skittish audience, it is imperative that your stories are information rich, perfectly structured and, if you want to keep them on your site, a compelling read.

Print readers, on the other hand, tend to be older and creatures of habit who probably pick up the same publication through familiarity and loyalty.

Rather than hunting aggressively for information, they are seen as passive and receptive. They may have more time and will sit down to read and absorb.

As a result, they may expect a more polished and considered product. They will be less tolerant of mistakes; even small slips of grammar can irritate.

Eye-tracking tests suggest they read more closely than online skimmers do but they do not linger as long on a story. If many are going to turn the page or go to another story on a page within a few paragraphs, it makes a brilliantly delivered intro and expansion essential.

. . . by ideology

Don't let anyone tell you that the news business is about fair, unbiased reporting, shedding light on the world's injustices for the greater good of mankind.

All news publications are skewed towards the ideologies of their readers, who, for better or worse, want to see their world view reflected back at them. Newspapers have long been echo chambers of their readers' prejudices; in the increasingly fragmented world of digital news, those echoes are deafening.

Take a controversial issue such as immigration. This data is extrapolated from an analysis in the *Daily Telegraph* in November 2014:

> In 2014, 4.9million (92.6%) working age benefit claimants were British while 131,000 (2.5%) were EU nationals. The number of recipients from outside the UK – but not from the EU – was 264,000 (5%).
>
> Likewise, in 2013, 3.9million (84.8%) families receiving working tax credits were British, 302,000 (6.4%) were EU citizens and 413,000 (8.8%) were from outside the UK.

How – and, indeed, whether – you report this data depends entirely on the ideology of your readers. They might feel a diverse society is a good thing; maybe they are supporters of the EU; perhaps they protest that Britain is overrun with migrants or maybe they are immigrants themselves. Hence, you may write:

> *A tiny proportion of European immigrants are claiming benefits, debunking claims that they are a drain on the British taxpayer, new figures show.*

Or maybe:

> *Hundreds of thousands of immigrants to Britain are claiming millions of pounds in benefits and tax credits every year, new figures show.*

They are both accurate. Let your audience take your pick.

. . . by geography

Where your readers live is a critical factor in story choice and writing.

If you are working for a British national news publication, then your audience is, unsurprisingly, going to be mostly British. Those who are not will expect a British flavour to the stories.

They are going to be concerned primarily with events closest to home – things happening in Britain or involving British people.

Of course, they are interested in world affairs. But the machinations of Australian politics or the struggles of mine workers in the Democratic Republic of Congo are more likely to attract attention if you can connect them to something closer to their lives.

> *It looks like British-born opposition leader Tony Abbott has overtaken PM Kevin Rudd in the polls with the election just two days away.*
> *ITV News, September 2013*
>
> *Picks, pans and bare hands: How miners in the heart of Africa toil in terrible conditions to extract the rare minerals that power your iPhone.*
> *MailOnline, October 2015*

Nonetheless, the world has shrunk. Londoners may have visited New York more often than they have been to Manchester. Many holidaymakers have spent more time on the Costa del Sol than they have in Brighton or Blackpool. Many have deep affection for the far-flung destinations across the world they have been to.

Furthermore, online publishing has knocked down national borders. Readers could come to a website from anywhere in the world. MailOnline, the world's most popular news website, is said to draw 70 per cent of its audience from overseas.

In that context, the parochial feel of the *One Briton among thousands killed in earthquake abroad* approach to a story ought to have had its day.

For national publications, the location of a story is rarely important enough for an intro or even the expansion. But that thinking is skewed online by search engine optimisation, where the setting is likely to be a key search term. Hence, you may need to use it within the first paragraph or two and probably in the headline and URL.

For writers working on regional newspapers or hyperlocal websites, geography is paramount.

These publications have a patch they cover, be it a county, city or a single town. By definition, they cover events happening on their doorstep or those involving people who live or work within that area.

Firm boundaries need to be imposed. There is no point in calling yourself the Townsville Express, selling most of your papers in Townsville, if you include material from Nextdoorsville, 30 miles up the road.

Local readers expect in-depth knowledge of the area, an appreciation of its history and a willingness to champion its industry, culture, community groups and sports clubs. They are less convinced by sensationalism, expecting implacably fair and honest coverage.

Your subject matter may seem parochial or low-key but it does not mean your storytelling standards should slip.

When writing you need to identify quickly the local connection to a story. If you are writing for the Townsville Express, you will need to make it within the first few pars. It doesn't need to be in the intro but it has to feel to your readers as if it is close to home. Avoid starting an intro with the hackneyed and bland *A Townsville man/woman*.

Undoubtedly, our baby fire rescue story would be a major event for the Burbton Herald and its website. In our story, we would want to identify the location quickly, ideally in the second or third par:

> *Her father, Joseph, who smashed the window to allow his wife, Mary, to leap clear before throwing his baby into the crowd, was trapped inside the property in Arcadia Avenue, Burbton.*

. . . by age and sex

To define an audience by their age and sex makes for some wild generalisations and seems slightly out of step with a modern world.

But publishers still see opportunity in targeting groups along traditional lines. As a storyteller, you need to be in tune with these expectations.

Older readers will expect news with more gravitas, covering conventional topics relevant to middle age and beyond in a more measured, formal and knowledgeable tone. They will expect your use of language to reflect that – clear, well-written sentences, high-brow only where necessary but largely free of slang and gimmickry. Wit and wisdom win out over crash-bang fart jokes.

Younger readers – likely to gravitate online – are probably looking for accessible news on lighter topics veering from information towards entertainment. They may not mind a looser style, less formal language and innovative approaches to storytelling. They are likely to be more tech savvy, fashion and lifestyle conscious, liberal leaning and more willing to respond and interact.

The idea that men are interested in football, beer and cars, while women cook, clean and knit should be dead and buried. But many publications are still orientated towards one sex or another. Make sure your storytelling fits the perspective of your intended readers.

. . . by interests

If there is a facet of life people are interested in there will be a publication – big or small, online or in print – to cover it.

Audiences coalesce around political and social interests, professions, corporate connections, culture, hobbies, sports and pastimes and all areas in between.

These audiences can run from a few dozen to millions. They cut across other boundaries, such as age and sex, and some readers may be members of several.

Furthermore, the audiences can be fractured, tribal even. Some caged bird keepers love canaries; others prefer budgies; while for another group nothing but a huge, talkative parrot will do. You can't devise a publication to please them all.

To write news in a specialist area, much like writing for a local audience, you will require immense knowledge of a subject. Your tone must be one of the expert among the experts – you won't be able to bluff.

At the same time, however, you need to be able to step back and be aware of the damage you can do to your storytelling by letting too much knowledge get in the way. Always view your subject, its history and its characters – be it ballroom dancing, student life or mobile phone technology – as the setting to a story, not the story itself.

How to write for different audiences

You are covering the launch of a new range of Slashburner electric guitars, the first models from the renowned instrument-maker Graystock for more than 15 years.

Their arrival has been eagerly awaited by guitar fans, many who hold the brand in deep affection. It also marks a renaissance for Graystock, once one of the best-known names in guitar-making but rescued from bankruptcy after being driven to the brink of ruin by competition from cheap Chinese imports.

The announcement is a great boost for the 40 or so craftsmen and other workers at their small factory on the outskirts of Townsville.

How you would write this story is all about audience.

It might pique the interest of a general, national news or business publication. Most of its readers will not be guitarists, so the interest has to be driven by a broader approach, playing on a forgotten star reborn with a bit of showbiz thrown in.

> *Revived guitar maker Graystock, whose instruments were played by legendary rockers Hank Humbucker and Buddy Pick, is set to win over a new generation of music fans.*

It is certainly a major news story for the Townsville Express. Its audience is Townsville residents, thrilled at their town's association with such a renowned brand, coupled with excitement at its revival and the economic opportunities it brings.

> *Guitar maker Graystock, whose instruments put Townsville on the world music map, is set for a revival with the launch of its first new range in 15 years.*
> *The company's long-awaited Slashburner guitars, hand-crafted in its workshop on the Fret Street industrial estate, will secure the future of its 40 staff.*

For the readers of rockingitup.com, the country's leading rock music magazine, the focus will be on the contribution of Graystock guitars to the genre.

> *The ba-boom is back. Graystock, whose bass-rich, full-bodied sound shaped some of the finest rock anthems of the 1990s, is back to take centre stage with its first new guitars in a generation.*

Guitars4all.com, a site for all levels and abilities of players, has been building up to the launch for some time and needs a suitably general, catch-all approach.

> *They're finally here. The much-anticipated Slashburner range of guitars from renowned maker Graystock was released this week to widespread acclaim.*

Over at guitgeek.com, where stories are aimed at younger, tech-minded guitar players with a love of the latest gear . . .

> *OMFG! The Slashburners from Graystock are finally here – and they're bursting with innovative features including revolutionary Uberres pick-ups and slide-drive tuning.*

And, of course, there is always the genteel allstrummers.com, where fans of acoustic guitars gather for their news updates.

> *Hidden in the hillside of hullabaloo over Graystock's Slashburners lies the real gem – a breathtaking acoustic version which takes the guitar maker's craft to new heights.*

One size does not fit all – and any storyteller who fails to keep his or her readers in mind risks having no readers at all.

Perfect reader

You have a vision of your typical reader but it doesn't mean all readers are equal. Some are fully engaged, most are surprisingly knowledgeable and others are more casual followers of news.

As you can't write a personal version of a story for each one, you have to standardise them.

So, **imagine they are all perfect**, avid followers of news, up to date with all stories on all subjects. They are intelligent, informed and able to infer. They recognise public figures and on a running story they are aware of the background.

Picturing this all-knowing reader gives you a **starting point** to frame your stories and give you the confidence to trust them to understand. It allows you to tell the story in the intro and expansion and leave the explanation for later.

Of course, there will be those who are not up to date but in those critical first five or so paragraphs you only need to give them enough information to make it comprehensible.

If you write for a perfect reader, you will avoid ponderous, safe, slow copy. You will be a better storyteller.

The importance of a style guide

Every publication should have a comprehensive style guide to help you establish the tone and approach.

It's not just to settle arguments over spelling and satisfy an editor's pet grammatical peeves. It will cover the language, tone and attitude you are trying to capture.

Even the basic style points say something about your publication. A preference for metric measures over imperial suggests a more modern, European outlook; strict use of honorifics conveys a formal and polite style over a functional and pugnacious one; free use of swear words or web abbreviations suggests a more liberal and youthful approach.

The best style guides are written for the readers – to connect with them by making sure you are talking their language. It's imperative you follow it.

Writing for agencies

If you work for a news agency – or as a go-it-alone freelance – you have a very different audience. You write for **other journalists**.

All major news outlets rely on agencies, taking feeds from the established ones, notably the Press Association for British news, plus Associated Press, Reuters and AFP for foreign coverage. They may also regularly take news stories from the many other regional and specialist agencies.

The emphasis when working for an agency in a news environment is to ensure **100 per cent accuracy**, get it **written quickly** and get it on to the wires and out to publishers as soon as possible.

Breaking stories rarely go out as a complete and finished piece. As soon as major news breaks, it will be published as a one-sentence snap, serving as an alert to newsdesks that a significant story is on its way.

This will be followed by a short first version or take. This will be followed by a succession of longer versions with new lines added as they arrive.

By the end of the process, there may be several takes – indeed, on the biggest stories, it could run to dozens of takes, each adding a few new paragraphs.

When the story has run its course, it may well be revisited and rewritten as a wrap or nightlead, pulling together the by now haphazard series of takes into a more coherent story, probably with an updated intro. As it may be several hours since the first break, the story will have moved on and may well focus on reaction or implications of an event, rather than the event itself.

It means your work will pass through the hands of newsdesks at other publishers and, as a minimum, will be tweaked to correspond to house style.

More likely, it will be heavily rewritten, perhaps with a completely different angle from the one you or your news editor chose, or combined with elements from other agencies and staff reporters to form a more complete version.

Publishers regard news agencies first and foremost as **suppliers of information** to be adapted to their needs. It is imperative that information is accurate and unambiguous.

The **implications are serious if you make any errors** which appear in the final published version. The publisher will point the finger at the agency; the agency editor will come to you for an explanation. It could be highly damaging to the agency's reputation and yours will take a pounding.

Clarity of writing is essential. If your words can be misunderstood or read several ways, then it is storing up problems for later. At best, it might require time-consuming check calls from recipients asking what exactly you mean. A separate clarification may have to be filed. At worst, an ambiguity could be misunderstood and the wrong interpretation will appear in publications whose editors don't have time to check.

Writing to length is also less of an issue. It may be better to **include too much detail rather than too little**. If it makes the copy a bit of a slog, then so be it. Your reader – other journalists – will be more prepared than a lay reader to plough through it as they cherry-pick the bits they need.

Better to be safe than sorry by filing an extra paragraph or three of explanation or background. Don't leave any questions unanswered, even if the questions seem of secondary importance. You must include the caveats, nuance and rebuttals – it's up to the publisher to decide what to do with them.

Although it's a competitive business, **sexing up a story to sell it is a curse** for newsdesks. Breathless prose, lurid tabloid-ese and exaggeration will probably serve to irritate rather than impress experienced news editors, who will see straight through it. Aim instead for a well-written, honest story with a bright intro, good pacing and a smooth flow.

With constraints of time and urgency on breaking news, presenting a beautifully crafted story in a perfect pyramid may have to be sacrificed. As long as the information it contains is complete, the polish will have to be added by the publisher. That **does not mean abandoning good habits** – there's still no excuse for bad sentence construction, poor punctuation and spelling mistakes.

For all the corners you might feel you need to cut in a time-pressed environment, there is still occasion for polished writing with skilful storytelling. Agencies pump out embargoed stories which are prepared well in advance with no significant time pressure. There is no excuse for clumsy construction with these.

It is also worth noting that more and more publishers, especially online, are **using agency words verbatim** or without significant editing.

This is another challenge for agency news writers. It demands not only that they produce their material at great speed but also that they make it of impeccable quality.

Nail the intro

One sentence, one chance. That's all.

Much like the opening sequence of a film or the opening bars of a song, the intro is the moment you have to hook the reader into the story. Blow it and all is lost.

By the time the reader reaches the intro, he or she is already intrigued by a headline or an eye-catching picture. Online, they have made the effort of clicking through from a social media or search engine link.

Yet it is extraordinary how often the storyteller's instinct then goes AWOL.

The reader is waiting. **Go for the kill**. Punch them between the eyes with the most extraordinary, jaw-dropping, dramatic, exciting, intriguing, relevant and up-to-date sentence possible. Pick the words you need to deliver this with the utmost precision.

So not like this:

> *Peru said Friday a Venezuelan man in Lima, who recently traveled through Colombia, had contracted the mosquito-borne virus Zika, in the Andean country's first confirmed case of the disease that is rapidly spreading across the Americas.*
>
> *Reuters, January 2016*

Or this:

> *The Electoral Commission has admitted that some EU nationals have been wrongly sent polling cards for this month's referendum – and in some cases postal votes – because of an issue with elections software used by a number of local authorities in England and Wales.*
>
> *BuzzFeed, June 2016*

Or this:

> *As Hertfordshire Local Enterprise Partnership waits for an announcement on government funds which could be used to revamp Stevenage railway station and begin the transformation of the town centre, Stevenage MP Stephen McPartland has claimed it does not have the backing of millions of pounds of private funds it has suggested.*
>
> *Stevenage Comet, December 2016*

Think **what impact you are trying to have**; is it to make the reader laugh, cry, feel teased, gasp, lust for more information?

Alternatively, consider how you will avoid baffling them, or worse still, making them shrug.

Then, give them everything that counts, **say it in the most colourful fashion** and don't waste a syllable.

Choosing the line

There are dozens of factors at play in picking the best line for an intro. Some, such as a gap in information, the extent of previous coverage or an editor's whim, may lie beyond the writer's control.

Otherwise, it is a matter of personal judgment. But, if you **think like a reader**, then the decision always becomes clearer. Start from the premise that what matters most to you as a person, not a journalist, will also be what matters to those you are writing for.

As we have already seen, **different audiences have different needs**. A local news site, a trade publication, a niche publisher or a national news organisation will take different approaches to the same story.

Also crucial is to **assess the stage a story is at**. In a sudden event, such as a plane crash, a crime or unexpected announcement, you will write as if it is the first time the reader has heard the news.

But many other stories are updates or follow-ups to previously covered events. Storytellers should **always strive for the now** – a fresh line that won't bore your readers by telling them what they already know. In an era of 24-hour TV and digital news, stories are becoming older faster than they ever have before.

If a story is being widely covered, always ask if you can **say something different**. Is there a detail, an intriguing sideline others may have overlooked which draws your focus? Online, amid all the noise and chatter competing for attention, that could be a critical point of difference which makes your story stand out from the crowd.

A complex story may involve many characters, plot twists and, if you land on it after years of developments, a lot of history and background. There may be several exceptional lines to choose from. You must be **bold in your choice** and have the confidence to stick with it.

What you choose as your line in an intro **sets the direction and tone**, becoming the focus through the expansion. Your intro is **a promise to the reader** that you have a story about this event or about this character. You must not break that promise and get distracted from it as you progress from your intro.

This intro gives the reader the wrong steer – it is not a story about Prof Cox, albeit he's a well-known figure. The intriguing figures are von Humboldt and the author who writes about him.

> *Professor Brian Cox has announced that a literary award described as "the Booker Prize of science writing" has gone to Andrea Wulf's biography of little-known scientist and explorer Alexander von Humboldt.*
>
> *PA, September 2016*

The basics of intro writing

Keep the intro to **one sentence**, preferably without clauses or complex syntax. Avoid long words, technical phrases and jargon.

Confine an intro to something you can say comfortably within one breath. For most of us that is a maximum of **25 words**. Once you have written it, a visual check is also a good idea – sometimes, it just looks too long.

> *A University of Exeter researcher based at its Penryn campus is campaigning to raise funds to help put out thousands of forest fires in Borneo, which she warns are causing a global ecological and social disaster and putting the future of orangutans, gibbons and other wildlife at risk.*
>
> *Falmouth Packet, November 2015 (48 words)*

Nonetheless, an intro **needs rhythm**, so do not make it so shorn of personality that it ends abruptly. Read it out loud to make sure that it trips off the tongue.

Keep it **active, not passive**. This suggests an event, with urgency and immediacy. Use the subject–verb–object style wherever possible. If you find yourself writing the word *by* in an intro, you have probably stumbled into the passive.

Avoid starting with **a passive clause**, which makes the reader wait for the new information. It's more effective to turn the sentence round.

> *At a news conference in Ft. Worth, Texas, on Friday, billed by Donald Trump as a "big announcement," New Jersey Gov. Chris Christie endorsed Trump for president, calling the businessman "the clear standout" among Republican candidates.*
>
> *BuzzFeed, February 2016*

Add a bit of flair

Be specific. The general approach rarely excites. For example, why say xx has criticised/slammed/attacked yy when you can say exactly what the criticism is. Here we should be told what Netanyahu said rather than that it was controversial:

> *Israeli Prime Minister Binyamin Netanyahu delivered a controversial speech directed against Palestinians living in Israel on a visit to the scene of a recent shooting in a Tel Aviv bar on Saturday.*
>
> *The New Arab, January 2016*

Similarly, here we should be told what the measures are, not that they are being introduced:

> *The council has revealed a number of new measures to try and tackle transport concerns for Bristol's new arena.*
>
> Bristol Post, April 2016

And here, the writer has used the jargon *challenging conditions* as a substitute for homes engulfed in flames, temperatures above 40C and fierce winds:

> *Firefighters in Australia have faced challenging conditions as they tackle more than 300 blazes near Melbourne.*
>
> Sky News, December 2015

Keep it simple to avoid **information overload**. Try to mention only one or two people or organisations. This is a test of patience.

> *The head of the referees' union, Prospect, said he does not know of any officials being asked to lie in their post-match reports to the Football Association, following former Premier League referee Mark Halsey's claims he had been put under pressure from PGMOL, the body in charge of Premier League refereeing, to falsely say he had not seen controversial incidents.*
>
> The Guardian, September 2016

By the same token, **only have one number** in an intro. Make that figure the largest or most extreme case, not a mundane average. Avoid percentages and round up or down to produce easy-to-comprehend mathematical concepts.

Leave out **extraneous details**. In an intro the reader does not usually need to know when, where, which or, indeed, why. This intro is wordy enough without adding a date at the end:

> *Theresa May has attacked the lack of black and minority ethnic officers and women in the police service, as North Yorkshire was named as one of the four forces with no black officers as at March 31.*
>
> Sheffield Star, October 2015

Leave in **tantalising details**. An intriguing titbit, such as the Star Wars mask here, creates an image for the reader and sets up the rest of the story:

> A sword-wielding attacker in a Star Wars mask killed two pupils and a teacher during an hour-long rampage in a school today.
>
> Yahoo News, October 2015

Choose an exciting first word

Some readers will switch off halfway through a sentence, not even halfway through a story, so you need an active, accessible, colourful word which conveys excitement.

Avoid starting intros with the following. They are abstract or ugly, so rewrite if you find yourself using them:

The government: Probably the most boring two words in the entire English language and guaranteed to get most readers yawning. Likewise, avoid *The Department of* . . . , *The Secretary of State for* . . . , *The Chartered Institute of* . . . and all such impersonal phrases

Europe/European/EU: Notwithstanding interest over the Brexit vote, most things to do with European government come under the distant, worthy but dull category

Members of the public: Patronising and distant. Try *people* or a rewrite

A man/A woman: Too general to create an image in the reader's mind and there is always a better way to describe someone. So *A woman was left to bleed to death in a hedge after having her throat cut yesterday* is improved by writing *A murder victim was left to bleed to death in a hedge after having her throat cut yesterday*

The: While it can be effective as a stylistic device, it is a passive word implying familiarity with a story. Use sparingly

Numbers: Looks odd when spelt out. *Thirty-three people were killed by a bomb blast in Baghdad yesterday* is better as *A bomb blast in Baghdad killed 33 people yesterday*

Arnold Schwarzenegger: It's not just Arnie – any long or hyphenated name is a challenging start for a reader. Also in print, the word may well be capped up and becomes too long for a column

Hyphenated words: As with a long name, hyphenated words can look bulky at the top of the story. *An xx-year-old boy* is better written as *A boy of x*

Researchers/scientists: Suggests something heavy and technical is coming

Consumers: You probably mean *shoppers*

British/Britain: While digital news is breaking down international boundaries, it is fair to assume all stories on a British news site or in a British newspaper are about Britain or the British. It can usually be avoided with a rewrite. An exception might be if Britain as a country is being compared with the rest of the world, for example *Britain has the worst hospitals in Europe* . . .

In this example, the intro starts with the least engaging element of the sentence:

> The Ministry of Defence has announced that the first British reservists have set off for Sierra Leone to help tackle the Ebola outbreak.
>
> *ITV, December 2014*

By turning it round we would focus on the heart of the story in the first few words:

> The first British reservists have set off for Sierra Leone to help tackle the Ebola outbreak which has claimed thousands of lives.

Avoid negatives

Always accentuate the positive and **ditch the negative**. Negatives require too much mental processing from the reader – they have to grasp an idea, or already be familiar with it, and then understand the reverse of it.

Rewrite if you find yourself using the words *no, not, never*. You are telling the reader something has not happened – the antithesis of news.

> Suffolk is under no immediate threat from terrorists, the county's police and crime commissioner has said.
>
> *Ipswich Star, January 2016*

> No issues have been found on Irish Coast Guard helicopters after manufacturers ordered immediate safety checks.
>
> *PA, January 2017*

Negative phrases are easily flipped into positive ones. *Does not* becomes *fails*, *does not have* (*lacks*), *does not include* (*leaves out/excludes*), *doesn't listen to* (*ignores*), *doesn't use* (*avoids*), *not many* (*few*), *not often* (*rarely*), *not unless* (*if*) and so on.

This example invites a shrug of the shoulders to the casual reader. It's about something not happening:

> *Security agencies will not be given powers to look at a suspect's website browsing history under new laws, Home Secretary Theresa May has said.*
>
> BBC, November 2015

And could easily have been turned into a positive:

> *Security agencies will be forbidden from looking at a suspect's website browsing history under new laws, Home Secretary Theresa May has said.*

Similarly, conditionals such as *could, may* or *might* are meaningless. *A bomb might go off today* suggests that it won't go off at all. You can lose conditionals by creating a positive scenario:

> *Shops might be stopped from opening longer on Sundays by a band of at least 20 rebel Tories, it emerged last night.*
>
> The Sun, October 17, 2015

> *Shops will be stopped from opening longer on Sundays if a band of at least 20 rebel Tories gets its way.*

Be original

Some intros get used so often they deserve to be packed off to a retirement home. They might sound newsy but these **off-the-shelf favourites** are best wheeled out only as a last resort:

> *Police/detectives have launched an investigation/are hunting for . . .*
> *. . . was slammed/blasted/attacked/lambasted/condemned . . .*
> *. . . was continuing/rumbling/raged on*
> *Mystery surrounds . . .*
> *Fears are growing/mounting . . .*
> *When . . . . little did he/she realise/think that*

. . . has gone viral / become an internet sensation
. . . it emerged / was reported / claimed / revealed / disclosed

Beware, too, throwing **journalese** at the intro in the hope of making it seem newsy. It can end up breathless but a bit silly:

> TRAFFIC chaos has erupted after the Forth Road Bridge was shut due to safety fears.
>
> *Daily Record, December 2015*

Back it up

Remember that **an intro has to be justified or explained** later in the story. As you set it as the theme in the first sentence, it should be the line built up in the expansion.

If you fail to do so, the reader is left with unanswered questions from the intro. Similarly, if a part-quote or a paraphrase is used in an intro, the story must contain the full quote to back up the claim.

Be prepared to **break the rules**. It's fine to write a negative intro or start with a dull word if you are looking for an original or humorous approach. Don't overdo it, however. It can kill the joke.

Suspended intros

A suspended intro, where the key point is delayed by a paragraph or two to give the reader a softer landing, is a superb device to lift flat copy, especially where the event that sparks coverage is less than the sum of the story.

It's a stock in trade for lighter or celebrity stories, **walking the reader into a subject** without trying to assail or shock them in the way you might with a gritty, hard news story.

However, the looser, more florid style has its pitfalls. First, it has to make sense. Too often, the writer thinks of something which sounds clever but, when you read it closely, it really isn't. Worse still, it doesn't properly connect to the story you are trying to deliver.

This example reads well:

> First it was "boomerangers", young graduates who moved back home to live with their parents after university while they tried to pay off their student debts and get a job.
>
> Now more than seven million "doomerangers" are hogging the spare room after their marriage or relationship has broken down.
>
> *The Times, May 2016*

But this attempt on the same page of the same newspaper has the feel of a soft lead-in plonked clumsily on top of a straight news story:

> *It is sexist stereotyping, uncomfortable, unfair and – it is claimed – prevalent in the city.*
>
> *A receptionist revealed her astonishment yesterday at being ordered home from one of Britain's biggest finance companies because she refused to wear high heels.*

There is no connection between the first and second sentence. The meaning of the *it* in the intro is unclear – is it the practice of making staff wear high heels, is it imposing dress codes or just picking on receptionists – and is made no easier to decipher as you read beyond the second par.

Likewise, in the same edition, another attempt goes astray:

> *When relatives tell you at great length about their angst over the leylandii next door, do you struggle to care?*
>
> *Scientists have found that paracetamol can dull the ability to sense pain and suffering in others.*

Again, the chatty first paragraph is not linked to or explained by the second except by a process of deduction on the part of the reader.

The second paragraph might have read:

> *If so, then maybe you have been taking too many paracetamol.*

After the intro

Think about where you are going after the first paragraph.

A story **needs to flow** elegantly into the second paragraph, which expands upon the intro. Do not write yourself into a hole, where you have to switch subject and lose your flow or come up with a linguistic contortion to stay on theme.

Another common mistake is to **repeat what you have said in the intro in the second paragraph**, albeit expressing it differently. Always move on, adding depth with each sentence so the story expands naturally.

> *David Cameron wanted to shut down controversial investigations of murder, abuse and torture by British soldiers in Iraq but was overruled by the attorney general, an MP has claimed.*
>
> *Johnny Mercer MP, a Conservative member of the Commons defence committee and a former army officer, said the former prime minister told him he wanted to shut down the Iraq historic allegations team (Ihat) but the move was vetoed by Jeremy Wright.*
>
> *The Guardian, September 2016*

> *Schools should be allowed to pay their governors, a think tank has recommended.*
>
> *Reform is calling on the Government to make it possible for maintained schools and academies to financially reward governors for their time and effort.*
>
> *PA, September 2016*

Make the intro **work with the headline and sub-heads**. While they may even be written by separate people, the reader sees them as part of a single package presented to them on screen or page. Avoid an intro that just repeats the headline, especially where the headline is lengthy and SEO-friendly.

4

Let it flow

You gotta have rhythm. It's vital to lifting writing from the mundane and functional to the exceptional.

Writing that flows carries a reader through a story by making it easy for them to follow, as well as adding personality that stands out from the crowd.

You can hear the **rhythm** of a well-written news story in your head. It trips along without a rough edge or a paragraph that jars.

As soon as the reader stumbles, hits an obstacle or has to go back over a section to make sense of it, you have lost them. If you lurch down a narrative side alley or a path that leads to a dead end where they have to U-turn to get back on track, they will get confused and give up.

The first par to second imperative

The first step is to **keep the subject of the sentence the same from paragraph to paragraph.** When you make a change don't lurch. Make it logical and smooth. It enables the reader to move through the story without stopping to think who or what you are writing about.

Make it an **unimpeachable rule** that you stick with the same subject from intro to second paragraph. That means the first character or organisation identified in the intro, usually in the first word or two, is the first character or organisation identified in the second paragraph.

In our fire baby story, the intro begins . . . *A baby* . . . and the second par begins *Six-month-old Daisy Tupper* . . . Had we kept with Daisy as the subject we could have continued the third par with *She* and so on. It's very easy to follow.

Apart from causing confusion there are **legal dangers** in muddling subjects.

> *Criminal defence lawyer David Edwards, 51, died when he was stabbed with a kitchen knife by new wife Sharon, 42, after the pair returned from Majorca, Manchester Crown Court was told.*
>
> *Edwards was described as 'domineering' and 'possessive'.*
>
> *Metro.co.uk, February 2016*

This is easily read as the victim being *domineering* and *possessive*. In fact, it was the attacker.

Similarly, this story wrongfoots the reader twice. The intro focuses on a prominent Muslim but, confusingly, he is the third character mentioned in the second sentence.

> *A prominent Muslim who claims he has links to MI5 is likely to die in jail for murdering a Syrian cleric who was executed in "cold blood" following a power struggle at a London mosque, it can now be reported.*
>
> *Abdul Hadi Arwani, 48, from Acton, west London, was sprayed with bullets from a MAC-10 sub-machine gun by Iraq war veteran Leslie Cooper on the orders of Muslim convert Khalid Rashad on April 7 last year.*
>
> *PA, October 2016*

Stay on subject

Switching the subject of sentences is a sign of a writer throwing down a series of facts rather than telling a story. It is a common error.

If you can keep to one subject through the intro and expansion, it will **help with your storytelling**. By focusing each sentence on a central character, for example, you will keep the story focused on them, too.

Again in our fire story, when we want to switch subject from the baby to the father, we keep the transition smooth by going from Daisy to *Her father, Joseph* . . .

If the subject remains the same, you will need to **find a fresh label** for it at the beginning of each sentence. Just repeating *Mr Tupper* will become dull. Use other identifiers, such as *the 29-year-old*, *the engineer*, *the keen footballer* and so on.

Don't come up, however, with **synonyms which sound ridiculous** – some writers call them knobblys – as this writer did when trying not to repeat the words *manhole cover*.

> *Massachusetts police are trying to establish what dislodged the chunky cast-iron disc.*
> *Sky News, February 2016*

Pronouns can be a lifesaver. If your intro begins *Game of Thrones fans were treated to* . . . , you could begin the second sentence with a synonym, such as *Viewers*, but it might sound awkward or forced, so stick to a simple *They*.

You are unlikely to be able to maintain the same subject throughout a lengthy story. Other characters and organisations plus background narrative will be needed.

But try to make a switch where the story has a **natural pause**, for example, after a breather. Elsewhere do so smoothly. For example, in a story about a politician, you could switch focus to a critic with a phrase such as *His biggest rival, Nelly O'Sullivan said* . . . Move the setting with phrases such as *In the next street* or *At a second meeting*. Soften the jolt by starting sentences with words such as *But, However, Meanwhile, Later, Elsewhere, Nonetheless*.

Avoid sudden jolts

Good flow sweeps a reader through a story. Never let the story hit the buffers with a **stopper sentence.** These are sentences which appear to be thrown in at random as the writer stops to inject a piece of explanation.

In this example, the intro focuses fairly enough on the effects of sugary drinks.

> *Drinking two or more sweetened drinks a day could increase a man's risk of heart failure by 23%, a new study has found.*
> *Huffington Post, October 2015*

The second par should go on to expand on the findings. But, oddly, that is delayed while the writer injects an explanatory sentence on heart failure:

> *Heart failure affects about 900,000 people in the UK. It can affect people of all ages, but it is more common in older people . . .*

While this is worthy background information, it's not critical to the story and should be used much later.

If a detail is needed to make the story comprehensible, then **weave it in as a clause**, rather than interrupting the flow of the story. Learn this technique in the next section.

5

*Tell now,
explain later*

Where does a news story begin? Rarely, if properly told, with . . . *In the beginning.*

With every news story, there is history and background. Even a sudden calamity . . . a natural disaster, a plane crash, a violent crime . . . falls within a context or a pattern of events.

> *A wife shoots her husband of 20 years dead*. Their story begins, we might reasonably feel, at the point where this couple first meet. *However, our story begins when she pulls the trigger.*
>
> *A politician decides to reform the education system.* The story begins with the problem he or she is trying to fix with the education system and society's increasing awareness of this issue. *A news story begins with the announcement of the new law and its significance.*
>
> *A football player is savaged on social media for making sexist remarks.* His story begins with his rise to prominence; it may be he has been in trouble before for similar stupidity. *Our story begins at the point Twitter tells him he is a chauvinist pig.*
>
> *A professor invents a breakthrough in treatment for cancer.* Again, the story begins when the disease becomes a problem society needs to tackle. The professor's story begins when he starts to research it. *A news story comes at the end of his many years of study, clinical trials and peer review, when he announces what he has discovered.*
>
> *A kitten is filmed in a very cute video playing with a mouse.* There is still context – cats like eating mice. *We break in at the point they play gently together.*
>
> *For*example

News is the significant or dramatic moment where we break into this chain of events. That is our story and it is always our beginning.

Burying the history

In news, there is, as the word suggests, one constant, one must . . . that it is *new*. It is the material the reader has not heard, seen or read before. Otherwise, the new is missing from our storytelling. It is also our seventh W – the **now**.

A secret government file is released after 30 years, an archaeological discovery or scientific research into the dawn of time are about events many years, even aeons, ago . . . but what we are learning about them now is the news.

On a **running story**, fresh developments may even have been published previously, perhaps many times. The coverage might go back decades or just a few hours.

Getting sidetracked into history and context is a **curse among news storytellers**. It is born of a fear that their readers are stupid and need everything set out in a plodding fashion or they won't understand what has happened. Bad writers forget the mantra – **tell first, explain later**.

The curse leads to **intro plonking.** Writers find the latest angle for an intro without too much trouble. Then, they should build on the intro – the key moment, the latest development, the news – in the expansion. But, having teed up a potentially interesting story they stop, reach for their security blanket and begin explaining. They have not created a story, they have **plonked a news intro on a recap**.

> *Planning permission for a 50-metre high wind turbine in the Green Belt near Nottingham was rightly granted, a High Court judge has ruled.*
>
> *Nottingham Post, December 2016*

In this example, the reader is told the latest development is from a High Court judge's ruling.

But no more is heard of this ruling until ploughing through four pars of history, explaining the turbine has been a bone of contention for years and recapping developments in 2011 and April 2016.

Instead, those four paragraphs should have been dedicated to detailing the judge's ruling and what it means for the turbine opponents.

Key is using our **timeline approach** from Chapter 5. It shows exactly the moment you need to focus on for the intro and expansion, your critical first four or five paragraphs. It guides you to what is happening now, what is the news – in the case above, the judge's decision. Everything outside this is secondary and can be explained methodically within the chronology.

You will lift this curse if you write for a **perfect reader**. Imagine they are intelligent and familiar with the context so don't need to have it explained. It will allow you to focus sharply on the exciting new information, not on something the perfect reader has heard before. Indeed, most of the readers of the Nottingham turbine story will have been following the developments for years.

Learn to weave

Of course, the perfect reader is a fiction, a sensible base point to help shape and focus a story. Most readers do not come with a cuttings file implanted in their heads. We have to make our story comprehensible to them. For this we need to master **the weave**.

The weave allows us to propel the story forward in the intro and amplification for those familiar with it, while making it comprehensible for those who need a reminder of past events or are joining it for the first time.

The weave does what it says on the tin – you weave in just enough background and explanatory detail around the new material so anyone can follow it.

Weaving is little more than adding clauses with contextual detail and background in the first few pars so it does not interrupt the flow of the story.

To do this unleash the full array of *which, who* and *when* **clauses** and unfurl **adaptor and linking** words such as *following, after* and *despite*.

It ensures old information is cleverly and stylishly tucked away rather than becoming the focus of **stopper sentences**.

On this running court story, the details of the crime were widely covered during the trial in March 2015. But, here, the writer resorts to explaining them again in paragraph two, rather than remaining focused on the latest developments – the sentencing and the judge's comments – which become scattered through the story.

> *Two teenagers who kidnapped then "tortured" a girl aged 14 by pouring salt down her throat and making her perform a sex act have been sentenced.*
> *The girl was taken to a flat in Waltham Cross, Hertfordshire last year by the strangers before being made to strip naked and sit in a freezing cold bath.*
> *BBC, May 2015*

It can be recast as far as the breather along the following lines. The woven details are in bold:

> *Two teenagers have been sentenced for **kidnapping and torturing a girl of 14 by pouring salt down her throat and making her perform a sex act**.*
> *Caylen Candy and Chyanne Powell, **who made their victim strip naked and sit in a freezing cold bath,** were sent to a young offenders' institution for six years and three months and seven and a half years respectively.*
> *The 18-year-olds were told they "showed a callous indifference to a visibly distressed victim who was pleading to be let go" **when they held her in a flat in Waltham Cross, Hertfordshire**.*

> *Sentencing them, Judge Stephen Warner said the girl's **17-hour ordeal, filmed on a mobile phone,** was "humiliating and belittling".*
>
> *He added: "What she was subjected to was nothing short of torture – physically and psychologically – done for your amusement and gratification."*

This version rounds up the newest information in the intro and expansion, weaving in enough to make it comprehensible to the new reader and leaving all the recapping until later.

By using the weave on the wind turbine story, we could approach it thus:

> *A 50-metre wind turbine built in the Green Belt near Nottingham was rightly granted planning permission, a High Court judge has ruled.*
>
> *The decision was based on a "pragmatic and sensible" report and Gedling Borough councillors were properly advised **when they gave approval in April,** said Mr Justice Green.*
>
> *Consent had taken into account the "practical realities" of business for Woodborough Park farm owner John Charles-Jones, **who said the turbine brought in more than £110,000 a year,** the judge added.*
>
> *The latest ruling scotches campaigners' hopes that the turbine, **a bone of contention for years and the subject of two costly court challenges,** will be taken down.*

Keep it simple

Life is complicated enough. Burdened and busy readers have enough challenges to distract and befuddle them.

Reading their news stories should not be one of them.

Storytellers must give them what they want in the easiest possible form to digest.

Sentences should be **direct and simple**. Use the subject-verb-object style and avoid impenetrable paragraphs such as these:

> *Several protesters were treated for minor injuries and a small crowd was briefly "kettled" by police at Great George Street, a short distance from Conservative Party headquarters, before large numbers of police rushed the surrounding crowd and most protesters dispersed towards the Palace of Westminster were flares and fireworks were set off and a small drone was flown into Portcullis House, where many MPs have their offices.*
>
> *Independent, November 2015*
>
> *Customers interested in the new service can fit a wireless 'electricity router', available for free from JE, to their roofs which will harness the energy, enabling them to run all household appliances without the need of plugs or sockets and Jersey Electricity will continue to monitor power consumption, which they say is unlikely to change under the new set-up.*
>
> *Jersey Evening Post, April 2016*

Watch your **sentence length.** Keep them to under 25 words or so they can be read in a single breath and stay logical. If a sentence gets too long, cut it in two.

> *The only sting in the tail from a win that saw Joe Root dominate with the bat, scoring 325 runs across two innings – including a career-best 254 – and Chris Woakes continue his golden summer with seven wickets, came with the injury to the all-rounder Ben Stokes that is likely to rule him out of the next instalment.*
>
> *The Guardian, July 2016*

The occasional staccato sentence can be used for stylistic effect but beware of using this device too frequently as it can strip writing of elegance.

Cut out the clunk

Avoid clunky phrasing such as this. It will save words, space and your readers' time:

> *His victory saw him beat off competition from fellow finalists Kellie Bright and Georgia May Foote. (16 words v 11 words for **He beat Kellie Bright and Georgia May Foote in the final.**)*
>
> *The Sun, December 2015*

*In the same interview, Jamelia also explained that the reason she decided to take part in 'Strictly' was to change public opinion about her. (25 words v 14 words for **Jamelia added she took part in 'Strictly' to change public opinion about her**.)*

Huffington Post, November 2015

The extent of injuries sustained by the cyclist are believed to be serious, they added. (*15 words v eight words for* **The cyclist was said to be seriously hurt.**)

Ipswich Star, January 2016

Clause celebre

Use only **one clause** in each sentence. Put the **clause directly next to the subject** to which it refers, otherwise you end up with nonsense notions such as a bus not a rant being captured on video and put online or Liam Payne buying the whole of Los Angeles:

A woman has been arrested over a racist rant on a bus which was captured by a passenger on video and posted online.

Sky News, October 2015

The pair are living in a multi-million-pound mansion in Calabasas, Los Angeles, which Liam bought from his One Direction earnings.

The Sun, April 2016

Don't dangle

Beware **dangling participles**, where you start a sentence with a passive phrase that is unconnected or confuses the information which comes after it. The dangling modifier at the start of this sentence, complete with typo, implies the taxi was crossing at the traffic lights.

Crossing the road at a set of traffic lights, a taxi suddenly slammed into her, sending her sprawling across the road.

Mirror Online, December 2015

Repeat offending

Nothing jars more than **repeating words, phrases or ideas** in the same sentence.

> *From April 2018, a tax of 18p or 24p per litre, depending on the sugar content, will be added to fizzy drinks depending on their sugar content.*
>
> *BuzzFeed, March 2016*
>
> *A new social media craze which sees women posting opinion-dividing letters to their boyfriend's ex partners has divided the internet.*
>
> *The Sun, April 2016 (note the apostrophe and hyphen errors, too)*

Avoid it wherever possible in consecutive sentences, too.

> *Police are appealing for witnesses to the incident, which took place between 8pm and 9pm and left three men injured. The fight broke out outside the Jenny Wren in Campkin Road, during which three men were injured.*
>
> *Cambridge Evening News, December 2015*

Although these sentences might have benefited from a more substantial rewrite, simply replacing the second *tree* and *suspension* with an *it* would have avoided ungainly repetition:

> *Ms Madichie said the council's planners indicated they had suspicions that the tree was causing damage to the property years ago – even while it was blocking the owners from felling the problematic tree.*
>
> *Mirror Online, March 2016*
>
> *Evans mounted an unsuccessful legal challenge against the suspension, but some of her allies have now launched a petition to get the suspension overturned.*
>
> *The Guardian, March 2016*

Information overload

Beware **overloading a sentence**. This has three clauses in a row:

> *Hirst, 50, below, who has a fortune of around £215million, began buying property in Ilfracombe, Devon, a decade ago.*
>
> *The Sun on Sunday, November 2016*

Likewise, this crammed-in clause implies it is Monmouthshire that does not smoke:

> *Emma Caresimo, 40, of Magor, Monmouthshire, who does not smoke and has never been to Wigan, had to pay £650 to save her car.*
>
> *Daily Mirror, April 2016*

This overloaded example is easily broken up:

> *Samuel Pozo, 35, from Malaga, who helped save the British holidaymaker's daughter, told a local paper: "If it hadn't been for me and the other people who helped by jumping into the sea or helping out from the rocks, the child would have died as well."*
> *Mr Pozo added: "The red flag . . ."*
>
> *Evening Standard, August 2016*

It could have been slimmed to:

> *Samuel Pozo, who helped save the British holidaymaker's daughter, said: "If it hadn't been for me and the other people who helped by jumping into the sea or helping out from the rocks, the child would have died as well."*
> *The 35-year-old, from Malaga, told a local paper: "The red flag . . .*

Junk the jargon

Jargon is the antithesis of good storytelling.

It slithers from the mealy mouths of those who want to sound much bigger and cleverer than they really are. Its purpose is to complicate the simple, to obfuscate, to disguise the negative as positive, to sidestep responsibility and to give false hope.

Sadly, even people in news publishing have started spouting it.

> . . . a [Trinity Mirror] *spokesperson said: "We are exploring alternative revenue streams across the publishing division as part of our ongoing strategy and we have seconded some resource as part of this."*
>
> *Press Gazette, January 2016*

For a while, even the Press Association, Britain's leading news agency, labelled itself *The UK's leading provider of multi-platform content solutions.* Maybe it was planning to start drilling for oil in the North Sea.

Our job, our mission, is to detect it and unravel jargon. Work out what the jargon-droppers are trying to say – or what they are trying to avoid saying – and write that instead. In these cases, the writers forgot to call a flat-bladed, wooden-handled implement designed for digging a spade:

> *Massey's death has been attributed as a causal factor in an increase of gun attacks in Salford, some the result of two on-going feuds between rival criminal gangs in the city.*
>
> *BuzzFeed, February 2016*
>
> *Breivik claims he brought this lawsuit because his forced separation from other prisoners and controlled access to visitors and correspondence is having a negative effect on his health.*
>
> *RT.com, April 2016*

> *They ruled that the explosion rendered both victims unable to exit the store as fire consumed the outbuilding and resulted in a fatal level of carbon monoxide.*
>
> *PA, January 2016*

Doctors are just what you want when you are sick and injured – but suffer from crippling jargonitis. They talk of a *healthcare delivery system* (health service) or a *negative patient outcome* (the patient died).

Likewise, unravel the words of other professionals – a **social worker** who advocates a *multi-disciplinary approach* (team effort) or a **teacher** speaking of a *daily act of collective worship* (assembly) or *intended learning outcomes* (what a pupil is supposed to know) – or a lawyer saying, well, pretty much anything.

Police are serial offenders. As officers are no longer allowed to beat up prisoners, they take out their rage by murdering the English language instead.

Today's police *apprehend* (arrest), *attend the scene* (go) to deal with *fatalities* (deaths) or those who are *fatally injured* (killed), some of whom may be *foreign nationals* (foreigners). They also *look for persons of interest* (suspects) who have *made good their escape* (escaped) by *fleeing on foot from the location* (running away). Their meaning is usually comically clear . . . but take *evasive action from* (avoid) repeating it.

Sadly, even when writing about misuse of jargon, some writers seem to slip into jargon:

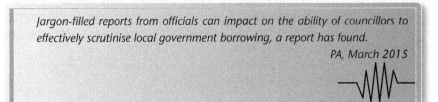

Jargon-filled reports from officials can impact on the ability of councillors to effectively scrutinise local government borrowing, a report has found.

PA, March 2015

Use simple words

Just as we should stick to simple sentences, we should also **lose the long words**. There is always a shorter alternative. It is better to substitute two or even three short simple words for one long, little-known one.

It is common to see approximately (about), attempt (try), concerning (about), consumer (shopper), cutbacks (cuts), demonstrate (show), establish (set up), eyewitness (witness), participate (take part in), utilise (use), underwent (had) surgery. There are countless more.

Take ownership

We need to be honest with readers. We need to tell them where our stories come from. **Attribution is key to accuracy,** as it provides a caveat which allows them to judge the worth of what they are being told.

Attributing **opinion, quotes and information which is vague, incredible or open to challenge** is a must.

However, too many storytellers use it to paper over the cracks. Phrases such as *it was reported* or *reportedly* or *told the Daily Times* allow you to cover what others have written. Yet, it is tacit acknowledgment that you do not own your story and provides no guarantee that it is accurate or legally sound.

Don't always attribute

Clear-cut, indisputable information **does not need attribution**. If you have faith in your reportage and your sources and believe what you are told, simplify your storytelling by **taking ownership** of that information and using it.

Remember, the reader wants **a story, not a report** – in other words, they want to know what is happening to whom and not, as a priority, where that story has come from. They should be able to trust your judgment as to its veracity.

If you attribute everything, you will have a series of disconnected statements from sources. It is not news writing – it is vomiting the contents of a notebook and leaving the reader to mop up the mess.

Online, use the gift of **hyperlinks.** If the reader wants to explore the background sources, they are only a click away.

Keep the intro clear

Strive to **keep attribution out of the intro** – on more dramatic stories, such as our baby saved from the fire story, you should be able to keep it out of the expansion, too.

This is unnecessarily guarded. Sadly, there was no doubt whatsoever that Arnie had played his last round.

> *Golfer Arnold Palmer has died, aged 87,* ***according to the US Golf Association and US golf media.***
>
> *Sky News, September 2016*
> *(The death had been confirmed and had even*
> *prompted a response from Barack Obama)*

In these examples, the writers waste words and slow down storytelling with unnecessary attribution:

> ***Police said*** *Farook and Malik, aged 28 and 27 respectively, were intercepted and a gun battle with more than 20 officers left their dark SUV riddled with bullets and both suspects dead.*
>
> *The Guardian, December 2015*
> *(Video, images and witness reports of the incident*
> *were widely available for at least 24 hours)*

> *He was famed for his **"gospel-infused southern boogie piano rock, blues, and country music", his website says**.*
>
> BBC, November 2016
> *(Was anyone claiming the late Leon Russell was renowned for anything else?)*

Learn to let go

Over-attribution is a **false security blanket**. Attempting to justify every sentence by distancing yourself from it does not protect the news writer's reputation or that of his or her publication. Rather, it smacks of a lack of confidence in your information-gathering, ability to judge its value and storytelling skills.

In this example, the humour is destroyed by attributing it to a *US environmental official* (as well as by ignoring the fact the dog was called Trigger). It suggests the writer does not believe it. In which case, it should be spiked, not slaughtered.

> *A woman in the US state of Indiana is recovering after being shot by her dog in a bizarre hunting accident, an environment official says.*
>
> *The woman, named as Allie Carter, 25, was hunting waterfowl on Saturday in the north of the state, Jonathon Boyd, an Indiana conservation officer said.*
>
> BBC, October 2015

It is not uncommon to see sentences such as:

> *The minister, in an interview broadcast on TV channel News 7, said he would like to see new laws introduced to curb drinking, the state news agency reports.*

Given that the interview was seen by millions of viewers, it seems ridiculously overcautious to apply all these layers. Get to the point and simply state:

> *New laws should be introduced to curb drinking, the minister said.*

Tell now, attribute later

To keep sentences vibrant, **put attribution to the end of sentences**. The active words should be the first ones readers see and phrases such as *according to, the jury heard, a charity claims, scientists said* should be at the end.

The points of these sentences are in the last few words and it's painful waiting to get there:

> *The Advertising Standards Authority (ASA) has said a TV advert for XLS-Medical Max Strength diet pills that BuzzFeed News first revealed was being formally investigated was one of the most complained-about ads of 2015.*
>
> *BuzzFeed, February 2016*
>
> *At a meeting of Plymouth City Council's cabinet on Tuesday, the head of the committee which runs the crossings said he expects traffic to grow by one per cent each year from until April 2019, so no increases in charges are expected during that time.*
>
> *Plymouth Herald, January 2016*

Security loophole

Remember, too, that having layers of attribution provides **no extra legal protection**, especially from libel. We cannot deflect criticism by pointing to the source and saying we were just repeating what was said.

It **won't even protect your reputation**. Even if you say information has come from government, police or official sources, the reader doesn't notice that. If it is later proved to be wrong, they will point to your story as the source. You're the messenger and they'll shoot you first anyway.

Make it add up

Numbers are dull. Impersonal, untouchable, at the top of the ladder of abstraction when we want to be at the bottom.

Readers do not like numbers. It reminds them of maths lessons and accountants. It's hard to fall in love with either of those.

Numbers even look awkward and daunting amid the text. They jar and readers tend to skip over them.

It's a truism, too, that journalists – by definition, writers and lovers of words and people – also don't get on that well with numbers.

Unfortunately, **numeracy is not optional for news writers**. And it is subtler skill than just being able to add up quickly or decipher tables of official statistics. It is about being able to assimilate and assess – to spot the story lurking in the pile of digits and write about it in an engaging way.

Make the most of numbers

Start by **looking for the headline figure** for an intro. Select the most surprising or eye-catching – usually, the very biggest or smallest. Don't worry if it is atypical or an occasional occurrence, as news is meant to be about the exceptional.

For example, house prices in Anytown may have risen by an average of 10 per cent, or £20,000, in a year. Hence, a perfectly sound intro may be:

House prices are surging ahead in Anytown, with the average property going up by £20,000 in the past year, estate agents report.

That might please those who like to be told their houses are worth more than they paid for them. But the report also shows that property prices in some of the most desirable parts of town have risen by 15 per cent, or £50,000. Hence:

House prices are surging ahead in Anytown, with property in some neighbourhoods rising by £50,000 in the past year, estate agents report.

That's better but there is a detail that might trump them all. For smaller properties, such as one- or two-bedroom flats, the rate has been 20 per cent. That gets to the core of the story, as it becomes obvious who is going to be worst affected.

First-time buyers' dreams of getting on the property ladder are receding fast as the price of starter homes in Anytown has soared by a fifth in a year.

Once you have cherry-picked a headline figure, stick with it. Think of that number as your story.

Focus on that number exclusively through the expansion. Try not to get distracted, even though you may have many statistics which are potentially equally valid and interesting.

Hence, we might go on:

They have seen the asking price of a one-bedroom flat climb from £100,000 a year ago to £120,000 while prices for two-bedroom flats are now £180,000.

> *Worse still, a shortage of properties for sale means those which do come up for sale are snapped up within days.*
>
> *Estate agent Brian Braces said: 'It's tough for your buyers at the moment. Some are scraping together the money for a deposit only to need thousands more a month later.'*

This keeps it very focused and simple for the reader.

Put them into context

A standalone total may be eye-catching because it is exceptionally large or small. But it doesn't necessarily tell much of a story.

You might hear from a charity that more than 10,000 people die every year in Britain from a certain kind of cancer. That sounds concerning but it only becomes interesting when it is put into context.

Maybe the rate is growing or falling sharply, or perhaps it has become one of the ten biggest killers in the country as a result. You could compare it by region or gender, or set it against countless other measures for myriad diseases. Totals are rarely empirical. They are a tool for asking these kinds of questions.

Less is more

Take care **not to overwhelm a numbers-based story with numbers**. This is hard to follow:

> *The AA said it had figures showing that nearly two-thirds of drink-drivers arrested in the run-up to and during the past three Christmases were at least almost twice the alcohol limit.*
>
> BBC, December 2016

In our house prices example, we have only a couple of figures in the first few paragraphs and the second is there only to expand the information we have given in the intro.

Try to use only **one figure in each sentence**. Try not to have sentence after sentence with a statistic in them. Break up the use of figures with quotes or narrative.

It can help to find a way of **expressing a figure in words**.

So, instead of:

> *The report said 96% of properties in Anytown had risen in value in the past year and 78% had gone up by at least £5,000.*

Try something like:

> All but a handful of properties in Anytown have risen in value in the past year while most went up by at least £5,000.

Look for inventive ways, such as a **chart or graph**, to present figures so they don't bog down the storytelling.

Make numbers real

Beware, too, of **the effect of extremely large numbers**. At first glance they appear mind-blowing and spectacular and so might be perfect for a headline or intro. But it's worth hesitating to ask whether readers can really grasp them.

Imagine a billion pounds. What does it look like? How much does it weigh? Where would you keep it? Now, imagine a trillion pounds. It's almost beyond comprehension. It might even make the reader shrug.

If possible, explain it to try to make it feel real. Scale it down to the personal:

> It is said the monarchy costs British taxpayers £40million a year. That's hard to picture. It is more comprehensible if you say that is £1.26 for everyone who pays tax, or 56p for everyone in the country, or a third the price of your morning latte. Readers can visualise a cup of coffee.
>
> **F**orexample

For years journalists have made comparisons to everyday, imaginable things when faced with very large or very small numbers. Enormous volumes are measured in Olympic-size swimming pools, vast areas are several times the size of Wales or Belgium and heights are compared with London buses or Nelson's Column. The microscopic are a tenth the width of a human hair, while long things stretch several times round the world or to the moon and back. Some have become cliches – but they are effective.

Always be conscious that **readers notice the one more than the millions**. Ask how you can **humanise a statistic**.

Readers tend to skip past a figure, even a shocking one, and take away only a vague understanding of the general scale of a problem.

They will struggle to connect to the news that hundreds of thousands of people suffer from a disease.

On the other hand, they will empathise with office manager Charlotte, a 35-year-old mother of two from Sutton Coldfield. She is fighting the disease, which has had a devastating effect on her life and those of her children, Rosie, six, and Robin, four.

She is a story, not a statistic.

How to avoid mistakes

If you are not a natural mathematician, then take extra care when dealing with figures.

Check and recheck your sums. If you really lack confidence, ask a colleague to confirm the maths.

Your main defence is **your common sense**. Some figures just look and sound wrong. And if they look wrong, they probably are. In this example, 2 million tonnes would be an enormous heap of ivory – it was, as the text made clear, only 2 tonnes.

> *2 million tonnes of ivory destroyed as Thailand steps up fight against illegal trade.*
>
> *Yahoo News, August 2015*

Ask yourself if a figure sounds plausible. Try working out a calculation, at least roughly, in your head or on paper, so you know the ballpark answer before using a calculator to confirm it.

Type them carefully – would the Serious Fraud Office have charged executives over a measly 250 quid?:

> *It comes after Tesco announced in 2014 that it had discovered a £250 black hole linked to a "problem with its accounts".*
>
> *ITV, September 2016*

Take care with noughts. In Britain, round thousands have three zeroes, millions six, billions nine. It is easy to misplace a nought or two.

One simple mistake, which occurs surprisingly often, comes when you are typing a **list**. Make sure you do not add or leave out an item:

> *The update, which includes four new reactions – Love, Haha, Wow, Sad and Angry – will be available to all users in the next couple of days.*
>
> *Mashable, February 2016*

Another common mistake is when dealing with **increases and decreases**. There are a number of ways of saying the same thing and this seems to cause confusion.

For example, a figure that has risen from 200 to 400 has doubled or has gone up by 100 per cent or twofold. You could say there are *two times as many*. However, avoid writing *two times more* as it will probably be taken to mean two times as many plus the original 200, so you would be implying there are now 600 rather than 400.

Falls are more straightforward but still need care – if a figure is down by a third, it has dropped by 33 per cent, or is at two-thirds of its previous level.

Percentage pitfalls

Percentages are just a way of expressing proportions in terms of hundreds, but throw the unwary.

It can be easy to get into a muddle over **increases or falls in percentages**. For instance, if the rate of employment goes from four per cent to six per cent, it has not risen by two per cent but is a *two percentage point* rise. In fact, the absolute number of people who are unemployed is up by 50 per cent or half, as six is half as large again as four.

Very low figures are rarely worth turning into percentages, as this can be meaningless.

> The number of people injured as a result of fires in North Ayrshire has dropped dramatically in the last year. The figure dropped by 90.9 per cent from 11 last year across North Ayrshire to one, according to the latest figures released by local fire chiefs.
>
> *Irvine Times, August 2016*

Convert with care

It is good practice to have an idea of the **common conversion rates**, such as the number of kilometres in a mile or dollars to the pound, so you can sense at a glance whether the figure you have generated is correct.

Beware using websites for **temperature conversions**. In this example, if the temperature outside is 0.5C it is 33F but a rise of 0.5C is a rise of 0.9F.

> Kerry said the move could help avoid a global temperature rise of 0.5 degrees Celsius (33 Fahrenheit) by the end of the century.
>
> *AFP via MailOnline, July 2016*

Number style points

If you use a figure in your intro you will have to **justify or explain it elsewhere** in the story, ideally before the breather. So, if you say *A third of husbands admit having an affair, a new survey shows* . . . you will need to give the absolute figure later, ie *In the survey, 60 out of 180 husbands said they had been unfaithful.*

Avoid starting sentences with a figure, especially if it is a large or hyphenated one.

Don't mix different styles of presenting figures in a story; it is confusing. For example, if you use fractions or one in four, then don't switch to percentages halfway through and vice versa.

Precision is not always an essential. It is sensible to round up and down. If you are told that *32 per cent of footballers are paid more in a week than most people earn in a year*, you can fairly assert that it applies to *a third*. Similarly, you can look a bit daft when being too precise:

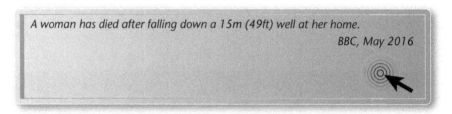

A woman has died after falling down a 15m (49ft) well at her home.

BBC, May 2016

As no one will have gone down the well with a tape measure, 50ft would have been fine as an imperial conversion.

Beware the **second largest** trap. While the largest and smallest are straightforward, the next in the queue is the largest after and not the second largest after.

Death is inevitable. So, **never say that the risk of dying increases or decreases** by whatever factor or percentage. The risk of dying is always 100 per cent. What you are probably referring to is the risk of dying early.

Make sure you **stick to house style** with figures. Even the basics, such as which numbers are spelt out or used as figures, whether to write 7 million, 7million, seven million or 7m and how to present weights and measures, vary from publication to publication. Check the style guide and be consistent.

*Knock out
the niggles*

Your story is accurate. Tick.

Your story is constructed well. Tick.

It has a spanking intro. Tick.

And it flows neatly from paragraph to paragraph. Another tick.

Yet it's easy to ruin things by overlooking the little things – those minor, yet avoidable slip-ups, which niggle readers and can stain your best work and harm your reputation as a writer.

Making sense

Writers always **get too close to their stories** – they research them; they immerse themselves in them; they pore over the best way to construct them.

As a result, they always understand what they have written because they know what they were trying to say. But they need to step back and ask, do their words make sense? And then ask again, **do they *really* make sense?**

> *She is believed to be aged 29, with whom he had enjoyed a close relationship since at least mid-2014, after the break-up of his marriage.*
>
> MailOnline, March 2016
>
> *Two Spanish villas thought to be hideouts for a British crime gang accused of plotting to kill a rival were raided last week and uncovered a haul of lethal weapons.*
>
> BuzzFeed, February 2016

In this example, the phrase should have been *Reading a hastily prepared statement*; instead, we have David Cameron racing through his statement at unseemly speed:

> *In a hastily-announced statement outside Number 10, the PM said he was delighted Theresa May would be the next Tory leader.*
>
> BBC, July 2016

And, if it's **difficult to decipher**, it needs rewriting:

> *The bid will be in two stages, the first of which should take around nine months will undertake detailed surveys, cost and further develop the project. The second bid will be for the works to take place, over the following two years.*
>
> Canterbury Times, January 2016

It's easy to read past **missing words** – and that can make nonsense of a sentence:

> *The clip sees a male sportswear being interviewed beside the conveyor belt at an airport.*
>
> *Express, March 2016*
>
> *Trust director said: "This opening marks many years of hard work and is testament to what can be achieved by several organisations working together . . ."*
>
> *Chronicle Live, March 2016*
>
> *Since the episode aired, fans have been ways in which Wylis may have turned into the Hodor we know and love today.*
>
> *Independent, May 2016*

Odd or clunky phrasing such as this may be just about comprehensible but leads to some inelegant sentences:

> *Ms Degutiene also took part in an exhilarating espresso race that saw her against the clock, producing seven perfect espressos in a minute.*
>
> *Worcester News, January 2016*
>
> *And after Gateshead's decision on Tuesday, one of the signatories of it, Blaydon MP Dave Anderson, said: "What's on offer isn't good enough . . ."*
>
> *Chronicle Live, March 2016*
>
> *A drama facility has been thrown into the battle between two proposals for the future of a town library.*
>
> *Hertfordshire Mercury, March 2016*

Using the **wrong idiom** or **mangled metaphors** can also produce some peculiar sentences:

> *Jennifer admitted that she is 'not even allowed to say' if she is in the TV episodes, but she did say with a smile in her voice: 'It would be great to work with David Lynch.'*
>
> *Metro.co.uk, March 2016*

> *The move comes as pressure hots up on fizzy drinks companies to take action amid concerns over the health effects of consuming too much sugar.*
> *BuzzFeed, January 2016*
>
> *Rafael Laguna, CEO of secure communications company Open-Xchange believes that this new form of 'Minority Report' style advertising is the beginning of the end for people's tethers.*
> *Huffington Post, November 2015*

Predictive text is a wonderful thing, except when it appears to have inserted the wrong word:

> *In addition, moving the library into the sports centre will require considerate* (considerable) *investment and cause disruption to both buildings.*
> *Northern Echo, May 2016*

Or substitutes the name of a popular singer for the name of a popular Spanish holiday resort:

> *Paramedics could do nothing to save her when they arrived at the apartments in the resort of Adele* (Adeje).
> *The Sun, June 2016*

Look out, too, for **misplaced clauses**, which mangle sentences:

> *She said she informed GoToGate about the instrument, which was booked in its own seat under the name "Chuck Cello", who told her to contact BA directly about the booking.*
> *Independent, August 2016*

Or leave them open to a completely unintended interpretation:

> *The actress and model teamed up with Rabbi Shmuley Boteach – an author, host and TV speaker – to write about the dangers of pornography in the Wall Street Journal.*
>
> *Sky News, September 2016*

Spelling fails

Inconsistency in spelling and style can spoil a story.

> *Bednest managing director, Mark Green, later reportedly apologised for the suggestion, and offered an unreserved apology to the Roseman family. But the girls' father, Gideon Rosemen, said the first he and his wife Esther had learned about it was via press reports.*
>
> *The Guardian, January 2017*

Watch out, in particular, for variations in spellings between the body text and captions, headlines and other elements on the screen or page.

> *The 18-year-old was caught when he shared material with an undercover police officer through a chat room.*
>
> *Metro.co.uk, February 2016*

But the caption says:

> *Andrew Picard, 17, has been spared jail despite sharing 'appalling' child abuse clips in chat rooms from his university room.*

This sentence might not win prizes for elegance but makes sense:

> *Jamie Price was enjoying a "usual Saturday night" with her two girls, when the blaze took hold at the Vauxhall Crescent property in Sturry at around 6pm.*
> *Canterbury Times, January 2016*

Unfortunately, the copy goes on to refer to her as *Jamie*, *Miss Price* and *Mrs Price* ... turning it into a confusing read.

Names are easily muddled. Here, the writer became confused because the name of the person paying the damages (Michael Jackson) was similar to that of his alleged victim (Jordan Chandler).

> *The case was settled with Jordan paying $22million to the Chandler family.*
> *The Sun, June 2016*

And here the source of the story was US park ranger Phil Strehle, who was unfortunately killed off.

> *Rescuers were unable to safely recover Strehle's body, due to the "volatile" thermal area and an incoming lightning storm. When officials returned the following morning, Scott's body was no longer visible.*
> *The Guardian, November 2016*

Wrongly spelt names look particularly amateurish:

> *Gary Linker, who followed in his footsteps to become a presenter on Match of the Day, wrote on Twitter: "Deeply saddened to hear that Jimmy Hill has left us."*
> *Sky News, December 2015*

There's little excuse for **spelling mistakes**, especially as most content management systems and word-processing software come with spell checkers.

The Neverland home was filled with games as well as dukeboxes and lifesize dolls
The Sun, June 2016

Sky News understands that moves will be made to remove the European Com-
munities Act from the statue book next year.
Sky News, October 2016

His closet rival, António Sampaio da Nóvoa, the main left-of-centre candidate,
polled between 22 and 25 per cent, the poll said.
FT.com, January 2016

Earlier the Cambridges had a two-hour jeep safari into the heart of Kaziranga
and gave a rhino a wide birth when they found it blocking their path.
PA, April 2016

It's inexcusable when the embedded tweet in the story has the word (resilient) spelt correctly:

"Life doesn't get easier or more forgiving," she posted on March 23. "We get
stronger and more resiliant."
ET Online, April 2016

Or you spell it differently in consecutive sentences:

Apple's new software for iPhones and iPads has left some older models unuse-
able. The update – released last week – brings with it a raft of new features and
improvements. But for owners of the iPad 2 and some other devices, it left their
tablets and phones completely unusable.
Independent, March 2016

Bad spelling can destroy your work. This example is in a story about a murdered child's sister, who gave a moving and intelligent interview on knife crime.

> *He peddled on for a few hundred yards before collapsing outside a swimming pool and bleeding to death.*
>
> *Evening Standard, September 2015*

The misspelling of the word *pedalled* creates a bizarre image of the stabbed boy going along the street selling things. It's ridiculous and the distracted reader ends up chuckling rather than crying.

Punctuate properly

Bad punctuation grinds readers' gears. Perhaps this writer should have listened to his or her teachers:

> *It went on to say the students are loyal proud of their academy and they follow teacher's instructions.*
>
> *Lincolnshire Echo, January 2016*

A missing comma can mangle a sentence:

> *Platforms across Sussex were packed with delays of at least 50 minutes across the county.*
>
> *Brighton Argus, June 2016*

As can a hyphen – it's unlikely police are chasing corrupt counters:

> *Police counter corruption unit faces report overhaul calls.*
>
> *PA, July 2016*

News writers need to have a dirty mind – otherwise they can miss unintended **double entendres**:

Lovely evening now, sun glinting off McIlroy's shaft as he goes down 12.
BBC, April 2015

Members of an Ohio family have been urged to take precautions after eight relatives were shot dead by a gunman who is still on the loose.
Sky News, April 2016

*Style*point

Final check

Your best defence against the niggles is to **read your work through**. At least once and preferably out loud.

If time permits, walk away for a few minutes, then re-read it. It will help you see it like a reader, coming to your story for the first time.

If an error slips through, learn from it and don't repeat it. Most are utterly avoidable but some are forgivable – it can be impossible to predict what will niggle a reader:

A feature about fans coping with boybands splitting up mistakenly said that the Bay City Rollers wore tartan socks. Although the band were fond of tartan garments, their socks were striped.
The Guardian corrections column, August 2015

10

Get set before you go

The final flourish to news writing has nothing to do with the words you write. It is how you make them look when they are published.

Setting the text so it looks attractive is a critical but surprisingly overlooked skill which is a fundamental part of the storytelling process – it makes it easy to read.

There is no point in assiduously researching a great news story, pouring your heart and soul into the writing and then seeing it plonked before the audience in an untidy and unappealing fashion.

Unwieldy blocks of text, mismatched fonts, ugly widows and orphans all pose a barrier to the readers. Their visual journey through the text must be smooth and badly set text is an irritant.

Setting in print . . .

. . . and let's begin with the first word.

Make sure it is in style. Some have the first word capped up but if it's too long it can look unsightly.

ANDREW LLOYD WEB-BER'S latest musical has broken all box office records after opening to sell-out crowds in London and on Broadway.

COMPOSER Andrew Lloyd Webber's latest musical has broken all box office records after opening to sell-out crowds in London and on Broadway.

Make sure the leading – the space between the lines – is correct. Most papers have a little extra leading to make sure the text looks open and is readable. If it gets changed or corrupted it can look too squashed:

A BABY was thrown to safety from the window of a blazing house during an arson attack which left her father clinging to life.

Six-month-old Daisy Tupper landed in the arms of a passing rugby player 15ft below moments before the room was engulfed in flames.

Her father, Joseph, who smashed the window to allow

by JAMES MOSS

bottom. 'The baby was in the air for ages, it seemed. When she was caught safely everyone cheered.

'The lad who caught her was a rugby player who told me he was on the way to practice.

'His mate was ribbing him because apparently he's normally rubbish and doesn't catch anything.'

But the cheers quickly died

LEADING IS TOO SQUASHED

Or too spacy:

A BABY was thrown to safety from the window of a blazing house during an arson attack which left her father clinging to life.

Six-month-old Daisy Tupper landed in the arms of a passing rugby player 15ft below moments before the room was engulfed in flames.

by JAMES MOSS

leapt to safety but injured her ankle as she landed awkwardly, witnesses said.

But as the flames grew fiercer, engineer Mr Tupper was forced to drop the baby from the window into the crowd.

'Time seemed to stand still,' said witness Alice Winter-

Orphans – single or part words left on a single line – look messy and a run of them makes copy look like a set of broken teeth. You can manipulate the text to avoid them, or sometimes it's just a question of rewriting a line:

He was pulled unconscious from the burning room by fire-fighters and taken to hospital where he was in a critical condition.

Police said the blaze was started deliberately and were hunting a ginger-haired suspect seen fleeing the scene shortly afterwards.

The fire broke out early yesterday evening in a two-storey, terraced house on a quiet suburban street in Burbton, London.

He was pulled unconscious from the burning room by firefighters and taken to hospital where he was in a critical condition.

Police said the blaze was started deliberately and were hunting a ginger-haired suspect seen fleeing the scene.

The fire broke out early yesterday evening in a two-storey, terraced house on a quiet suburban street in Burbton, London.

It was started when the arson-

If you make adjustments, also check you don't leave lines that make text look too squashed or stretched:

The fire broke out early yesterday evening in a two-storey, terraced house on a quiet suburban street in Burbton, London.

The fire broke out early yesterday evening in a two-storey, terraced house on a quiet suburban street in Burbton, London. It was started when the arson-

Ungainly widows are also a no-no:

A BABY was thrown to safety from the window of a blazing house during an arson attack which left her father clinging to life.

Six-month-old Daisy Tupper landed in the arms of a passing rugby player 15ft below moments before the room was engulfed (in flames.)

Her father, Joseph, who smashed the window to allow his wife, Mary, to leap clear before throwing his baby into the crowd, was trapped inside.

He was pulled unconscious from the burning room by firefighters and taken to hospital where he was in a critical con-

Check for horrid hyphenation. A word should break in a logical place that does not make it too hard for a reader to follow. A good rule of thumb is that when the hyphenation breaks a word it should leave at least three letters on either side of the hyphen. Two letters on their own look odd:

But the cheers quickly died away as the bedroom was engulfed in flames and Mr Tupper disappeared from view.

A firefighter wearing breathing apparatus climbed a ladder to get in the bedroom and brought him out a few moments later.

But the cheers quickly died away as the bedroom was engulfed in flames and Mr Tupper disappeared from view.

A firefighter wearing breathing apparatus climbed a ladder to get in the bedroom and brought him out a few moments later.

Ragged text looks better without hyphenation. If the house style is to have no hyphenation, make sure that it has not been used. Also take care when text is running around a narrow obstacle such as a headshot – it may take some tweaking and the use of soft returns to make sure it looks neat and tidy.

Watch how one leg of text runs on into another. If you end a paragraph at the bottom of one leg, a reader may not realise there is more of the story to come in the next leg, especially if, to continue reading the story, the eye has a long way to travel from the bottom of one leg to the top of the next:

A BABY was thrown to safety from the window of a blazing house during an arson attack which left her father clinging to life.

Six-month-old Daisy Tupper landed in the arms of a passing rugby player 15ft below moments before the room was engulfed in flames.

by JAMES MOSS

Her father, Joseph, who smashed the window to allow his wife, Mary, to leap clear before throwing his baby into the crowd, was trapped inside.

He was pulled unconscious from the burning room by fire-fighters and taken to hospital where he was in a critical con-

Often the fix is simply to delete a paragraph break so the sentences run on into each other. If it creates a two-sentence paragraph, that is probably better than an awkward switch from one leg to another:

A BABY was thrown to safety from the window of a blazing house during an arson attack which left her father clinging to life.

Six-month-old Daisy Tupper landed in the arms of a passing rugby player 15ft below moments before the room was engulfed in flames. Her father, Joseph, who

by JAMES MOSS

smashed the window to allow his wife, Mary, to leap clear before throwing his baby into the crowd, was trapped inside.

He was pulled unconscious from the burning room by firefighters and taken to hospital where he was in a critical condition.

After making any alterations, check the alignment of legs of text. If you are working in page editing software, such as InDesign, it's easy to knock them out of line, which looks amateurish:

ankle as she landed awkwardly, witnesses said.

But as the flames grew fiercer, engineer Mr Tupper was forced to drop the baby from the window into the crowd.

'Time seemed to stand still,'

Miss Winterbottom, a 26-year-old financial analyst, said she might have seen the man running away. 'He bumped into me. I'm sure it was him. I wish I'd realised and done something to stop him.'

Your final adjustments should not leave a line short (see middle example in figure 7.20) or the copy too long, so there are words (overmatter, right example in figure 7.20) which the reader will not see:

26-year-old financial analyst, said she might have seen the man running away.
'He bumped into me. I'm sure it was him. I wish I'd realised and done something to stop him,' she added.

said she might have seen the man running away.
'He bumped into me. I'm sure it was him. I wish I'd realised and done something to stop him,' she added.

← LINE SHORT

Miss Winterbottom, a 26-year-old financial analyst, said she might have seen the man running away.
'He bumped into me. I'm sure it was him. I wish I'd realised and done something to ← OVERMATTER

As a final check, lean back from your screen for a moment and half close your eyes so the text goes out of focus. You should then just see the shapes it forms. If it looks neat, full-bodied and pleasing, then the setting is probably right.

Setting online

Much of the above has little relevance in online publishing.

Screen size tends to determine how text appears, so, for example, there is little point in spending valuable time sorting out bad word breaks on your screen when they will not appear on most other screens.

Most websites set their text in **single columns** across the screen and have **hyphenation turned off**.

Simple **sans serif fonts** – ones without curly bits – are generally preferred and type is usually set at a bigger size than in print to make it easier to read.

Content management systems for online publishing tend to be simple and intuitive.

All the settings – from font sizes to styles, to leading and spacing between para-graphs – are likely to be predetermined with **limited manipulation** available to those inputting copy.

Some design features, such as the automatic need to place a picture or break-out quote at a certain point, may also be preset.

It is important to make sure that you **complete all the required sections** before publishing – this can make it feel more like form filling than journalism as you tick the boxes, set the tags and enable comments, but it is part of the publishing process and you would not want to create a story which fails to open properly or appears incomplete to the reader.

You may have to complete **several versions of a headline** – one for the home page, one for the story and even one to create a search-friendly URL – but, given the vital role this plays in bringing readers to your work, this is worth spending as much time on as possible.

On the page itself, you will need to **embed** video, pictures, graphics and social media posts carefully, as well as create links to sources and other stories.

Check a **preview** before pressing the publish button to make sure they all appear properly and that links are working.

Readers are daunted by **long chunks of text**. It's even more onerous while squinting at a smartphone screen or a tablet.

So, you will find news websites have an **open feel** to their text. That means keeping paragraphs short and to the point and using just **one sentence per paragraph**. There is always space between the end of one paragraph and the start of another.

Some sites, such as the BBC, want **clauses kept to a minimum**, occasionally at the expense of elegance in writing.

Text is run in **one leg** as readers scroll down a screen – they wouldn't want to go down a story and then back up to the top to continue reading.

It is usually **broken up every few pars** – using pictures, video or social media embeds, for example. Apart from helping break down text to bite-size pieces, it has the bonus of keeping readers scrolling through to get past the images and increasing the time they spend on a page.

Although not widely used, **sub heads** can help to break up text. In print, they are used merely to break up long legs of text or to fill out a space when copy falls short.

Online, however, they are more useful. Online readers tend to **skim**, alighting on keywords and speeding past other chunks of text. To maximise this, you can use sub heads as an **index**, checkpoints in a reader's journey which can help them to settle on the critical sections.

In a similar vein and although rarely seen in news websites, keywords and phrases can be made **bold** in the text to catch the skimming eye. However, along with underlining, it is a tactic usually reserved for setting hyperlinks.

Lists are more commonly used in web copy than in print. As they offer a lot of detail in a short format, this plays to the reader's tendency to skim while they hunt for information. They are a particularly handy device when working on a round-up of a complex story with lots of different angles.

Make sure, though, that they are set neatly, ideally with **each bullet point confined to one line**. If that's not feasible, try to make each of them roughly the same length so they occupy the same number of lines.

The SEO factor

Search engine optimisation is crucial to online journalism – there is little point in crafting a brilliantly researched story if no one can find it.

It is, however, an **art, not a science** and the goalposts are often moved.

There are said to be more than 200 criteria which determine where a published story appears in a Google ranking. It, along with other search engines, is striving to move away from the writing-for-robots school where news was judged not on its clarity or elegance but on its ability to stuff text with keywords and waymarkers.

Today, ranking is weighted towards **reputation**, linking to and from other sites, citation and its shareabilty through Facebook, Twitter and other social media.

Increasingly, the emphasis is that **quality writing** and journalism should trump attempts to manipulate the ranking system.

Personality counts, too. The more you work over agency and third-party source material, the more it will stand out. Using a barely disguised lump of wire copy won't cut it.

You don't always get what you deserve for journalistic effort but it's a long game, so the more your content stands out for its **reliability and readability**, the more you inch yourself towards the treasured top spot in a search engine ranking page.

However, while writers should not distort to accommodate the robots, they still need to play the SEO game.

You need to include **keywords and phrases** in a story. Think like a reader looking for a story and the terms they would type in a search engine to find it. Make sure they are included in the story; repeat them as appropriate, make sure they are not buried too deep in the copy and, of course, make sure they are spelt properly.

They should be **written out in full** at some point. Nicknames and short forms, such as RPatz and RiRi, may be fine for second reference but Robert Pattinson and Rihanna are needed.

You might consider putting **geography higher** than is ideal – even in the intro and where it adds nothing to the storytelling – if you think it's a crucial search term.

Remember **hyperlinks**, which are part of the reputation building. It's a two-way thing, with a you-scratch-my-back-we'll-scratch-yours philosophy of linking to and from third-party sites.

Do the work at the back end of your **content management system**. Add tags and meta tags and use the alt text function for pictures.

The big SEO winner is the **headline**, which needs almost as much care as the story itself (see Chapter 8). The robot tends to win over style or clever wordplay.

With more readers now coming to stories via social media rather than through search engines, writing a tempting **social media pitch** is a craft you will need to master, too.

Remember, though, that for all the theorising about how to promote material through search engines or social media, readers still want to arrive on a **compelling story**, brilliantly told.

They have invested time and effort in clicking through to your work – make sure they are never disappointed.

They are golden rules – observe them.

1   Accuracy
2   Know your audience
3   Nail the intro
4   Let it flow
5   Tell now, explain later
6   Keep it simple
7   Take ownership
8   Make it add up
9   Knock out the niggles
10   Get set before you go

*Key*points

Typesetting terms

Ascender: Portion of a lower-case letter that sticks out at the top

Banner: A newspaper headline stretching across the width of a page, usually at the top. Also called a **screamer** or **streamer**

Bleach: Where colours in an image or text are washed out to create a faded effect

Bleed: Type or an image which goes into the margin outside the main area of a page

Body type: The main typeface or font in which stories are set. Headlines are often set in a different type for contrast

Bold: Black type used for contrast or emphasis

Breaker: Any typographical device, such as sub-head or break-out quote, used to break up chunks of text

Broadsheet: Large-format newspapers such as *The Times* and the *Daily Telegraph*, with a more serious and formal style

Bust: When a headline or copy is too long for the space available

Caps: Capital letters

Centre: To set a headline or text in the middle of a column

CMYK: Colours – cyan, magenta, yellow and black – used in typesetting and printing. Mixing the four colours in various percentages creates different colours and shades. Colours can also be set by RGB (red, green, blue) from computer screen settings and Pantone, which uses numbered swatches

Crop: To trim a picture so only the most eye-catching portion remains or so it fits a given shape

Crosshead: Small headline used to break up or fill out copy. Also **sub-head**

Cut-out: Removing the background from a picture to make it stand out or to remove clutter

Deck: Old-school subs get in a lather about this. Many contend it refers to one of a series of headlines stacked on top of each other but it is misused to refer to a single line within a headline

Descender: Part of a letter, such as the tail of a p or a q, which sticks out below the line

Dingbats: A collection of arrows, blobs and other symbols used to decorate text

Drop shadow: Type set with a shadow background, slightly misaligned, for effect

Em or en: A unit of measurement for type. Nowadays, used in the context of an **em dash**, ie a long one, or **en dash**, which is a shorter one. For the record, an em is also one pica or 12 points, or about 4.233mm; an en is half that width

Flush left: Typesetting style where the type is aligned to the left of the column but ragged to the right, also known as **range left** or **ragged right**. Usually set so words do not hyphenate

Flush right: Typesetting style where the type is aligned to the right of the column but ragged to the left, also known as **range right** or **ragged left**. Usually set so words do not hyphenate

Font: The size and style of letters used to set text. Traditionalists say **typeface** is the correct name for the lettering design

Frame: Rule drawn around an object, usually a picture

Full out: Type which fills all lines of a paragraphs, except the final one. Also known as **justified**. May also refer to type where the first word of a paragraph is not indented

Glyphs: Set of special characters and symbols available within a font

Gutter: The space between columns of text or between pages in a spread

Hanging indent: Text where the first line of a paragraph is set full out but subsequent lines are indented

Image area: The page without the margins (or **bleed**). Technically, this is the only part of the page which should be printed but designers often use the margins and page gutters for effect or to link two halves of a spread

Indent: Text set in a few spaces from the left-hand margin

Italics: Sloping type, used for emphasis or contrast

Leading: The space between lines of text. The higher the leading, the more open text will appear. In lower-case type, leading is not usually set lower than the size of the font or ascenders and descenders will crash into one another

Leg: Column of text

Lower case: The usual form of letters

Orphan: A single word or a part of a word left on its own in a line of type

Pasteboard: The area outside the image area and margins of a page. Used for putting aside handy bits of text, artwork or imagery which might be used in the finished page design

Pica: Unit of type measurement

Pierce: Where another picture or text is overlaid on a picture. Also called an *overlay*

Point: Unit of type size. Still widely preferred, as it is more precise than using millimetres. There are 72 points in an inch or about 28 points to 1cm

Roman: Generic word for the most commonly used types of plain, upright type

Rules: Lines used to separate stories from one another

Run-round: Type which flows around an object, such as a picture or break-out quote

Sans serif: Generic word for plain, blocky type without frills. Commonly used for tabloid headlines and for both headlines and text online, as it is easier to read

Screamer: Exclamation mark. Affectionately(?) known as a **dog's cock**

Serif: The decorative frills added to type faces and a generic word for the kind of typefaces it creates. Commonly used for body type in newspapers and headlines in broadsheets or feature sections

Shy: Headline which is short of the space available

Stroke: A rule around an object or letter

Tint: Lightly coloured background panel which appears pale as only a proportion, say 10 or 15 per cent, of the full colour is applied. A **graduated tint** (or **gradient** in some page design systems) is one where the colour becomes gradually lighter or darker from top to bottom, from one side to the other or in a circular pattern

Transparency: Part of a design which is meant to be invisible. The **opacity** setting will determine whether it is fully see through or whether a screen effect is created

Upper case: Capital letters

Widow: The last line of a paragraph which sits on its own at the top of a column of text. Can be a single word or several words but always looks ugly

Wob: Short for white on black, ie white letters on a black background.

8

HEADLINES, QUOTES AND PICTURES

Writing headlines

Coming up with the perfect headline is an art. Online, there is more than a dash of geekiness involved, too.

Without a winning headline, who will notice your carefully researched, brilliantly written story? It's your sales pitch, so spend as long as you can polishing and perfecting it.

Headlines as lures

The headline is a stopping point, a lure to catch the eye.

So think like a reader. What would make you click through or stop and read? Emotive and challenging words infused with a sense of drama, conflict or humour — much as they are vital to a story, they breathe life into a headline, too.

You are selling the story with a headline, so it should contain the **strongest angle possible.** It is little different from writing an intro — find the gee-whiz moment, the biggest figure, the exceptional rather than the ordinary to capture the reader's attention.

Always grab the most **eye-catching figure**, be that because it is frighteningly large or worryingly small. There is no need to be precise, round up or down appropriately — for example, 296.8million in copy can reasonably be called 300million in a headline.

Be bold and **be specific**, so rather than the plodding and predictable — *Home secretary wades into row on gay marriage* or *Home secretary slams gay marriage plan* — go with what the home secretary actually said: *Gay marriage plan is an abomination, says home secretary.*

Use **keywords** in the headline to give the reader clues to what the story is about. Try to be specific: so (obvious as it seems) if the story is about a strike, then use the word *strike*, if it's about tennis then say *tennis* and so on. If it is about a personality, then it should include his or her name.

> You only require precision for effect £1.06: *that's all the royal family costs you*. Using figures, ie 7 rather than seven, is more effective in headline fonts, and single-figure numbers would not need to be spelt out even if starting a sentence, *7 hopefuls join battle for train contract*. Avoid using more than one figure in a headline, otherwise it will look like a maths question.
>
> ### *St*y*le*point

Writing headlines is a **creative challenge** and the thought process can be exacting. If you are stuck, walk away for a short break. A great headline often comes to you when you are least thinking about it. The longer you stare at the space you need to fill, the less likely you are to have that eureka moment.

Don't **repeat the intro** in the headline. Each is a selling point and you waste an opportunity if they say the same thing. One tactic is to adopt the sidestep (see Headline categories). Also try to ensure that the headline and any picture caption do not repeat.

Accuracy is all. Much like your story, a headline falls at the first hurdle if it is not a fair reflection of the story.

Those readers most likely to make complaints often react to the headline because it is in the largest type and is a brutally short version of the story, often without nuance or balance.

Ask yourself if every element of the headline can be justified by the words beneath. If the story says something *may* happen or is laden with caveats, is it fair to imply in a headline that it *will* happen? Have you taken something which might be implied or alluded to and made it fact?

Always **check the basics**. Does it contain the right figures; for example, does the copy say millions and you have written billions, do sums of money or death tolls match? Does it have the same names with the same spellings?

> A headline must strike **the right tone**. It's poor taste to put a punning or light-hearted headline on a story where someone has been killed or badly injured, even if the circumstances may be bizarre or the result of their own stupidity. Similarly, a light-hearted, celebrity or gossipy story is rarely well served by a straight headline. If an occasion is joyful or one of celebration, then don't be a curmudgeon. For the personal and human interest, the watchword is empathy – the headline is part of the process of telling the subject's story, not for making judgments or mocking. Be strident when you wish to campaign.
>
> ### *St*y*le*point

Headlines in print

Trying to define what makes a great newspaper headline is like trying to catch the wind. Everyone has their personal favourites, much as one man's £20million Rothko is another man's blotchy, dark squares.

What's not to like about this superb headline over a rather dry story about experts claiming that wind power was the only economic, rational answer to the nation's energy needs? *The answer my friend . . .* It's funny, clever and fit in a very tight space.

But while some readers might have had the tune stuck in their heads all day, critics will point out that the reference to a 50-year-old lyric would have passed many by. You can't please 'em all.

Headlines are impossible to categorise . . . but we can try.

Does what it says on the tin: Straight, to the point. *Man walks on the Moon.*

The updater: For running stories or follow-ups, where the art is to explain the background while making the update the focus. Hence, *First Moon landing astronaut admits it was filmed in a studio*

The negligee: Reveals enough of the story to entice but leaves something to the imagination. *Moon landings: The truth about those fascinating discoveries*

Partner in crime: A headline which works only when seen alongside a picture, sub-head or even the intro. *Gee, mum, the views are amazing* alongside a picture of the Earth taken from the Moon

The sidestep: A clever tactic for a story where straight feels too literal, limp or risks repeating an intro. *Astronauts win thousands of dollars in Moon bets* becomes *Did we have a good time on the Moon? You bet*

The 'Aah, I see': A rare gem, so subtle it mugs the reader without them realising. It gives pause; there is a moment of hesitation but then the penny drops. *Come see, come sigh* over a picture of rows and rows of millionaires' yachts at a boat show in a French resort. You'll get it in a moment . . .

The screamer: A tabloid speciality, usually set in a very large font, across the top of a page or a spread. The more melodramatic the better. *We're walking on the Moon!*

The wringer: Every ounce of emotion and drama is wrung out of a story. *Doctors said I would never get out of my wheelchair, now I'm dancing on the Moon*

The walkie-talkie: A wordy walk through the essence of the story. *My wife kissed me on the cheek as I left for the launchpad. By the time I got back from the Moon she'd left me for my cousin*

The punfest: Dog owners whose pets are *feeling ruff*, Easter events that are *eggstraordinary*, award-winning plumbers who are *flushed with success*, hairdressers who are *a cut above*, how Angelina had a *Jolie good time*; the list is groan-inducingly long. Made-up words, sometimes with arbitrary hyphens, *We had a Brazil-iant time in Rio, Goalden times ahead for striker, My inkredible tattoos* are also all-too frequently sighted. Try to be original or use sparingly

The twister: The groan-up version (geddit?) of the punfest. Take a well-known saying or title and rework to produce memorable headlines. Essex libraries with empty shelves, *Book lack in Ongar*; seabirds getting high from cartons of drugs which spilled from a sinking boat, *No tern left unstoned*; and *The Sun's* best headline of 2016 on Tom Hiddleston and Taylor Swift, *Tinker Taylor snogs a spy*.

Setting headlines

In print, it's a basic requirement that a headline **fits the space** allotted to it.

A single-line headline should never fall short or have its font be crudely manipulated to fit.

If there is more than one line, the words should, ideally, be of the **same length** and fill every one of them. Tweaking the font or the spacing between letters (kerning) is usually permitted but don't leave one line looking abnormally squashed while another is stretched out too far.

If not all lines fit precisely, it is better to have a **shorter bottom line**, drawing the reader's eye naturally down to the text, than it is to have a longer bottom line, which creates a visual block to the text below.

Don't pad a headline to fill. Adding an *a* or *the* or ellipses to make it fit may ruin the flow and it is better to rewrite.

Supermarket deal brings 1,000 jobs

FIGURE 8.1   Headline with words crudely squashed and spaced

Football stars seal stadium deal

FIGURE 8.2   Headline with wrong shape

Sex pest prime minister to face charges

Medal for life-saving doctor

FIGURE 8.3 Headline with breaks in phrases and names

Avoid **breaking names,** titles and clearly linked phrases across the lines of a headline, as it interrupts the rhythm. Hyphenated expressions and names should also be kept to one line:

Make it sparkle

Lose the source – *court, council, ministers, report, survey, scientists, experts* and so on are dull, procedural words. It is always better to say *Wind power 'will save our dying planet'* rather than *Wind power will save planet, says report.*

Just as you would with an intro, **keep it active.** The subject-verb-object style is the classic – and most concise – construction for a headline, as it suggests action and immediacy. *Man walks on Moon* is better than *Moon walked on by man* or *Man has walked on Moon.*

Avoid writing a headline without **a verb,** even if you only have two or three words, otherwise it will feel more like a label from an information leaflet.

Stick to **short words**. If you have anything with three syllables or more, try to find a shorter alternative.

A **headline needs rhythm**. If it does not roll off the tongue when you say it, then it will be hard for the reader to absorb. Alliteration and cleverly used rhymes are a winner but beware letting the wordplay get in the way of the flow.

Turn **negative** headlines into positive ones. *No refunds for passengers delayed on planes, We won't change stance on tax reform, insist Tories, Brilliant Jones can't secure England win.* They are all enhanced by indicating something *has* happened: *Passengers denied refunds for plane delays, Tories rule out tax reform, England lose despite brilliant Jones*

Similarly, avoid using **conditionals** such as *may* or *could*, as they also imply uncertainty. *Tories may help poor with tax reform* implies they probably won't.

Headlines should be written in the **present tense** – it adds urgency and a feeling of being up to date. Hence, *House prices break through £1 million ceiling*, even though it is based on a report from the end of the financial year; *Mudslide traps 200 miners*, even if some may be freed by the time you publish; and *Farmers feel pinch from dry summer* even if you are now well into winter.

*S*ty*le*point

Throwing so many nouns and adjectives at a headline in a misguided attempt to squeeze in detail will destroy the rhythm and create a **crossword clue effect** – a jumble for the confused reader to try to solve. It will be further confused when you throw in a verb which can also be read as a noun: *Fence row backlash dogs election blow council leader, 'Death-trap' claims restaurant in red-tape battle survival plan; Better headlines call editor 'a hopeless drunk'*

Punctuation slows down the rhythm of a good headline, so keep it to a minimum. Commas and clauses are to be avoided, as is the American approach of using a comma to replace the word *and* as in *Trump, Clinton fight goes to the wire*.

Single quotation marks are used in headlines to convey an opinion or claim. *Sugar tax 'will wipe out obesity once and for all'*. They do not provide legal protection but it is accepted practice to use them when headlining with unproven allegations from a court case.

It is common to drop the quotation marks if it is clear who is speaking, as in *Corbyn: I dreamt of being a milkman, My dream was to be a milkman, says Corbyn* or, where a picture or sub-head makes it obvious who is the subject, *Father made me give up my dream of being a milkman*.

Avoid putting quotes round an entire headline, as you risk losing a sense of narrative. Hence, *'Knifeman walked naked through city before stabbing victim'* becomes *Knifeman walked naked through city 'before stabbing victim'*

Use **question marks** with great caution. They suggest you are covering up a thin story and the answer is usually a resounding No. *Is Korea building a nuclear arsenal to destroy civilisation? Can Witheringthorpe Athletic win the FA Cup this year? Can Fido become the first dog to study astrophysics at Cambridge?*

For some, **exclamation marks** are overused and grammatically incorrect, often thrown at the page to tell the reader 'look at me'. Yet they are a red top's stock-in-trade and even if, as Mark Twain put it, they are like laughing at your own jokes, there is some evidence from online analysis that they persuade readers to look at the story.

Brilliant headlines are often built round **cultural references**, such as film or song titles, but before patting yourself on the back, make sure you are not trying to be too clever.

Ask yourself will every reader get it? Is yesteryear's advertising slogan, such as the much-overused *P-p-p-pick up a penguin*, likely to be widely remembered? While you will probably get away with a Beatles standard or the current No.1, a headline echoing an obscure 1990s dance anthem will go over most readers' heads.

*Style*point

The best headlines will **work on any level** – in other words, they are straightforward enough to understand without knowing the reference.

For a belt and braces approach, you can include an explanatory line in the text. Hence, for a story on singer Adele topping the celebrity earning charts, you might offer *£50m Adele is rolling in the green* and in the text say *Adele, whose hits include Someone Like You and Rolling in the Deep, has topped the charts all over the world.*

Sometimes you have to rein yourself in – you may be trying **a bit too hard.** Is there really any benefit in referencing the lyrics of a Queen song in a story about rail infrastructure, or a Monty Python sketch on a story about CCTV cameras?

And before pressing the publish button, make **a final check**. Read it out loud to yourself, slowly and word for word. Nothing is more embarrassing than a typo in a headline, especially on your splash:

> *Public reassurred over future of doctors' surgeries*
>
> *View from Beaminster, November 2016*
>
> *Uni fights absestos payout for Albert, 86*
>
> *Exeter Express & Echo, July 2016*

Or if you are having a pop about standards of literacy:

> *And in this furious indictment Sarah blames liberal education dogmas for creating a generation of hopelessly ill-equiped teachers*
>
> *Daily Mail, September 2014*

Online headlines

The online headline needs to follow many of the rules for those in print – but it also has to feed the algorithms which power internet search engines. **Functionality** has replaced wordplay and wit as you appease the robot.

Online, straight is supreme. Many of the most memorable newspaper headlines – from *Gotcha!* to *Zip me up before you go-go* to *Headless body found in topless bar* – would have been a flop online. Out of context, they don't tell you what the story is about.

Hence, in a piece on the influence of the song Jack Your Body on house music, the print headline was the rather smart:

> *The Jack that built house*
>
> *The Guardian, January 2017*

But the online version was prosaic:

How Jack Your Body began house music's squelching electronic revolution

Online headlines are waymarkers, **aids to navigation** that bring readers to a story from Google or other search engines. They have to tell readers what they will find when they arrive or give them a purpose for clicking through.

Moreover, when a headline appears on an internet search results page, the reader only sees a few words – it is their only clue – so the key information has to be contained **in the first few words**, too. In a Google News results page, for example, readers only see the first 55 characters, about eight words or so.

Think what a reader will type in a search engine when looking for a story. If they want to read about Jennifer Aniston getting married they will type, well, *Jennifer Aniston* and *marry* or *wedding*. On a controversial plan to build an eco-friendly, cow-dung-powered supermarket in Milton Keynes, they will type *Asda, Milton Keynes, cow dung*. If they need to find out when a new iPhone goes on sale, they will type . . . yes, you've guessed it, *when is iPhone on sale*.

Hence, the relative lyricism of *Marriage beckons for loved-up Jen* might become *Jennifer Aniston to marry actor Justin Theroux in Hollywood ceremony*. You have answered most of the questions people use for searches, the *who, what and where*.

This runs **counter to what newspaper headline writers are told**. Want to hoodwink readers who don't care a jot for Milton Keynes that a new Asda getting planning approval on the outskirts of the town is of interest to them? You don't mention Milton Keynes. Hence, your headline in print, pun included, might be *Cow-dung-powered supermarket wins pat on the back*, while online you might go for *Asda wins approval in Milton Keynes for store run on cow dung* or even *Milton Keynes: Asda wins approval for store run on cow dung*.

There is a little room for manoeuvre; search engines are now smart enough to recognise near misses with keywords, for instance, it will understand *iPhones* for *iPhone* or *killing* for *kills*.

Use **short words,** as readers are not going to type long ones in search engines. Make sure proper names are written out fully – so *Jennifer Aniston*, not *Aniston* – and, of course, make sure they are spelt correctly.

Lesser-known people may need extra identifying factors. Take Dave Budd? Who? Dave Budd, the mayor of Middlesbrough, of course. Google *Budd* and you may well be reading about a South Africa–born runner whose notorious flirtation with British athletics ended in tears. You might also get yourself tangled up with a little-known New York Knicks basketball player. And maybe another half-a-dozen or more Dave, David and Davy Budds whose exploits have in some way brought them to the attention of the internet. For precision, your headline is going to have identify him as *Middlesbrough mayor Dave Budd*.

What is the **right length** for an online headline? If you want the answer, look at the front page of the two most-clicked news websites in the world.

The BBC is the epitome of brevity; its front-page headlines, constrained to just four or five pithy words punching straight at the subject. They are exquisite on a mobile phone screen. Click inside and the headline on the page may breathe a little more with SEO-friendly additions but is still admirably tight. MailOnline sprawls out like a gangly teenager with ungainly headlines running to three or four lines or more and containing every keyword you could stuff in them. Click on the story and there are several sub-heads, all equally wordy.

In short, it is all a matter of style.

*Style*point

Unlike in print, a **question mark** can be a winner. It chimes with the notion that online readers are news hunters, looking for answers. When readers are in that search mode, questions evoke a powerful emotion to be tapped into – curiosity. They hold back information until the reader has clicked through. Hence, rather than *Halle Berry named the Bond girl we would most like to date*, you could try *Bond girl survey: Which one would we most like to date?*

Questions can also be **conversation starters** which invites feedback, such as *Churchill, Thatcher or Blair – who is the greatest prime minister? Why does Apple always win the PR war?*

While robots don't do jokes and clever wordplay, there are ways to **get round some of the limits of SEO**. When assessing headlines, search engines look at the HTML or page title, the stream of hyphenated words which appear in your browser when you click on a story. Many content management systems are set up so the story headline used on your site is used as the HTML headline by default. But it is sometimes possible to set the HTML headline manually; it can just be a random collection of SEO-friendly keywords, leaving you to write a snappier, witty and more reader-friendly headline. Bear in mind, however, that whatever headline appears on your site is used by Google News, regardless of your HTML headline.

*Style*point

If you are looking for humour, **make a virtue of literalism**. A style of headline has emerged which simply takes the says-what-it-does-on-the-tin approach to a droll extreme. Click on these stories and you know what you will get. *Photographer gets too close to 10ft bull shark, shark reacts badly; Man wears pink hat to the office for a month and no one comments; Woman in high-heels meets shiny floor, pain and embarrassment result.*

It's also worth remembering that Google and other search engines **don't just rank stories on headlines** and keywords. They are trying to place more emphasis on factors such as quality, reliability, hyperlinking, shareability and citation, as well as popularity.

Another factor which may force a further change of course, is the rise of **digital assistants,** such as Siri and Cortana, which respond to voice commands. It is likely that we will ask them to find stories in a different, probably more complex and colloquial, way than how we might type them.

The clickbait debate

All online headlines should be clickable. We want to tempt and tease as many readers as possible so they can be hooked in to our story.

It's tough because a headline has to persuade a reader to take an affirmative action – clicking on a link, often from a list of other equally alluring headlines, to get to a story.

So clicky headlines invite conspiratorially, like a gossipy friend saying 'Pssst, you'll never guess . . .'

Hence, the appeal of headlines such as:

> *You'll never believe what . . .*
> *The 17 most incredible/amazing/outrageous . . .*
> *The 17 things you should never say/will need*
> *This one thing will . . .*
> *This will really surprise you . . .*
> *What we really feel about . . .*
> *These suggestions/ideas/comments are truly hilarious . . .*
> *The internet was asked and the response was totally predictable . . .*

They work. They're simple, chatty and they get clicks.

But they don't please everyone. Critics worry we are on a dangerously slippery slope when editorial teams become content factories pouring valuable resources into getting clicks and promoting shareability above 'quality' journalism.

In August 2016, Facebook, the foremost distributor of online news, declared war on clickbait, saying it would use its algorithms to suppress stories containing phrases such as those examples above, in users' news feeds.

It defined clickbait thus: 'Pages should avoid headlines that withhold information required to understand what the content of the article is and headlines that exaggerate the article to create misleading expectations . . .'

Facebook may be doing us a favour – most of these formulaic approaches have been flogged to within an inch of their lives. They are clichés and, as the online audience matures, they will need to become smarter.

However, there is nothing wrong with a headline being clickable – that's the point, after all.

What turns the clickable into clickbait is what the reader finds when they land on the content to which they are directed.

This is why the quality of information gathering, writing and storytelling becomes paramount. It must give what is promised.

There is nothing more irritating for a reader than clicking on a story which promises information which is *amazing/incredible/outrageous* if it's not. Or something that is supposed to be *really surprising/unbelievable/hilarious* but is distinctly ho-hum. Or if the 17 things are little more than a badly cobbled cuts job unearthed with a bit of Googling. Or the *one thing you absolutely need to know* is something you and pretty much the rest of the world knows already.

A clickbait headline also leads you to advertisements or poorly signposted sponsored content. Clickbait takes you to a post which is slow to load, awkwardly presented or makes navigation a chore as it corrals you down an online cul-de-sac. Clickbait leads to a news page so overwhelmed with ads that it is almost impossible to find the story you are trying to read.

Clickbait leads you to a story which is wrong, poorly researched, old, badly structured, sloppily or lazily written or without linguistic flair. Clickbait leads you to stories which are just a poor rip-off from another site.

In short, clickbait leads you to a story that disappoints. If it disappoints it won't get read to the end. It won't be shared. It won't do your reputation as a writer any good. Readers will dodge your site in the future.

Clickability is the goal. Sell your story and sell it hard. But do not promise what you cannot deliver. Then, it is just clickbait.

Social media as headlines

Social media is indispensable as a source of stories.

But it is also the place to **make your sales pitch**, the digital era version of the news vendor in the street, yelling, 'Read all about it!'

Your goal is to get your social media headline heard above all the other vendors, some with more powerful voices, yelling just as enthusiastically to sell their wares.

First, remember your posts are, like an online headline jostling for attention in a search engine results page, **a waymarker for the reader**.

Your first goal is to use the limited time and space – and attention span of readers – to **persuade them to click through** to find out more.

Second, you want to build up an **audience of followers** for your publisher's accounts as well as your personal ones. Once they have read your story, you hope they will see you as a trusted and capable storyteller and will share it with their social networks, too.

There are times when a post needs to be no more than **an announcement**. Social media is the first place where breaking news appears. Don't waste the advantage over other sources – get it posted quickly without fuss or dressing. You have to believe that the immediacy or importance of the event is enough to entice.

Once it is posted, it is important to **keep updating.** On Twitter, in particular, it is possible, once each detail emerges, to let a story unfold through a series of tweets. Ultimately, you want them to visit a finished story, so don't forget to include **a link**.

Strike a sensible balance, though, making sure each update adds a layer to the storytelling and is not just an attempt to look busy. You are striving for **vibrancy** while remembering that quality is too easily diminished by quantity. Facebook and Instagram, for example, are less dynamic platforms and need updating regularly but not incessantly.

As with writing a story, **remember your audience** and keep the tone appropriate. For example, Twitter is a faster, more aggressive platform, beloved of media types, LinkedIn is for serious-minded professionals, Snapchat is dominated by teenagers and most users of Pinterest are women.

*Style*point

Even on those media which allow you more than 140 characters, you need to **be succinct**. Keep the headline and any summary tight. Why not discipline yourself to an arbitrary word or character count so you give the reader just enough to intrigue but leave them with a reason to click through to your site?

If you are trying to intrigue don't give everything away. It's the digital equivalent of the negligee. Hence: *Train company gloriously fires back at customer's rude complaint, The Nigerian Under-17 football squad are the most successful young side ever – just one problem, The only country which prefers Trump over Hillary won't surprise you.*

Wherever possible use an **image** – it's known to boost engagement. Video, graphics, maps, gifs and memes are just as valuable.

Always **give the reader a reason to click** – it might be the promise of valuable or up-to-date information (*What the Pope said when he was asked what causes terrorism*), something that benefits their life (*If you have a penis you must stop doing this immediately, 8 words that you should never, ever use on your CV*) or just something of great entertainment value (*People are suggesting their own Olympic sports for consideration and they're hilarious*).

Social is the keyword in social media – so strike a **conversational tone**. Create a sense that you are co-conspirators around a piece of information.

Use **simple, informal language**, yet remember you want an emotional response. Your headline can challenge convention (*Boris Johnson doesn't deserve our mockery for calling out Saudi Arabia – he deserves our admiration*), or attempt to stir up outrage (*Iran opens theme park where children get to dress up as soldiers and pretend to attack Western enemies*) – and never underestimate the power of animals and children (*The internet is sobbing after this dad texted his daughter all the reasons he loves her mum*).

*Style*point

Using quotes

Quotes – or, as the grammar fiends would have it, quotations – are essential in any story. Without one a story feels incomplete.

They **add authenticity**, directing the reader towards a source for the information you are putting before them.

A quote can be the story. A few carefully chosen words, an off-the-cuff quip or unguarded and outrageous remarks can change a nation's mood, generating outrage, dismay or laughter.

Follow-up stories are often built around reaction and comment especially when there is no significant turn of events.

Spotting a great quote

It's a necessary skill to be able to spot a great quote and to use it to its maximum effect. The pithy, punchy and rhythmic are best.

They should be **succinct yet powerful**, a pithy, emotional, passionate or humorous aside which adds another layer to the storytelling. The best are a dramatic statement of how someone is feeling, the description of an event in a way which brings it to life, or the statement of an obvious truth in an honest and simple way.

They should leave the reader with an ahh-say-no-more feeling.

These are not quotes:

> *Chris Warne, director of the Resistance Studies Network at the University of Sussex, said: "This is an exciting opportunity for the Resistance Studies Network and the University of Sussex to bring the importance of resistance to a wider audience and to explore the significance of locally born individuals within the wider resistance story."*
>
> *Brighton Argus, June 2016*

> *Professor Mike Grocott, chair of NELA and council member of the Royal College of Anaesthetists, which led the report, said: "Shortfalls in the perioperative care of these patients before, during and after major surgery may be negatively affecting patient outcomes and use of resources."*
>
> *PA, July 2016*

Use them sparingly

Quotes are **rarely the best way to tell a story.** Your interviewees should inform you so you can put it in your own words.

The words of those we interview are often ungrammatical, incoherent even. It is a **lazy storyteller** who writes a few paragraphs and then plonks a stream of quotes down and calls it a story.

There are exceptions, such as a dramatic first-hand account where the speaker has been involved in something extraordinary and their words are shot through with an emotion which you would struggle to replicate in narrative.

But these occasions are few and far between and it is better to **take ownership of what you are told** and write it as a narrative or reported speech.

Hence, *Camilla's spokeswoman said: 'Following the operation Her Royal Highness will remain in hospital for several days, followed by a period of recuperation for six weeks.'* is not much of a quote.

It's a piece of information wordily stated. It's much better to trim it back to *Camilla would be in hospital for several days and needed six weeks' recuperation, her spokeswoman said.*

Beware, too, of repeating yourself. Many quotes just say the same thing over and over again. The speaker is only making one point, so select the best example.

Another common error is to use a quote to repeat narrative, which is pointless.

Cook remains optimistic though, believing that the public and press backlash to the bill will mean that the right decisions get made. "I'm optimistic. When the public gets engaged, the press gets engaged deeply, it will become clear to people what needs to occur."

Huffington Post, November 2015

Eric Moseley, 69, who lives opposite the care home, said he heard "two or three bangs", but at the time put it down to military testing on nearby MoD land. "I did hear two or three bangs. It was probably the gun," he said. "I put it down to the testing we hear quite often."

The Guardian, December 2015

Use one or the other but not both.

This has a new iteration when quoting from Twitter or other social media. The writer will say: *Mr Johnson took to Twitter, saying: "I am disgusted and appalled by what has happened. #heshouldbehung"* above an embed of the tweet. Instead, try a cleverer means of introduction, along the lines of *Mr Johnson was among those to voice their disapproval.*

It is good practice to **attribute clearly before using the quote.** If the character has already been introduced, then a *he/she said* is enough. Don't launch into a quote and then introduce the fresh speaker at the end. This is a particularly confusing example:

> *Howe said the player "handled himself with real dignity throughout the process".*
> *"While people maybe grieve in their own way, I found it easier to come in and play and try and do everyone proud," Arter said.*
>
> *BBC, December 2015*

To edit or not . . .

It is a point of some debate whether to rewrite or tidy up a quote or to use only the words – solecisms, hesitations and all – that the speaker has used.

You can sidestep the debate completely by using clumsily worded quotes as narrative or reported speech.

Otherwise, the test is whether you are changing the meaning or intent of what the speaker is saying. Removing extraneous words or adding one for clarification is safe practice. It is likely that the speaker will be grateful for you making them sound more coherent.

It is a preferable – and cleaner – approach than using square brackets within quotes to explain a meaning, as in '*He [the rodeo rider] was killed because he was a stupid hick who didn't know his saddle from his stirrup,*' *Mr Jones said.* The use of [*sic*] to correct speakers is pompous.

Social media is riddled with semi-literate comments. If you are lifting, it is probably best to use them precisely because your version can be checked against a published original. However, make it clear where they are from, with a phrase such as *Writing on Facebook, Mr Smith said . . .*

Curse of one-word quotes

One- or two-word quotes make copy look spotty and cluttered, especially online, and add nothing to the meaning of what you are writing. They are comfort blankets for bad writers trying to deflect ownership of a sentence to a character in their story.

In these examples you can remove the quote marks and the sentence is just as effective, if not more so:

> *Mr Stevens' fiancee, Sarah-Anne Allen, said all charges were dropped and the Canadian will return to his home country "soon".*
>
> *Sky News, December 2015*

The Oscar-winning director told the LA Times that claims he was a "cop hater" were attempts to "discredit" and "intimidate" him, and called them "slanderous". BBC, November 2015

They "may" be tested regularly

> *BuzzFeed, January 2016*

He added that he does not wish his daughter to be "distanced" from the family home in Gatcombe Park Estate, Gloucestershire, and would rather she was educated "nearby".

> *Telegraph, June 2016*

He said it had been "a long time coming" and was "recognition" for 50 years of charity work.

> *The Sun, December 2015*

The rare exception might be where the word itself is extraordinary, made-up or wildly out of context and deserves added emphasis. Keep to one such quote in a sentence.

Where to stick them

Make sure you use the quote at the **right point in the story**.

Generally, they might be considered embellishment or colour and can be confined to the chronology.

Only use a quote as an intro if you are looking for a stylistic effect.

However, if you pin your intro on something being said, for instance, in an announcement, speech, press release or public forum such as a meeting or court hearing, then you will probably need to bring a quote in as part of the expansion to justify your intro.

In our pyramid, it is a great device to round off the expansion before you take a breather.

If you use a fragment of a quote in an intro or even within the first few pars, then **the full quote is needed later** in the story so the reader knows where it is from.

Hence, *A 'shocked and appalled' mother is demanding an apology from sports centre bosses after her disabled son was barred from a trampoline session* cannot leave the reader hanging without later using, preferably before the breather, *Mrs Hough said: 'The staff's behaviour and attitude towards a six-year-old boy was terrible and left me shocked and appalled.'*

Quotes make great pay-offs to lighter stories. If it is a light-hearted story, the droller or drier the quote the better.

> *"Unknown offenders approached a local authority car park and removed a large pay and display car parking meter and made off with it," said the spokesperson.*
>
> *Lancashire Evening Post, November 2015*

However, beware the **cheesy or scripted PR quote**. The words spoken should sound authentic.

> *He said: "Thanks to the fantastic work at Cancer Research I was able to beat cancer and return to full health."*
>
> *Falmouth Packet, March 2016*

Final checks

If you are supplied with a written quote, **read it before cutting and pasting** it into your story. It's surprising how often they have typing errors or might puzzle the reader:

> *The company administrator RSM Restructuring Advisory LLP said: "All coin assets of the Company were either banked in their local jurisdiction or disposed by specialist agents, and dealt with in accordance with the Joint Administrators' legal advice. Further details are included in our reports to creditors which are in the public domain and are attached for your ease of reference."*
>
> *Brighton Argus, June 2016*

And, of course, make sure you type your quotes correctly:

Asked what he made of it, he said: "If you don't read the newspaper you're uniformed. If you do read it you're misinformed."

Independent, December 2016

Finally, check if you use a **well-known quote**. They are frequently misquotes, misattributed or were never said at all. *It's life, Jim, but not as we know it, Beam me up, Scotty* and *Damn it, Jim, I'm a doctor not a* . . . are routinely worked into stories about Star Trek but were never said in the original series.

A note on quotation marks

Quotation marks are ugly things. Use them sparingly – but correctly.

Online, it is better to use double quotation marks, as they are easier to pick up than the tiny fleck of a single mark. A few newspapers prefer single quotation marks.

In headlines, single marks are most widely used.

The guide below, based on double marks, would be a standard – and sensible – approach, keeping punctuation to a minimum. If you prefer single quote marks, then reverse the usage.

Always consult the house style guide for any variation.

Full quotes

One par:

> *Sir Brendan Barber said: "This long-running dispute has clearly been an extraordinarily difficult period for the NHS."*

One par, the speaker's name at the end:

> *"This long running dispute has clearly been an extraordinarily difficult period for the NHS," said Sir Brendan.*

Two pars, speaker's name at the end:

> *"This long running dispute has clearly been an extraordinarily difficult period for the NHS," said Sir Brendan.*
> *"So I am glad that all the parties are strongly committed to tackling together the bigger, wider challenges facing the NHS."*

Full quote (NB no need to include attribution in each par):

> Sir Brendan Barber said: "This long-running dispute has clearly been an extraordinarily difficult period for the NHS.
> "So I am glad that all the parties are also strongly committed to tackling together the bigger, wider challenges facing the NHS."

Part quotes

At end of sentence:

> Sir Brendan said it had been "an extraordinarily difficult period for the NHS".

In middle of sentence:

> Sir Brendan said it had been "an extraordinarily difficult period" for the health service.

With attribution at the end:

> It had been "an extraordinarily difficult period for the NHS", said Sir Brendan.

Part quote with full quote run on:

> Sir Brendan said it had been "an extraordinarily difficult period for the NHS. So I am glad that all the parties are strongly committed to tackling together the bigger, wider challenges facing the NHS."

Although this is clumsy and is better written:

> It had been "an extraordinarily difficult period for the NHS", said Sir Brendan. "So I am glad that all the parties are strongly committed to tackling together the bigger, wider challenges facing the NHS."

Alternatively, break them like this:

> Sir Brendan said it had been "an extraordinarily difficult period for the NHS".
> He added: "So I am glad that all the parties are strongly committed to tackling together the bigger, wider challenges facing the NHS."

Quotes within quotes

Full sentence within a quote:

> Sir Brendan said: "When I informed the health secretary, he told me, 'Thank God, it's finally over.'"

Full sentence within a quote, then carrying on:

> *Sir Brendan said: "When I informed the health secretary, he told me, 'Thank God, it's finally over,' and then he broke down in tears."*

Part quote within a quote:

> *Sir Brendan said: "When I informed the health secretary, he said he was 'absolutely gobsmacked' that we had reached an agreement after all this time."*

Part quote within a quote but at the end:

> *Sir Brendan said: "When I informed the health secretary, he said he was 'absolutely gobsmacked'."*

Working with pictures

What makes a great news picture? The most memorable capture a moment in time – the dramatic, the original, the emotional, the amusing and the life-affirming. They tell a story in that instant.

In newsrooms, you may have a picture desk or picture editor with expertise in assessing and choosing images. However, it is becoming more common, especially online, for writers to select and place pictures to illustrate their stories.

Online, every post will require a picture, even if it's just a placeholder in a preset design.

Choosing the right picture

Writers must think how a picture choice **complements the storytelling**.

First, check it's the **correct picture**. Read captions closely to make sure you have the right place, subject or person. If you are lifting a single person out of a group shot, ensure you have lifted the right person. It's easy to muddle up relatives, especially if they have similar names. What about an Austin-Healey car for Austin Healey, the former England rugby player? It's been done.

Be **precise in your choice** to make sure the picture is **relevant**. If it's about cross-country skiing, don't use downhill skiing, if it's a story about fox hunting don't use a shooting party, if it's about India don't use a picture of Pakistan. Readers spot technicalities, such as mislabelling a piece of military hardware or a breed of dog, and will soon question your intelligence in the comments below the line.

If you use a head shot of someone, make sure they are mentioned in the story to explain its inclusion.

A picture works with the words and headline as part of a package. Think how the picture will look to the reader and make sure it **enhances, not contradicts**. You have a story about how a high street has been revived . . . don't use a picture of two old people stumbling along a near-deserted scene.

Ensure it is the **most interesting image available**. Movement, drama, facial expressions, clever juxtapositions, bright colours or use of contrast and lighting all contribute to making an image eye-catching. Remember, you are trying to get a reader to click on a story or hesitate while flicking through a newspaper.

Think carefully if you have **a choice of frames** – the most animated or best composed should win. A story on health spending might justifiably be illustrated with an image of the health secretary but it may not be as dynamic as a picture of surgeons performing an operation.

Make sure the image is **appropriate.** If it's a gloomy or sombre story, don't use a picture of someone grinning to illustrate it. Likewise, upbeat stories need happy images.

Pick photos that **fit the space** available. If you have a preset shape to fill, make sure the picture will crop into it comfortably. A tall, thin person will look odd cropped in a letterbox shape and, likewise, a picture of an aircraft rarely fits a portrait shape.

Crops should be tight, with as little dead or wasted space around the main focus of the image, especially when using head shots. If you use a sequence of head shots, make sure the faces all appear the same size.

In news, **people make pictures**. However, choose ones that show them doing something. Avoid pictures of grey-haired, middle-aged men (politicians/business people/dignitaries) in suits looking important but standing stiffly in a line. While a well-composed portrait can look stunning in close-up, it is best to avoid oversize head shots of people staring grimly at the camera.

Use as up-to-date an image as possible to **make it current**. A picture of someone in his 30s with a beard may be irrelevant or misleading if he is now in his 50s, balding and clean-shaven.

Be sure that you **have permission** to publish the picture, especially if it's being taken from social media or other online resource. Never lift the image and re-use. Remember that the copyright always lies with the person who took the image, not the person who uploaded it.

And don't forget to **caption it properly** ... see page 168. Remember to **include credits**, especially those required under the terms of use.

Writing to images

Sometimes, however, the pictures or video *are* the story. Here you have to make your words complement and provide context to what the readers can see for themselves.

A story may be built around a single eye-catching frame. **Let the picture be the star** and don't crowd it with words.

To take best advantage of a one-off picture, make sure the image is not used for a social media post or in a home page trail which might be seen in a Google search. The reader may not want to click through if they have seen it already. Tempt them with a headline promising an image they just have to see. Perhaps crop the image for preview so readers can only see a portion of it before clicking through for the big reveal.

Writing to video

Similarly, you should **be sparing with words when writing to a video**. Generally, you will only need a few paragraphs to set up the story and explain the context.

It is worth remembering, however, that **not everyone is going to watch the video**. They may be hampered by a poor internet connection or not be able to turn the sound on, while many are put off if they have to watch adverts, known as *pre-rolls*, before the footage kicks in. Video also struggles to hold attention if it runs for more than a minute or so, research suggests.

Quality may also be an issue – it may be difficult to see what is happening in poor definition, wobbly mobile phone footage or fuzzy CCTV images.

Hence, it is good practice to include in your story a summary of what is happening in the video.

Many standalone videos – from basketball trick shots to cute animal fails – are meant to be **entertaining and shareable**. Any words you write alongside them should be introductory and in the conversational style. A few chatty paragraphs will probably be all you need.

Increasingly, edited video packages contain explanatory captions so they can be watched with the sound off. Check them for inaccuracies, spellings and other inconsistencies with the accompanying text.

Picture spreads

In newspapers, images might be used to create a visually appealing page or even double-page spread. Typically, it might be an array of images from a town show or fireworks display, a collection of photography competition winners, unusual artworks or a spectacular set of landscapes from a less travelled part of the world. The pictures will catch the eye of the reader – your words need to tell the story of how they came to be taken and to provide the context.

So, you have a collection of spectacular wildlife shots from a photographer who likes getting up close and personal with nature and has just returned from her latest adventure. The best five or six are used big and bold to create an eye-catching double-page spread.

Your words must work with the pictures. If the pictures are being used because they are spectacular rather than obviously newsy, then a straight approach rarely works.

Instead, try walking the reader in:

Molly Wright has been lying motionless on her belly for two hours under the heat of the African sun. The adventurer and photographer knows any movement will ruin her chances of getting the shot she has been waiting for.

Finally, the lioness and her cubs wander up to the water hole for a drink. Molly knows danger awaits them, as this oasis in the parched savannah is full of crocodiles hoping to pick off easy prey.

And, as the crocodile pounces, she is poised with her camera.

Another approach may be to walk the reader through the images themselves:

> *As the sun sets across the savannah, a lioness approaches a water hole with her cubs, unaware a deadly presence lurks just beneath the surface.*
>
> *Suddenly, with a mighty thrash of its tail, a 12ft crocodile leaps from the water, jaws gaping . . .*

Your words should work as **commentary**. It should be measured, dramatic but, most importantly, enhancing, filling in details and colour which are not always obvious from the images themselves. Put yourself in the shoes of the reader; they do not need to be told what they can see, they need layers of extra detail. What led up to the image, what was the outcome (did the cubs get away?), what is this part of the world like, who took the picture, why was the photographer there and so on.

Think holistically so you do not leave gaps in the finished offering to the readers. Make the main (biggest) picture the principal subject of your story – it will seem odd if the reader's eye is drawn to one image while you are writing about another. However, make sure you cover all the pictures in the spread, either in the text or using the captions to explain them.

Try to say something different in each caption, even if the pictures are on a similar theme.

If pictures are in a sequence, make sure they are used logically, reading either left to right or top to bottom.

Online galleries

Using a selection of pictures online is a different proposition. The reader will not be looking at them in one spread but rather in a gallery, slideshow or long scroll down through a page. It means that the reader cannot readily cross-reference text against the images.

Your approach will depend on how the pictures are presented. Typically, however, you might need to write a brief introductory piece – think the first three or four paragraphs of our pyramid – with separate, explanatory captions for each picture.

However pictures are presented, don't dash off the words – our ABBC of good news writing can't be abandoned. Readers may be admiring the pictures but they will be watching the words.

Writing captions

Writing a picture caption is too often seen as a chore and dashed off at the end of the writing process.

Yet, it is integral to the telling of your story. It requires **thinking like a reader** to consider how the picture, story and other elements work together on the screen or page.

Most captions are a **short sentence**, either underneath or alongside an image used with a story. In some publications they begin with a kicker – a one- or two-word phrase and a colon to tee it up, followed by a few words of explanation.

A **head–shot caption** may require no more than a name, or a kicker and a name. Sometimes, there is no caption but the word *pictured* or *left, right, below* or *above* is in the story text.

In print, on a standalone (or *filler* or *gash*) picture you will need to write a self-contained caption running to a sentence or two to tell the entire story.

When you write a caption, don't just plonk down a label. Make it a vibrant piece of text which **describes what is going on** in the picture.

Hence this image:

FIGURE 8.4 Theme park photo.

Source: author

A game of chess at Chumps theme park

. . . is a label. Instead, this describes what is happening:

Check this, mate: Kieran Reynolds, 11, takes on his sister, Alice, in a game of chess at a celebration of the opening of Chumps theme park

Use the **present tense** in captions to give them animation. Include all **names** if space permits. Identify who is who by using *left* or *right* as the reader sees them, unless it is obvious – for example, the chess image is clearly a boy and a girl. If you don't have enough room for every name of everyone in a group shot, just focus on the central character. For example:

> *Kate Middleton joins six young gymnasts for a training session on the parallel bars*

If you do include everyone's name, check you have not left anybody out – don't have seven people in the picture but only six names.

A little creativity may be needed to make the link between picture and story. This can be a challenge, for instance when using a file picture.

If you have a picture of the event itself:

> *Rihanna beams with delight as she achieves a lifetime achievement award*

But if you only have a picture of her performing on stage a week earlier, then:

> *Rihanna shows the style which has earned her a lifetime achievement award*

This is a particular challenge online when the design of a website demands that every story must carry a picture at the top of the text. There may be no alternative other than to accompany a breaking crime story with a stock image of a policeman, while a financial survey always seems to be accompanied by a picture of a pile of notes and coins and a mental health story with a silhouette of a woman clutching her head.

In these cases, break the 'say what you see rule' and write a generic caption, maybe lifting a line from the story. The reader will make the link.

Captions, should **say something different** from the headline and the intro. Find another detail to use. Hence, if the headline is:

> *Girl kicked to death by muggers*

. . . and the intro is:

> *A girl of 12 bled to death in the street after being set upon by a gang of muggers who stole her iPhone*

. . . then the caption should refer to something else along the lines of

> *Future star: Murder victim Jade Nash was a promising gymnast on the fringe of the national under-13 squad*

Caption style points

If you have a set of similar-looking pictures – many websites use several frames simply as a means to break up chunks of text and to keep readers scrolling on mobile devices – **say something different** under each one.

If your pictures are a **sequence of images**, perhaps taken from a video or CCTV footage, then help the reader by placing them in logical order and numbering them or linking the captions with ellipses.

Check **photographers' captions**. Cameramen are not writers and can be less than diligent at checking names. Sometimes it works the other way and photographers who visit events get the names right because they ask the subjects themselves.

Make sure all spellings are **consistent**. It is baffling to the reader to see a name spelt one way in a caption and differently in a story.

Include a **photographer's credit**, wherever possible. They are undervalued and deserve it. Check if it is a requirement to include an agency credit. Be diligent if using a photograph under a creative commons licence, where the only restriction on use may well be on giving a credit and failure to do so will cost goodwill at best and a few hundred pounds at worst.

Online, you must include the **alt text** description of the picture. This is to help those with poor eyesight who use text readers to describe pictures. It's a must for search engine optimisation, too.

In print, give a thought to the **text setting** of a caption, too. Just as you wouldn't set a line of text with an orphan, don't do it in a two- or three-line picture caption – fill out the final line with extra detail if necessary.

Spend as long on a headline as you can – it's your selling point
Online, headlines also act as waymarkers – make sure readers can find them
Always use a quote – but make sure it is the best one
Pictures and captions are more than an afterthought – think like a reader to get the most out of them

*Key*points

9

TACKLING DIFFERENT SUBJECTS

You're a political animal but don't have much interest in sport? You love celebrity gossip but got a D in your science GCSE? You love gadgetry, geekery and social media but are not so sure about interviewing the victims of crime? Well, tough.

News reporters have to be jacks-of-all-trades. Or, better still, they have to be masters-of-all-trades.

There is no hiding place. As a generalist, you will have to tackle everything a newsdesk can throw at you.

Enjoy it. It's a healthier way to be – you will be a better reporter, a better writer and a better human being if you are ejected from your comfort zone.

Back to basics

If you feel challenged working on a subject you are unfamiliar with, go back to basics.

Your story will hinge on the depth of the research you carry out, your ability to connect with people and to take a genuine interest in their worlds, the skills you have as an interviewer and your willingness to keep asking questions.

Don't be afraid to tell an interviewee that you are not a specialist and to ask them to explain in as simple terms as possible.

Don't be afraid to call or email back for clarification if you are unsure. Do it again if you are still unsure.

Don't write anything until you understand. If you don't, your reader never will.

Once you have the details and quotes you need, then remember our mantra. You are a **storyteller**. Your job is to gather information, assess it and then produce the most compelling copy you can find.

Story v setting

Above all, remember the speciality is no more than the setting.

Your story will not be about politics, a court hearing, science or the mechanics of a business meeting. Your story should be about the characters who are part of these worlds, the conflicts within them and about how we who do not inhabit them are affected or influenced by those events.

In films, plays, TV or books the settings may be interesting; we need an understanding of how they work and what we see or read sheds light upon them.

But it is the people we put in those circumstances and the challenges they face which enthral us. Saving Private Ryan is not about war, A Beautiful Mind is not about mathematics, The Karate Kid is not about karate, The Walking Dead is not about zombies and Field Of Dreams is not about baseball.

Always get on with the telling and **don't get bogged down with explaining**. Because the background may be technical, writers fear they must walk the reader through very slowly and painfully. Invariably, the result is plodding, dull copy.

Think of an obscure Olympic sport in which a Briton is challenging for a gold medal. You don't have to understand every nuance of every rule of the competition to enjoy watching it.

So it is with news – build the story and the reader will come.

Celebrities

Readers love 'em, editors love 'em, you need to love 'em too.

Celebrity culture is rampant. Newspapers have fed off it for decades. Online, where the merest mention of side-boob sends visitor numbers soaring, celebrities equal eyeballs.

But no matter how irritating, self-serving, talentless and vacuous many of the 'stars' seem to be, you **cannot shut yourself away from it**.

You need to know your Arianas from your Elbas, your EastEnders from your Emmerdales and your Khloes from your Kendalls. Intellectual indifference is not an option.

Think of celebrity news as **soap opera**. It details the lives of a cast of personalities with whom readers feel they are familiar. Just like their on-screen characters, many of them grow up, get married, have children and die before our eyes.

We are so familiar with some of them they do not even need surnames, even in an intro:

> *Gwyn and Chris's "consciously uncoupling" was one of the friendliest separations in Hollywood history.*
>
> *Mirror Online, April 2016*

Celebrity news changes our storytelling convention. The focus shifts from action to **character** – from the what to the who.

By definition, celebrities are – or should be – **interesting people**. They have unusual jobs, many are talented and entertaining, they are also wealthy and move in rarefied circles. Your stories should give an insight into this sometimes fantastical world. It is necessary **escapism**.

In many celebrity stories, the **events are relatively trivial**. It is who they happen to be which makes it of news value. Would any of these major celebrity stories of the past couple of years have attracted any coverage had ordinary people been involved?

> *Jeremy Clarkson suspended by BBC: Top Gear presenter 'punched producer because he didn't have dinner ready'*
> *(Independent, March 2015, Impatient man slaps workmate)*
>
> *Johnny Depp and Amber Heard in marriage split*
> *(BBC, May 2016, Fractious couple divorce)*
>
> *Royal baby: Duchess of Cambridge gives birth to baby girl*
> *(The Guardian, May 2015, Unemployed couple have another baby)*

Elsewhere, stories are built around **what the rich and famous say** as they reveal snippets about their lives. They are frequently culled from **social media,** recycled from in-depth interviews stars have given to magazines or TV shows or taken from **press junkets** and pre-arranged **events** where stars promote their work or receive awards.

Inevitably, the celebrity is using their fame to **promote something** – a new film or book, a fashion line or even a charitable cause. If the project is legitimate, it may be enough to focus on that for your story.

So, you enter a Faustian pact – a puff for them in return for a snippet, an insight into their working or personal lives. Focus on this to fashion a story and **keep the puff buried** as an aside in the copy.

Celebrity meanders from news to content, from serious to trivial and back again. As such it fits **any writing format**. We can be straightforward with a classic intro and build a pyramid:

> *Angelina Jolie has filed for divorce from Brad Pitt after two years of marriage, a lawyer representing Jolie has confirmed.*
> *Independent, September 2016*

Or use a walk-the-reader-in conversational approach:

> *They have been Hollywood's starriest couple for more than ten years.*
> *But today it emerged that Angelina Jolie has filed for divorce from Brad Pitt.*
>
> *Mirror Online*

Or even a commentary style:

> *It is the shock split that has sent social media into a meltdown.*
> *And although some seem genuinely upset by the news of Angelina Jolie and Brad Pitt's impending divorce, others have delighted in sharing Jennifer Aniston memes.*
>
> *MailOnline*

Often your writing needs to walk round the lack of meaningful action. Adopt a **chatty, gossipy style**, as if you are telling readers about a personal friend.

> *Let's be honest, nobody liked the idea of Taylor Swift and Rihanna having beef with each other.*
> *So most were actually jumping for joy when the pair were spotted hugging it out at Coachella over the weekend.*
>
> *Mirror Online, April 2016*

Many of today's celebrities take a deliberate choice to turn their lives into a public spectacle and are **complicit in the attention it brings**. Stories are staged or at least highly managed – romances are faked, spats and feuds are dreamt up and wardrobe malfunctions are contrived.

As a news writer, you invariably choose to play along but you need **a healthy dose of scepticism**, too. Bear in mind that your readers can spot the fakes a mile off.

> *Dramatic footage captures moment Olly Murs performs Heimlich manoeuvre on choking woman.*
>
> *Evening Standard, December 2, 2016*

> **"** *That video of Olly Murs is a PR stunt at its worse, I'm sorry if someone is choking the last thing you grab for is a mobile phone to film it.*
>
> *Twitter user Fiona May, December 2, 2016* **"**

> *Olly Murs admits video of him saving a choking woman was really just an Alan Carr comedy sketch.*
>
> *Metro.co.uk, December 3, 2016*

Use celebrities as **a cultural reference point** on hard news stories. Connections to the well-known can lift the everyday, even if it is milking the definition of celebrity.

> *The brother of a Boney M singer has been jailed for life after hiring a hitman to kill his rival following a bitter dispute over control of a mosque.*
>
> *Sky News, October 2016*

Just because you are writing about the well-known, **don't forget the basics** – include ages as a matter of routine, mention significant others if relevant and check the spellings. Look out for the quirks and stylised names, such as *CeeLo Green, Meat Loaf* (two words), *Guns N' Roses* and so on.

For all their courting of the media, celebrities can be surprisingly thin-skinned. Make sure your **sources are reliable**, particularly if the resulting story is likely to be perceived as negative.

Celebrities can, with much more justification, be protective of their families and those who are famous only by association. Their children, in particular, are off limits – only involve them in stories with **clear consent**.

Not only are they quick to take umbrage if something upsets them, they also have deep pockets to pay for expensive lawyers.

> Some global stars, as the showbiz cliché goes, need no introduction. But it is still worth reminding readers in the story that Madonna is a singer, George Clooney is a Hollywood actor and Kim Kardashian is . . . well, whatever she is.
>
> *Style*point

Other stars are not universally known and you will need to state sooner in a story, even in the intro, why they are well known: *Saturdays singer Mollie King, Strictly contestant Ore Oduba* or *reality star Sam Faiers*.

Also, celebrities with **long careers** have different identities to different audiences. To one generation Ian McShane is Lovejoy and Diana Rigg is an Avenger and a Bond girl. Today they are Game of Thrones stars.

Courts

The world of news writing is split into two camps; those who master court stories . . . and those who don't.

Courtrooms are places of great theatre. Think of all the fictional legal dramas, from The Crucible to Twelve Angry Men to John Grisham. It's easy to fashion the highly readable and entertaining from the events played out in front of a jury.

Drama, conflict, settings, colour, humour, characters, a beginning, middle and an end – the court story has them all, wrapped up neatly in one place and played out in front of reporters given the best seats in the house.

It would be a crime to make a mess of it.

Detecting the story

The key to court stories is **unwrapping the story from the legal process**. It is rarely important where the case was held, who is prosecuting, defending or judging, how many charges the defendant is facing, how they plead or even what they wear in the dock.

In criminal cases, what matters is the **story of the crime** alleged to have been committed. In civil cases you need to dig out the **story behind the dispute** before the judge.

Courts are the conduit to the story. The events that play out are wrapped in legalities dressed in formal and daunting language – but that has to be set aside.

You must **rebuild a picture of the events** which are being replayed before judge, jury or magistrate. Therein lies your **story** – from drunken driving to serial killings, from the multimillion-pound business dispute to the neighbours bickering about a fence. It is your chance to say what happened, how it happened and why.

Be ruthless

It's **easy to be overwhelmed** in court. A lot can be said in the course of a day. Many strands of evidence are examined, sometimes in immense detail. Step back to see the bigger picture. Several hours of a witness's technical evidence might boil down to very little of wider interest. For example, a forensic expert may spend some hours explaining a test he or she has carried out but it amounts to no more than an assertion that it places the accused at the scene of a crime. That may be all you need or have space to tell.

With a notebook full of material, **you need to be ruthless** to reduce thousands of words spoken in court down to a few hundred. As you make notes, mark those remarks that stand out to you as important as you go along. Underline the best quotes.

Always **pick a focus and stick to it**. On the opening day of a criminal trial it is likely to be an account of the allegations and the evidence against the accused. As the trial goes on, however, you will hear more and more detail. Pick one and run with it through your intro and expansion. Don't try to cram in tangential material.

Using pyramids

Once you have picked your focus, court copy **fits our pyramid perfectly**. Spot an intro and then build it through an expansion:

> A conman who likened himself to gentleman thief Raffles tricked wealthy widows out of hundreds of thousands of pounds of jewellery, a court heard.

Much of the art of court writing is in making it look like it isn't a court story. So we go on:

> Well-spoken Reginald Young was said to have befriended lonely women online before wooing them with expensive meals, gifts and weekends away.
>
> After winning their trust, the 48-year-old convinced them he was a high-class jeweller and wanted to take their most expensive pieces away to value them for insurance purposes, the jury heard.
>
> Young, who told some of his victims he was a minor aristocrat called Lord Leech but was really a twice-divorced mechanic from Bognor Regis, allegedly then vanished without a trace.
>
> When police finally caught up with him, he was said to have joked with officers: 'Indeed, I'm like Raffles, you know. A gentleman thief. I never hurt anyone, just separated a few old fools from their money.'

This (imagined) story has only one reference to court and one to a jury, flows well and yet is legally sound.

Moreover, it is **highly focused**. We introduce only one character and **tell his story**, keeping it simple. There will have been lots of twists and details which we have left until later, or left out altogether. It steers clear of any complexities.

After our intro and expansion, we find the appropriate point at which to begin our chronology:

> *Young, a child actor who never got over the disappointment of failing to make a go of his stage career, found his victims on Matchmeup.com, Anytown Crown Court was told . . .* and so on through the story in a simple progression.

After the prosecution opening, the case enters a second phase by hearing evidence from some of Young's victims. We can write a fresh story with a new focus:

> *A wealthy victim said she was lonely and desperately looking for love when she fell prey to an alleged trickster who stole her £20,000 diamond necklace.*
>
> *Isobel Rankin admitted she was easily taken in by Reginald Young when he told her he was a wealthy jeweller from an aristocratic family.*
>
> *The 68-year-old, whose City stockbroker husband died ten years earlier, told a court she fell head over heels for the politely spoken stranger and felt safe handing over the diamond and emerald necklace.*
>
> *When her lover disappeared with the necklace, a wedding anniversary gift from her husband 30 years earlier, it left her devastated, she said.*
>
> *She added: 'Reggie was so kind and charming. I was smitten. But now I realise I was just a lonely old fool, desperate to find love.'*

And we take a breather.

> *Mrs Rankin was giving evidence on the second day of Young's trial . . .*

Again, we have kept it very focused. She might have been one of several victims who gave evidence but she was the most colourful. We tell *her* story. It's just two characters, stripped clear from the court setting.

Notice, too, how there has been **no stopping for a lengthy recap** of the evidence or any of the court procedure from our earlier story. It doesn't need it to tell the story of a lonely, gullible widow. Too much court copy falls into this trap as writers forget the mantra – **tell now, explain later**.

We may get several more days of evidence, including the defence and, ultimately, if Reginald Young is found guilty, the sentence. On each occasion, start it as a new story with a new focus.

The **sentencing** – or ruling in civil cases – is where court copy can go awry with too much backtracking. The intro is usually straightforward:

> *A conman who compared himself to gentleman thief Raffles has been jailed for ten years for tricking wealthy widows out of hundreds of thousands of pounds.*

The sentence is a moment of theatre. It will also be what is fresh about the proceedings – the new in the news. So, having set it up with the intro, this is what we expand upon in the next few pars. Do not launch into an immediate recap.

> Reginald Young was told he was ruthless and heartless for the way he deceived his lonely and vulnerable victims over the course of seven years.
>
> Sentencing him, Judge Sebastian Wigg said police were sure he had targeted other women who were too embarrassed to come forward.
>
> 'You likened yourself to Raffles in one police interview. But let me tell you, you are no Raffles,' the judge said.
>
> 'Raffles, if you remember, was a thief but a thief who had a shred of human decency. You had none. You cared nothing for anyone but yourself.'

This is sharply focused on the sentence. There is just enough backstory to make it comprehensible to a reader coming to it for the first time but it's kept fresh for those who have been following it.

There may yet be **further developments**, especially in high-profile cases, as victims, their families, the police and prosecutors, maybe even the defendant's friends and relatives, or even the defendant if he or she is acquitted, have their say after the case is done. If you focus on the reaction in the intro, stay with it and don't recap until you get beyond the breather.

The **approach is the same for a civil case**. Treat each update – through the claimant's case, evidence, defence and judgment – in the same way, picking a line, focusing on it through the expansion and avoiding lengthy recaps. Civil cases can be notoriously complex, with cases hanging on a technical definition and fine legal judgment. Don't let it distract from the bigger picture.

Some simpler cases, especially in a **magistrates' court**, may be done in a day. You will probably need to write only one story and need to decide whether the sentencing, the details of the offence or even something from the defence is the most important angle.

> The mitigation or explanation for a crime can often be the most intriguing part of a story, as it explains why someone has broken the law.
>
> GRAEME Swann was on a mercy mission to rescue his cat when he was arrested for drink-driving, a court heard yesterday.
>
> *Express, August 2010*
>
> A JOKER said he told a court security guard he'd planted a bomb in a court room as an "ice-breaker".
>
> *Plymouth Herald, January 2015*
>
> ### *Style*point

Legal requirements

If a defendant has been found guilty or admitted to a crime, then you can treat the allegations made in court as proven. This can help you move coverage further away from the courtroom. There is little legal need to qualify or attribute claims, although some mitigation or defence should be included for the sake of balance.

There are plenty of legal niceties which must be observed – they apply to both civil and criminal cases. Don't, however, let them wreck the flow of the story.

- Obey all the judge's orders and restrictions on what can and can't be reported. Observe strictly the rules on preserving anonymity, notably children and sex offence victims. Some writers like to include a line saying a character *cannot be named for legal reasons*, although it isn't necessary
- Behave yourself in court. Be professional, listen intently and don't disturb the proceedings. However, don't be intimidated. You have a right to details of defendants and charges, no matter how unhelpful court officials may be. Also, you are entitled to question rulings which affect your right to report the case. Magistrates and their clerks can be wild in their interpretation of laws protecting identity and so on. Send a note to the judge if you are unsure what his rulings mean and especially if you think they may be too onerous. The judge will want to explain what he or she expects of you and your coverage
- In most cases you can tweet from the courtroom. But don't use your device to record proceedings or take pictures
- Always state whether a defendant denies or admits a charge – even if it is towards the end of the story. Use the line *The trial continues* at the end to indicate a case is ongoing
- Ideally, you should include all the names and addresses of all the defendants and what they are charged with. However, including a lengthy list running to several paragraphs may not be practical where space is limited. If you have referred to no defendant by name or just one or two, then conclude with a sentence such as:

> *Twelve men, aged between 18 and 42, deny charges of theft, fraud and money laundering. Another defendant has admitted theft.*

or:

> *Jones and six alleged accomplices deny a total of 15 charges of murder, arson and theft.*

- Always state what the charge is but use your common sense if it is a hugely wordy and technical offence under an obscure act. You can slim it down to say, *He denies six offences under 18th-century gamekeeping laws.* Nonetheless, be precise when describing offences – theft is not the same as robbery or burglary, for instance

- Again, always state what the sentence is but it can be slimmed down — for instance, *He was jailed for a total of 15 years*, or *He was fined a total of £2,000 with £300 costs* rather than spelling out individual penalties, especially if space is tight. Always check your maths and do not muddle fines and costs

- Identify the defendant fully. An age and town should be enough without a house number or street name in national publications, although a regional publication would probably want a fuller address. If it is a common surname, such as Jones and Smith, identify the defendant as closely as possible to avoid implicating anyone with the same name

- Always make it clear that allegations or, indeed, anything which might be disputed is attributed or clearly identified as a claim. Phrases such as *the jury/judge was told, the court heard and allegedly* or *was said to* will cover this. Use common sense, though, as mundane details are unlikely to be disputed

- Say in which court a case was heard but, unless geography is important, weave it in later during the chronology

- It is necessary to make a story from a foreign court fair and accurate. However, for newspapers which do not circulate in the country any legal restrictions may not apply – for example, on naming of juveniles and so on. Online coverage may need to be more restrained because your story will be widely accessible

- Give the story one last check to ensure you have covered all the necessary legal details – it's easy to knock them out with a last-minute rewrite. And, of course, it is necessary to be entirely accurate. Slip up here and no lawyer will save you.

Death and obits

Death can be underwhelming . . . and, when the life which has gone before it is far more interesting than the moment of leaving, it presents a problem for storytellers.

Old people die all the time, often peacefully and without ceremony. From the factory worker who spent 60 years in the same job and a lifetime in the same modest rented cottage, to the glamorous celebrity with a jet-set lifestyle among the rich and famous, we want to tell the story of their lives.

Their deaths provide writers with an entry point but their passing may have been expected and unremarkable.

These would be perfectly sound intros:

> *Actress Mandy Makepeace, who won an Oscar for her portrayal of a one-legged cowgirl in Hopalong Cassie, has died at the age of 93.*
>
> *A factory worker who helped to build a code-cracking machine which turned the course of the Second World War has died.*

Given that Mandy, who hasn't been in the public eye in recent years, shuffled quietly off this mortal coil in a nursing home in Wisconsin, it is where to go next that many writers stumble.

They revert to **plonking the intro** on a life story, which, while full and exciting, begins more than 90 years ago and may have reached its zenith before most of your readers were born. It is, therefore, by definition, old news.

We need to adopt the weave and to remember the trump card is what is new, not what happened many years ago. Telling the death and reaction to it leads into a retelling of a life less ordinary.

> *Actress Mandy Makepeace, who won an Oscar for her portrayal of a one-legged cowgirl in Hopalong Cassie, has died at the age of 93.*
>
> *The star died, surrounded by family and friends, in the retirement home where she had lived for the past 15 years since her film career faded.*
>
> *Her family said Makepeace, whose flirty on-screen relationship with co-star Reg Macho delighted audiences in the 1950s, was cracking jokes to the last, telling them she was 'exiting stage left'.*
>
> *Son Michael said his mother's appearances in more than 100 films, including The Showstopper and Farewell My Lovelies, 'had earned her a place in the canon of greats from silver screen'.*

We are now at our breather and ready to resume with the story of her life, beginning with her childhood and going through her struggle for success, her accomplishments and the controversies through her career. Further tributes from friends, family and associates might round it out.

And likewise . . .

> *A factory worker who helped to build a code-cracking machine which turned the course of the Second World War has died.*
>
> *Reg Overall, described by his grandson as one of the unsung heroes of the battle against the Nazis, had been battling cancer.*
>
> *He died in the modest cottage where he lived all his life and just yards from the former site of Blitz Engineering, where he soldered some of the 6,000 electrical connections in the Mysteron machine.*
>
> *As the last surviving worker, his death marks the end of Anytown's links with Blitz, which closed shortly after the war.*

This is not the same as writing an obituary, commonly a longer piece which is an appreciation of someone's life in a logical order and in its historical context. It is written without the news trimmings and reflects on their accomplishments, successes and failures.

Politics

Many news writers have politics in mind when they think of a career in journalism. It has substance, tackles the big issues and offers a chance to hold the powerful to account.

Bad storytellers, though, make politics achingly, mind-numbingly dull.

Get out of the bubble

Politics is the easiest of all the subjects a news writer will have to cover.

There's lots of it; it's easy to find. The subject matter is, for the most part, worthy, public and impersonal, so getting people to offer an opinion is rarely troublesome. Politicians want to be heard. They expect to be asked questions. They like journalists.

Many news writers struggle to turn this stream of easy-to-obtain material into **engaging stories**. The worst get trapped in a bubble with politicians, detached from what most of us really care about.

The first step with political stories is a backward one. **Stand as far back as possible**. Ask if you are writing about something because you think it's important or because it's interesting to your readers?

Stepping back will help you explore the **effects, implications and significance** of political discussion and decision-making. These, rather than the mechanics of politics, should lie at the heart of your storytelling.

This is the intro to a 900-word to-and-fro between politicians over the structure of a budget. It's important but, written like this, it isn't a story.

> *The Scottish government has been accused of cutting nearly £330m from council funding to help pay for education and social care spending in next year's draft budget.*
>
> *The Guardian, December 2016*

It's typical of too much political reporting. It's about politics and politicians. It's stripped of colour; it lacks humanity and relevance.

Other versions were equally unengaging:

> *Scotland's finance secretary Derek Mackay has pledged a funding increase of £240m for local services as he set out his draft budget.*
>
> *But opposition parties said the amount of cash going direct to councils will be cut in real terms.*
>
> *BBC*

> *Opposition parties have slammed Derek Mackay's Scottish budget.*
>
> *ITV*
>
> *A row has broken out over council cuts following the announcement of the Scottish budget.*
>
> *STV*
>
>

That's a shame because it does matter; it affects the lives of millions of people.

An intro based on a quote used five paragraphs later in *The Guardian* story might have rescued it:

> *Ministers were today accused of ripping the heart out of public services by cutting hundreds of millions of pounds from council budgets.*

Forget the forum

Focus on **what is said**, rather than the forum in which it is said. A speech, a report from a committee of MPs, a council agenda and a parish council meeting are there to be mined for stories. But they are your source, a starting point. So . . .

> *Sajid Javid, business secretary, has called for emergency corporate and personal tax cuts to avert a Brexit slump, confirming that cutting the deficit was no longer the priority.*
>
> *FT.com, July 2016*
>
>

. . . becomes:

> *Emergency corporate and personal tax cuts are needed to avert a Brexit slump, Sajid Javid says.*
>
> *They have become more of a priority than cutting the deficit, the business secretary insisted.*

In this case, the source of the announcement is both obvious and irrelevant . . .

> *The Ministry of Defence has announced plans to sell off 13 military sites to raise £225 million and provide land for up to 17,000 homes.*
>
> *Belfast Telegraph, September 2016*
>
>

. . . and is better written thus:

> More than a dozen military sites are to be sold to raise £225 million and provide land for up to 17,000 homes.

The aliens have landed test

Imagine the announcement is made on the TV or radio that aliens have landed on earth. What matters most to the audience – the arrival of aliens and the likely consequences for humanity – or the name of the person who reads the announcement?

Even when the person saying it is important, the content can be of greater interest. This intro needs turning round:

> Chancellor George Osborne has announced that the government will almost double its investment in cyber security initiatives over the next five years, spending an additional £1.9bn.
>
> *City AM, November 2015*

The announcement has resonance for every taxpayer, as well as the countless businesses which are threatened. It's not a story about Mr Osborne:

> An extra £1.9bn is to be spent on protecting companies from cyber attacks by terrorists and other criminals, chancellor George Osborne has announced.

Inject personality

Wherever reasonable, turn a dry clash of ideology into a personal conflict. It should not be the *economic policy think-tank* versus the *Department of Men In Suits*. It should be *a group headed by outspoken former Communist Bill Fingerjabber* taking on *political nemesis chancellor Henry Austerity-Redbox*.

Make it a habit to **use names rather than titles**. For example, rather than *the prime minister has announced*, say *Theresa May has announced*. It becomes personal to her, not the office. Elsewhere, try using *health officials* or *ministers*, rather than saying *the Department for Health* or *the government/cabinet*. It suggests human beings are involved.

> The Department for Transport has announced that it will conduct its own investigation into car emissions, the latest twist in the Volkswagen scandal.
>
> *City AM, September 2015*

Just changing *The Department for Transport has announced that it will* to *Transport officials are to* or even *Ministers have ordered their own tests* . . . would have lightened this for the reader.

Don't be afraid to focus on the **dynamic and divisive characters** – think Boris Johnson, Nigel Farage and Donald Trump, who owe their high profiles to charisma, warts and all, rather than to their political ideologies. They give us a recognisability factor, an entry point for readers who would otherwise have no interest in what they are saying.

Cut out as many names of political organisations as possible. They are faceless, abstract entities, which put off readers.

> *The Nuclear Industry Association has welcomed the Government's decision to press ahead with Hinkley Point C, providing a major boost for the UK's nuclear industry.*
>
> *Politics Home, September 2016*

It might have been better focused on what was said, not the obscure group which was saying it:

> *Pressing ahead with Hinkley Point C has given a much-needed boost to Britain's nuclear sector, industry leaders say.*

Avoid using more than one abstract entity in a sentence. Once you have introduced an organisation, don't repeat the full name – so the *Department of Energy and Climate Change* becomes just the *department*.

Avoid repeated use of acronyms, as they can be distracting dotted through the copy. Capital letters carry an unappealing formality – use them sparingly.

Political theatre

In our storyteller's pyramid, it is the colour rising to the top.

It is seen every week during the posturing and showboating of prime minister's questions. Debates can become overheated during the most sedate of council meetings, lifting discussions about yellow lines into something newsworthy. Machiavellian behind-the-scenes manoeuvrings, with the plotting and backstabbing amid talk of dethronings and coronations is the time to break the guidance on avoiding the mechanics of politics.

Avoid intro plonking

Political stories are particularly prone to **intro plonking**.

Most political stories are twists to a longer-running narrative. Some are based on reaction to emerging events, a new comment or a new entrant to a debate.

The intro is straightforward – it's the latest development. But so many writers then go wrong, afraid that the context is not fully explained and plodding through the background which has been reported previously instead of staying with the latest news through the expansion. The mantra of **tell now, explain later** is abandoned.

Consider this imagined (if unlikely) story:

> *Plans to close the weakest secondary schools will be put on hold if teachers ensure all pupils pass at least five GCSEs, education secretary Pauline Bunn said today.*

So far, so good.

Here, though, having hooked the reader in with this tempter, the nervous writer feels the need to go through a lot of context.

> *Ms Bunn last month proposed hundreds of closures, saying she wants to pour the resources into those which produce the best exam results.*
>
> *She has spoken of a vision of super academies where thousands of pupils are taught by only the most skilled teachers with the best facilities as part of her Better for All programme of reforms.*
>
> *Opponents say she is tearing the heart out of communities up and down the country, throwing thousands of teachers out of work for a system that will do nothing to improve standards.*
>
> *They say it is a cover so she can save £3bn a year from the education budget.*
>
> *But now Ms Bunn has offered a compromise where schools which pledge to raise standards within three years will be spared from the axe.*

Unfortunately, paragraphs two to five have all been public knowledge for months. The writer has just repeated what has been said in many reports and lost most of the readers in the meantime.

In political news, the latest statement by a politician or the latest reaction is often all that gives us the new part in news. If you have **strong quotes**, build your story around them.

Don't waste your first few paragraphs explaining the background to what is being said – that can come later. Use **the latest remarks as your intro and carry them through the expansion**. Include a pithy quote to round off the expansion before a breather.

Hence:

> *A 3,000-home plan for the outskirts of Shiresville will be a greasy, pus-filled car-*
> *buncle on the beautiful face of the town, MP Jeremy Slime has said.*

The intro is the MP's colourful response to the proposal, which we have covered several times before. Don't stop the story in its tracks to spell out what he is talking about. Stick to the theme:

> *Pretty Pastures will bring nothing but traffic chaos, crime and a wave of unwanted*
> *migrants with its 500 low-cost starter homes, the Tory MP said.*
>
> *Instead, it should be redesigned as an upmarket, gated community with secu-*
> *rity guards, swimming pools and a spa to attract 'the sort of people we really want*
> *in Shiresville', according to Mr Slime.*
>
> *He said: 'I don't know what nincompoop thought this was going to be a good*
> *idea.*
>
> *'As it is proposed, with its cheap, ugly little blocks of affordable homes, it will*
> *become a pus-filled running sore, a carbuncle, on the face of beautiful Shiresville.'*

We have a breather – now on to the explanation in the chronology:

> *The plans were put forward last year . . .*

> Beware **legal traps**. Just because politicians accept, even enjoy, the cut and
> thrust of debate and accept personal attacks as part of the game, does not
> mean the gloves are off. It is convention – but not a legal protection – that a
> politician doesn't run to the courts when he is under personal attack.
>
> There are many legal protections when covering parliament, councils and
> public meetings and elsewhere but care is still needed. Bone up, too, on the
> extra restrictions which apply when **covering elections**.
>
> Politics **can be a style minefield**, too. Check your style guide carefully –
> even seemingly trivial issues such as when or if to cap up *mayor, Foreign Sec-*
> *retary* or *the government* need to be consistent.
>
> *Style*point

Press releases

Press releases are a blessing – and a curse.

Resource-starved newsrooms have come to depend on them to fill space quickly and cheaply. Savvy PRs know this and it's a weakness they gleefully exploit.

They pump out press releases to puff up products, protect reputations and put a positive spin on even the most damning evidence. An excoriating exposé of industry practice, for example, becomes 'an excellent opportunity for further dialogue to improve our service'.

Challenge the spin

For you, the storyteller, the key is to try to **wrest back control**. Most press releases contain information that has news value. However, they are issued on the senders' terms – they determine what a release says, when it is said and how it is said. Do whatever you can to turn that on its head.

If there are missing pieces of information or unanswered questions, **fill in the gaps**. It means asking questions of those who sent it or others with pertinent information or contrary views to offer.

Don't be afraid to **challenge the information**. If your common sense tells you the claims or even the statistics look flaky, then they probably are. If they are vague, ask for specifics. It is easy for an organisation to say it is the best, the greenest, the most open, the most efficient but make sure it can give you an example or two to back it up.

Also, **challenge the language**. PRs know they can obfuscate with jargon and generalities. If they use a phrase which seeks to play down or dehumanise, then ask them to explain precisely what it means. Take them out of their comfort zone by bringing them down the ladder of abstraction.

The **more you ask, the more you will get**. Even if you feel a press release has everything you need, it's always worth going back with more questions or to asking to speak to one of the characters mentioned in it. You may unearth a fascinating detail that was overlooked and find a new approach; at the very least you will have some different quotes from those other news outlets may use.

Devil in the detail

Don't just read and regurgitate a press release – study it, analyse what is really being said rather than what appears to be the message. Make sure the headline figure or claim is properly substantiated.

The best line may not be the one the sender suggests – you may find a better one well down the release. Go mining for other gems in the pile of any appendices or tables of figures which come with it.

Press releases are masterpieces of trying to **bury bad news**. Read past the positive spin – the company may have turned a corner, it might have improved efficiency, or seen an uptick in sales in crucial departments or the CEO's quotes may be unfailingly optimistic but somewhere in the 15th paragraph it will have to state that it made a £100 million loss.

Find the conflict

To make a worthwhile story from a press release, **you will need to find conflict**. Most press releases will contain one view, slanted towards the interests of those who issued it. Seek other opinions to provide proper context or an assessment of its consequences and implications to generate conflict. If a press release makes disputable claims, give the right of reply.

There are, of course, some **realities** here. A major announcement in a press release might need to be taken at face value as you tweet or produce a first draft for publishing as quickly as possible after you receive it.

Also, there is value in positivity, too. Softer stories might tell better if they are accepted for what they are, rather than analysed to within an inch of their lives, even if it means giving a PR a little more licence than they probably deserve.

Crucially, though, remember **you want a story**, not to act as an information conduit for a PR department. Just because you have a press release which seems important and appears to offer a convenient way to file some copy does not mean you should drop all basic news values. If it is not newsworthy – maybe it's just a reiteration of what has been said countless times before or too technical or dull to appeal to your readers – then **don't be afraid to spike it**.

Worthiness warning

Charities, campaign groups and community organisations all have an agenda and want publicity. Of course, everyone feels for the plight of the vulnerable and down-trodden but that does not mean a general press release saying more needs to be done to stop it has much news value. The reader is compassion-weary and you want a story, not well-intentioned words, to engage them.

We may be grateful for press releases as a source of stories and want to play our part in helping worthwhile causes but **be wary of making them into free adverts** for the organisations behind them. There is questionable value in inserting phrases such as *for more information visit the website* and *make donations at* for charities, or phone and crime numbers at the bottom of police appeals. All of that can be covered online with a hyperlink.

Writing them up

You have scrutinised the press release and made your follow-up calls. The writing should hold no terrors.

Give it structure – as ever, a well-focused pyramid is perfect for straight, hard news – and follow our golden rules.

Focus on what will interest your audience, which may or may not be what is suggested by the release. For example, a press release may talk in general terms about the decline of wildlife. Your readers live in a city and two-thirds of the way down the press release you spot some details about the migration of resilient species to 'urban environments'. That angle will work better for you – these are the creatures your reader might now be seeing. Once you have that line, stick with it, as ever, through the expansion and don't get sidetracked.

Use your own language and **don't allow your story to become infected by the phraseology in the press release.** The PR speak and officialese can seep too easily into copy, causing you to fail in your mission to make things as simple and as clear as possible for your readers. Sidestep the jargon – so don't use *urban environments*, write about *towns and cities*. If you must use a technical phrase, then explain it.

Whatever you do, **don't lift and repeat** chunks or even all of the press release. It should be a matter of professional pride that you rewrite to put it into your own words. PRs are astonished how often their releases and reports now appear word for word in publications, without any significant editing. Even if it is a harmless or soft story, it is a frightening abdication of responsibility and one that turns us from scrutinisers to churnalists. Spot the difference:

> **"** *A 41-year-old woman was walking to her vehicle after leaving The Shant pub in Crown Road at about 9.30pm on Wednesday 18 January.*
>
> *As she reached her car, she was approached by another woman who assaulted her and stole cash. The victim's car was also damaged during this incident.*
>
> Press release, Avon and Somerset Police, January 2017 **"**

> *The 41-year-old victim was walking to her vehicle after leaving the Shant pub in Crown Road, Kingswood around 9.30pm on Wednesday, January 18.*
>
> *As she reached her car, she was approached by another woman who attacked her and made away with her cash.*
>
> *The victim's car was also damaged during the incident.*
>
> Bristol Post

It's worse still when the chunk you copy incorporates a lot of business babble:

> **"** *Since joining the James Paget University Hospital's executive team in 2013, Liz has championed workforce development with the aim of inspiring nursing staff to maximise their potential and think innovatively – all with the ultimate aim of maximising the quality of patient care.*
>
> James Paget University Hospitals press release **"**

> *Since joining the James Paget University Hospital's executive team in 2013, Liz has championed workforce development with the aim of inspiring nursing staff to maximise their potential, think innovatively – all with the ultimate aim of maximising the quality of patient care.*
>
> *Northern Echo, December 2015*

It saves time to **cut and paste quotes** but do check them. It's surprising how often they are mistyped in the press release and you can do your PR contact a favour by correcting them.

Don't **get carried away** with the claims made in the press release. This research from Shelter extrapolated a relatively small survey sample to come up with a national figure of 3.7 million households. This report has gone a bit far:

> *Around 3.7 million households said they have been forced to reduce spending on essentials, with almost one in 10 parents saying they had to skip meals in the past 12 months.*
>
> *The YouGov survey questioned 1,580 working parents, and found that one in five (19%) said they cut back on buying their children new clothing or shoes to pay housing costs.*
>
> *ITV, September 2016*

Science

Scientists are notoriously nervous communicators. It's a shame because there are countless extraordinary stories lurking behind the lab coats.

Their awkwardness is compounded by newsrooms full of journalists who are equally nervous when it comes to writing stories about science. Some make it a badge of honour to announce they failed their chemistry GCSE.

It means a rich vein of material which affects every one of us, every day, goes unrecorded or misreported.

Understanding is all

Space travel, rocket launches, new inventions, technological breakthroughs, science prizewinners and so on make for excellent copy. Most just need to be treated in the same way and written using the same techniques as any other newsworthy event.

You cannot bluff, **you must understand** what is being said if you are to communicate it to your readers. That means reading and re-reading potentially complex papers, checking and asking questions and getting the experts to simplify as much as possible.

You may not wish to go into great detail in your story but if *you* are not clear on what is meant then you cannot write about it with authority. Avoid phrases such as *complex science*, *revolutionary new device*, or *high-tech equipment* – it is a sign you are pasting over the cracks.

As Albert Einstein supposedly said: 'If you can't explain it to a six-year-old, you don't understand it yourself.'

Find a reference point

Writing science is about making it accessible and engaging to those who might otherwise struggle to understand it.

Your story **needs a reference point** that makes it relevant to your readers' lives. It might be something about human behaviour or how we live our lives, an effect on their health or about the wonders of the world around them. If you can't find one, then it is probably drifting into the realms of science for scientists and the story might need to hit the spike.

This piece of research showed that parrots once lived farther north than anyone realised – not a piece of information most of us would find essential. But the popular references engage us:

> *To borrow a phrase from Monty Python, this bird has ceased to be and gone to meet its maker.*
>
> *But the dead parrot in question surprised scientists by shuffling off its mortal coil in Siberia more than 16 million years ago.*
>
> PA, October 2016

While you need to simplify, **beware of treating the reader like an idiot**. You may need to walk the readers through some of the complexities with a passage of explanation but they will understand if you write with clarity, using plain English.

Lengthy technical names and sets of initials are off-putting. Use them sparingly and explain them in as simple and vivid a way as possible, such as here:

> *A study of white blood cells taken from individuals afflicted by spots showed they had longer protective caps on the ends of their chromosomes. Called telomeres, the caps can be compared with the plastic tips that stop shoe laces becoming frayed.*
>
> *PA, September 2016*

Personality is often hard to inject into science stories. Wherever that veil is lifted – and it may not happen very often – it is gold dust for news writers. This is a lovely nugget in a story about Scottish-born Nobel Prize winner Fraser Stoddart:

> *Growing up on a farm in Scotland without electricity or any modern-day conveniences, he occupied himself doing jigsaw puzzles, a pastime that helped him recognise shapes and see how they can be linked together. His fascination with shapes continued in his research.*
>
> *AFP, October 2016*

> Make a good start by not beginning a story with the words *scientists* or *researchers* or even *A study of . . .* They can be off-putting and it probably means you are writing about the science and not about what the **science means to your readers**.
>
> *Style*point

Using journals

Many scientific stories are **based on research published in academic journals**, where one paper can be the culmination of years of work. Those reports are technical, written to scientific standards and, for the layman, difficult to penetrate. Universities and other research institutions will promote them through press releases and press conferences, which vary wildly in clarity.

To write about them, journalists **need to understand the way scientists work** and think. Their research – if it is to have any value – is subject to peer review, a supposedly rigorous process by which the methods and findings are verified. It is only then that it can be published in an established journal covering their speciality. Science without peer review is considered worthless.

Researchers do not like to push their claims too far. Any finding is **covered with caveats** and a call for further research to be carried out. It is a challenge for writers to carve through the hesitancy, yet remain fair.

For news writers there is a frustrating **gap between the what and the why**. Research may show, for example, that most people with a disease have a particular gene. However, it does not mean, as far as the scientists are concerned, that the gene causes the disease – what they call a 'causal link' between the two. They may have their suspicions but if their research does not prove it they may be reluctant to draw any conclusions. Don't make that link for them.

Remember, too, that scientific **research is incremental,** building over the years and involving many teams working in the same field all over the world. There is rarely a eureka moment, no magic bullets and no 'we've cured cancer' announcements. For news writers, it means the latest research, even the most exciting, may be little more than a step forward in a long race rather than breasting the tape.

Scientists can be picky, too. They care deeply about what they do and can see publicity as a dumbing down of their heavily nuanced findings. For writers it means that balance, accuracy and, moreover, a degree of restraint is critical if they want to avoid scientists' scorn.

Focus on the findings

Writing science stories based on research should **focus on the conclusions** and, critically, **how it might affect your reader**. Lab tests on mice might show that a new drug has potential for delaying Alzheimer's – clearly a finding of great importance to those who have the disease, as well as to those caring for them.

In your intro and expansion, you need to tell readers what has been discovered and how it might change readers' lives. You do not need to say how the experiments were carried out, who carried them out, where they were carried out or any of the caveats. Save that for later.

It may be helpful here to apply the **timeline approach**. It begins with a problem (finding a cure for multiple sclerosis), or a question (why do frogs jump so far?) or a theory (black holes are not really black). But, as the timeline (figure 9.1) shows, we don't usually break in until the newsworthy stage – the conclusions of the latest research.

Adopt the intro-expansion style to tell it. This is based on a low-key press release from October 2014:

> *Eating together as a family helps stop teenagers becoming obese.*
>
> *Having a family dinner even once or twice a week means children are more likely to eat healthier, better balanced meals, new research suggests.*
>
> *Six in ten adolescents who never ate with their families were overweight and three in ten were obese. The figures were about ten percentage points higher than those for all children.*
>
> *The trend was even more marked among black families than white, the US study showed.*
>
> *'Informing parents that even having one or two family meals per week may protect their child from overweight or obesity in young adulthood would be important,' said researcher Dr Jerica Berge.*

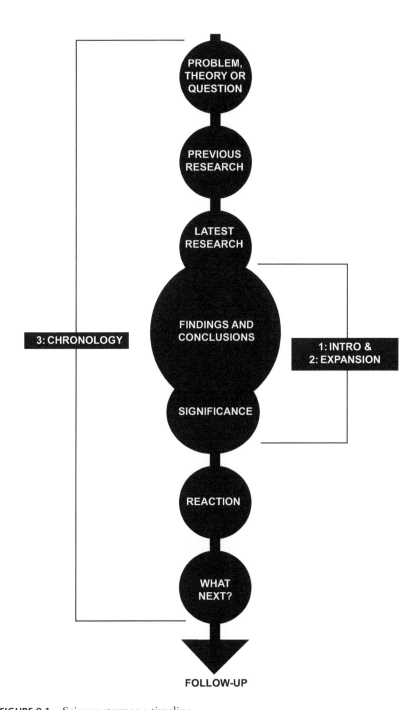

FIGURE 9.1 Science story as a timeline

Then we have a breather and resume with a chronology – an explanation of the scale of obesity (the problem in our timeline), the methodology (carried out over ten years with 2,000 subjects, analysing data from questionnaires), more on the findings (the effects of family meals) and the significance (that we should all eat together). Note how the story to the breather focuses only on the last two of these – the unspectacular methodology is buried beyond the breather.

Occasionally, the experiments, however, are so **bizarre** they become your angle. You only need to look at the annual Ignobel prizes to see the silly lengths some researchers go to. The 2016 winners included one who put trousers on rats, another who built prosthetic legs to walk on four legs like a goat, another who ate worms while trying to live like a badger and an American team who made up gibberish sentences to determine if bullshit was real. In these cases the conclusions matter far less than the ridiculousness of the research.

A trick to make it flow

Keep **attribution to the end of sentences** – it will help you focus on the story. If you find yourself writing *A study* or *scientists* as the first two words of a sentence, then try again. The scientists are not the story, their findings are. Hence, this second paragraph of a story . . .

> *Scientists writing in the Journal of Endocrinology found that cows given a "happiness" chemical have higher calcium levels in their milk.*
>
> *Daily Express, July 2016*

. . . should be:

> *Cows given a "happiness" chemical have higher calcium levels in their milk, scientists say.*

And . . .

> *A new study has found that new mothers have less sexual desire for male partners who express empathy.*
>
> *indy100, October 2016*

. . . becomes:

> *New mothers have less sexual desire for male partners who express empathy, a study has found.*

> The convention is to record, preferably at the end of the story, in which **journal** the research was first published. Scientific readers like this as they can then easily find the full study. However, it can happily sit at the end of the story. Where space is tight, it's enough to use phrases such as *according to US researchers* rather than something clunky such as *according to researchers from the Institute of Applied Mathematics and Physics at the University of Maryland in the US.*
>
> *Style*point

Surveys

If a PR wants cheap coverage, then the easiest way is to commission a survey.

Amazingly, no matter what the question being asked, respondents overwhelmingly agree with the conclusion the organisation behind the survey wants to reach.

The anti-taxation pressure group makes the startling discovery that we all think we pay too much tax; the pension company discovers we don't save enough for our retirement; the gym group finds that we need to do more exercise.

Picking them apart

And so, the first rule for dealing with surveys is to apply a **healthy dose of scepticism**.

The most interesting will shed light on our life and times but plenty are little more than a shameless attempt to get us to mention a chocolate company on Valentine's Day.

The temptation when a survey lands on your desk is to bash it out quickly – in a hard-pressed newsroom it may be all you have time to do. There is even a worry that scratching too hard at the data might leave with you nothing.

But you should pause to **apply the same scrutiny** to a survey as you would to any other story.

Examine the figures closely. First, check the basic maths – it's extraordinary how often there is an error in the press release. Make sure you interpret them correctly:

> *Just one in five people back a return to fox hunting, a poll has found, despite Government plans to give MPs a free vote on the issue.*
>
> *Telegraph, September 2016*

The second paragraph tells us, however, that the survey found *84 per cent of the public do not want a return to fox hunting.* That makes it 16 per cent – fewer than one in six – who do.

Second, **ask what figures may be missing**. If 40 per cent are happy or very happy with a situation, that means 60 per cent are not, which may be more newsworthy. Ask for the spreadsheets of the original research – it may be more illuminating than just following what's in the press release.

Third, **settle upon your angle**. Judge what really stands out from the data. It may well not be the finding suggested by the provider. It could be you can spot something which is more appropriate for your audience. Once you have the angle, line up the facts, figures and quotes behind it.

Work out what **information you can ignore**. Some surveys come with so much data it is overwhelming. Regional breakdowns, breakdowns by gender, age group and so on may be included but probably aren't that illuminating. If you want to give the material an extensive showing, it might be better turned into a graphic or data visualisation.

Keep numbers in check

A survey is most likely a numbers story (see Chapter 7) – so **select a headline figure** and stick with it through the intro and expansion.

The straightforward intro can be produced by rote:

> One in three British adults check their smartphones in the middle of the night, research has found.
>
> *Evening Standard, September 2016*

It's safe but predictable, while requiring the readers to get their heads round an abstract figure. A more engaging approach may be:

> If your smartphone is the last thing you look at before you go to sleep and the first thing you look at when you wake up, you are not alone.
>
> *Huffington Post*

It is often better to focus on the significance rather than the raw number:

> *The staggering number of elderly Britons who feel TRAPPED in their own homes has been laid bare – with many too frail to undertake minor household tasks, according to new research.*
>
> *Express, March 2016*

You must, of course, **back up your intro** or headline figure somewhere in the story.

Hence the *Express* story goes on:

> *One in five people over the age of 70 is unable to go up or down the stairs without harm, and almost a third are not using their kitchen.*

Beware the **extrapolation**. It is a trick of those who commission surveys to take the results from a modest sample and turn them into eye-catching ones.

If a poll shows one in ten people have taken selfies of their bottoms and, given that there are 65 million people in Britain, it is easy to say 6.5 million people are likewise obsessed. The survey may *suggest* this is the case, but it has not proved it.

On the other hand, this writer inexplicably went for a very modest *thousands* when the proportion was more than 40 per cent, giving an extrapolation of about 20million.

> *Thousands of Britons believe a robot uprising is inevitable and live in fear of a Terminator-esque future where artificial intelligence (AI) presides over humankind, a survey has indicated.*
>
> *iNews, October 2016*

Also, remember *one in two* looks odd and means *half* and *more than half* is *most* (not *the majority of*):

> *The future of Scottish parks is at a "tipping point", with one in two park managers predicting further decline over the next three years, a survey has found.*
>
> *Herald Scotland, September 2016*

Writing them well

The **focus of the story** is always the findings of the survey. Use this for an intro and carry it through your expansion. Don't worry too much on who carried it out, the methodology, the numbers of people interviewed. All that secondary information should be buried beyond the breather.

Hence, using the robot survey, we could have structured it thus:

> *A NIGHTMARISH future in which hyper-intelligent robots will rise up and destroy the human race is looming, millions of us believe.*
>
> *The dystopian scenario, plucked from the realms of Terminator movie fantasy, haunts four in ten of us, a new survey shows.*
>
> *Many of us fear a world in which artificial intelligence begins to evolve beyond our understanding and takes over society, the research suggests.*
>
> *At the very least, most of us expect human and robot interaction to be commonplace in the next 50 years.*
>
> *Robotics experts Professor Noel Sharkey, who was a consultant on the study, said: 'It'll all happen very gradually over the next 20 to 30 years until we don't even notice they're among us.'*

The copy is deliberately thin on statistics and the story lies in painting a picture of a future world and how we are troubled by the prospect. It is intended to **create an impression** that will be remembered rather than a befuddling list of statistics.

From here, having set up a doomsday scenario, we take a breather. Then, we can enter a chronology by setting up some background.

> *The survey findings echo the worst fears of cosmologist Stephen Hawking and space rocket pioneer Elon Musk, who see artificial intelligence as the biggest threat to mankind.*

And now we can flesh out the figures from the survey, who carried out the survey (Sky Atlantic), why (to promote a new series, Westworld), how many people were questioned and so on.

Make sure your **sentences are story focused**. This sentence takes a long time getting to the information that matters:

> *New research by insurance firm SunLife looked at 3,000 UK households and found that 25% of us are in the red each month, and 21% admit to having no savings whatsoever.*
>
> *The Sun, September 2016*

It might read better as:

> *A quarter of us are in the red each month and a fifth admit to having no savings whatsoever, according to a survey of 3,000 UK households by insurance company SunLife.*

As with any stat-based story **do not overwhelm with numbers** – even the re-written sentence above has three, which is probably too many. It's better to use a pithy quote before the breather rather than piling in another statistic.

Get tenses right

Survey stories look livelier when written in the **present tense**. They are a snapshot of the times we live in.

> *Online gambling by teenage boys across Europe is becoming a huge public health concern with one in eight now gambling frequently, according to a Europe-wide survey of school students aged 15 and 16.*
>
> The Guardian, September 2016

But do not muddle your tenses within a sentence.

> *The survey found* (past tense) *serious concern among frontline nurses that the rationing of access to care and shortage of beds are* (present, use *were*) *so acute that young people risk* (present, use *risked*) *harming or killing themselves.*
>
> The Guardian, October 2016

> Surveys may *find, show, reveal* or *suggest* but they are inanimate and cannot *say* anything. It is the *report* based on the survey which might *say* something.
>
> *Many* is a great word which can work well through its inexactitude and to help avoid bogging down the story with another figure.
>
> *People, users* or *shoppers* is preferable to the jargon word *consumers* or the oddly formal *adults*. Give pause before using the word *Britons* or *Brits* on a survey which is about British people and to be included in a British publication. Again, *people* will probably do.
>
> Finally, building sites, views and wreckage may be *surveyed* – people taking part in surveys are *questioned* or *asked*.
>
> *Style*point

Sport

Sports writing used to be pretty simple. Turn up to a game, watch it, write about it, then let 'em read about it.

Reporters were the eyes and the ears of readers who were not at the event.

Now it has become, ahem, a whole new ball game.

Live TV and online coverage means everyone has seen the match. When the final whistle blows at 4.50pm on a Saturday, anyone with a TV set, computer or smartphone will know who won, who scored, who was injured, who starred and who disappointed. Stats, performance charts and league tables are updated instantly.

It has left sports reporters with a challenge . . . by 6.30pm, live coverage is done and they must offer something different.

The answer – they must become **storytellers**.

Find a theme

Sports writing hinges on finding a theme, a hook, a sell, a key moment – in other words, for sports reporting read **sports stories**.

The focus must switch from the events played on the court, the pitch or the greens to **analysis, outfall and reaction**.

Maybe a player has performed spectacularly well or spectacularly badly. What is he saying about the wonder goal or his recovery from two sets down? How does the captain feel about the dropped catch that changed the course of the game? Can the swimmer go faster still and break the world record?

Look behind the action and **pick out the consequences** of what has happened. Has a player recovered form? Is the manager doomed? Is the injury serious? Will team selection need to be reviewed?

Personality has become all. It's not just the players – attention is focused on the officials, the managers, the coaches and even the backroom staff.

The treatment of Chelsea team doctor Eva Carneiro prompted plenty of headlines during 2015 and 2016. Even something as trivial as football referee Mark Clattenburg getting tattoos was deemed worthy of coverage in August 2016.

Have a conversation

Fan is short for **fanatic**. And sports followers are that and more – obsessive, passionate and unbreakable. Their favourite pastime is not so much watching their beloved sport; it is talking about it. Endlessly.

Once the action on the field has ended, the discussion begins: in the walk from the stadium, on the train or in the car home, in the bar, in TV studios, on radio phone-ins and internet fan forums. Passionate, heated, emotional – and often pointless – debates.

Every detail is talked about. Not so much the **minutiae** as the micro-minutiae.

> *A rapt audience was listening to the football journalist Jonathan Wilson wistfully lament the homogenisation in recent years of goal nets.*
>
> *The Guardian, September 2016*

As a sports writer, it is your job to poke that dragon and **get the conversation started**. There are any number of devices, from comment or analysis pieces on performance, players and tactics to player ratings, listicles of other great/terrible/ extraordinary moments, the game in numbers or statistical analysis, picture galleries, tips, hints, ones to watch and round-ups of quotes.

You can expect **knowledgeable feedback**, as you are talking to a unique audience.

If you write about politics, then a very small proportion of your readers is actively involved in politics. Many sports readers will be players, too, so they have had the experience of winning and losing, of being in a dressing room, of talking tactics and teamwork. This gives them a perceived ability to relate to those at the very top of their game.

You **cannot bluff it**. In these days of instant reader comments and feedback, someone will find you out. Any detail, no matter how trivial, will be picked over as a sign of your utter stupidity.

Become a nerd

Basic reporting skills remain crucial: do plenty of research, build up contacts, polish your interview technique so you can ask incisive, open-ended questions.

Above that, you will need to become **immersed in your subject** – presumably, if you want to write about sports you are already a sports fan. Good. Now, you will need to take it further and become a sports nerd. Then you will need to become the nerdiest of all the nerds.

But **not just a one-sport nerd**. You will need a broad appreciation of all sports. Although it can dominate coverage, it is not enough just to enjoy football. You will need expertise even beyond those mainstream sports, such as motor racing, rugby, cricket and tennis, which command huge followings.

Sports once considered unique to a single country, such as American football and baseball, now have plenty of eager supporters outside their traditional homelands. If you are lucky enough to be sent to cover an Olympic games, how is your knowledge of dressage, taekwondo or canoeing? Coverage of women's sports and disabled sports is growing.

Be aware that readers often **take sports more seriously** than anything else in their lives – their jobs, their relationships, even their health. Furthermore, they are resolutely tribal and will defend their countries, their favourite teams and players with never-to-be-dimmed fervour.

Their passion means their comments can be vitriolic. You will need a thick skin.

(Informed) comment is free

In news reporting, it has long been the convention to put up a pretence of being impartial. It's a chimera, of course, but it has provided a starting point for generations of journalists. To maintain this, personal opinion was off limits.

In sports writing, that approach would border on the bland. Your writing needs **informed analysis**.

While in news reportage you would leave it to others to say that a politician has performed poorly in a debate, a sports story might point out who has played badly, where a manager went wrong or what caused the defeat.

But these views need to be **supported by evidence**. **Statistics** are the most powerful weapon, even if the number of points scored, missed first serves or three-putts only tell part of the story. Observation and examples are less empirical but at least show the opinion is informed.

It has, of course, to be comment without prejudice. You cannot let your **own sporting loyalties** interfere. Even a United fan has to give City credit now and then.

With grass roots sports reporting – perhaps on a local paper or website – it plays well to adopt a **supportive tone**. Although you have to be fair to the opposition, your role is akin to the club cheerleader (without the pom-poms). Take the side of the fan whose only desire is to see their club do well but who won't be taken for a fool.

Beware, too, of being **unduly scathing** in the disappointment of defeat. The reality is that often one side enters as hopeless underdogs and, no matter how much you and your readers want them to win, it was never going to be.

Graciousness in defeat is a commendable quality. Recognise the flaws in the defeated but also the dedication and hard work which players and coaches commit to reaching the highest level. Seventh or eighth place in an Olympic final may seem like a crushing disappointment but it is an achievement few of us will ever experience.

Speed counts

Online sports coverage has to be **instant**. If you are live blogging it needs to be updated as quickly as humanly possible. Delays are frustrating for the fan eagerly waiting to find what has happened. Final reports, even if not fully formed – and indeed if they are little more than a two-par summary of who won – need to be ready to be published as soon as the final whistle has blown. And all the time you will need to keep posting updates on social media.

Even in print sports often push the deadlines more than any other kind of writing. Many games are played in the evening when pages have to go to the printers. Nothing can be more challenging than a late comeback, last-minute goal or final-round knock-out requiring a major rewrite with minutes to spare.

Experienced writers learn to produce their report as they go along. Any recap of the action on the pitch is prepared as the game is being played. The final words written will be the intro before the next few pars almost as the winning volley is struck, the final ball is delivered or the last putt is sunk.

Think of this process as setting down a chronology in our pyramid first and adding the intro and expansion at the last moment.

Reporting the action

Now for a U-turn – reports of the death of traditional match reporting may be exaggerated.

Such is the appetite of sports fans that they still like to read accounts of what they have just seen. They seek verification or the chance to relive:

> *This was true of most matches that I "watched" in my childhood. To me, they only materialised when they appeared in the newspaper the next day.*
> *Cricinfo.com blogger Anand Mamidipudi, December 2016*

Moreover, there are many people who do not get to a game or who are unable to watch it on TV or follow it closely online.

To meet these demands, you cannot ignore completely what has happened on the pitch.

If you are compiling reports on events such as a Sunday league football game, a swimming gala or a hockey match for a local newspaper or website, the only people who saw what happened were probably those who took part or officiated.

You will need a network of club representatives to send in match reports which you will have to adapt for publication. The reports will almost inevitably focus on what happened – you will need to build on these straightforward details to fashion a story to pass on to readers.

Even a major sports event which has been televised and widely covered online needs to **include a recap** of the highlights. **Don't make it the focus** of your story but it still needs to say who scored the goals, describe the pivotal putt or explain how a photo finish separated the first and second place.

Live blogging

Live blogging is where online coverage can really score.

The mixture of reportage, pictures and video, readers' comments, social media and graphics brings together every format in one place.

It should have the **feel of a TV or radio commentary** but the embellishments and level of interactivity means it can surpass its broadcast rivals.

Try to create the sense of a **group of like-minded sports fans** watching a game in one giant room, bouncing ideas, comments and wisecracks off one another as they follow the action.

In truth, many live blogs are compiled by **office-based** writers who follow the game on TV, occasionally with support from a reporter at the ground to provide insights missed by the cameras.

First, it can avoid rights issues, as live coverage from the ground is a prized asset and strictly controlled by sports bodies, clubs and the TV companies, who pay a lot of money for exclusivity.

Also, using TV coverage gets you closer to the action than a view from a distant press box. You can see close-ups, replays and take soundings from the commentators which help you frame your text.

There is so **much to juggle** – following the action, checking picture wires, following social media – all while throwing out words at breakneck pace. It is another reason why a comfortable set-up with your familiar screens and a reliable fast internet connection is preferable to working remotely.

In most sports, the action comes thick and fast and there is no time for elaborate writing. Instead, **get the information up** as quickly as possible. Add the decorations as time permits.

Accuracy remains imperative – there is little time for review and correction. The odd typing mistake will probably be forgiven by readers, who will understand that material is being published in a hurry. However, that is still not a licence for carelessness, missing words and endless spelling mistakes. Readers still expect professionalism.

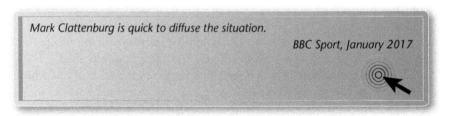

Mark Clattenburg is quick to diffuse the situation.

BBC Sport, January 2017

Stats and scorelines need to be **up to the minute**, as many readers will dip in and out of coverage, coming back just for a check on the score. If you have headline paragraphs or bullet points at the top of the blog, make sure they are up to date, too.

Live blogging is a two-way process – your reportage **starts a conversation** with readers, fans and other commentators. Throw out **opportunities for feedback** . . . ask for views on tactics and performance but also ask the trivial, such as if anyone can remember a better ginger-haired, left-handed tennis player or for readers to pick their top all-time sportspeople whose names begin with the letter Z. Readers love to show off their sense of humour in return. You act as the chair of the discussion.

Humour is important, too. Sports may be an all-encompassing passion to many people but, when all is said and done, it is a game. It is meant to be fun and a distraction from the drudgery of life.

Beware of being too **blokey**. Some sports are still male dominated but the wrong tone of voice will be exclusive, not just to women and families but also to men who dislike the barroom banter level of discussion into which sports conversations can descend.

Sporting pyramids

You work as a sports writer for the St Maragret's Times and its website stmaggies.com, covering the thriving town of St Margaret and surrounding area.

It is the height of summer and the following report arrives from the press officer for St Margaret's Cricket Club, the main team in the area and one which features regularly and prominently in your publications.

> St Margaret's travelled to Longville on Saturday needing a win to keep alive their championship hopes in the Prenderghast Builders Premier Division.
>
> Having lost the toss, St Margaret's were surprised to be put in on a very good-looking wicket.
>
> The Longville opening bowlers toiled hard and removed Johnny West early on to a loose drive but struggled to make further inroads.
>
> The wicket got easier to play on and, as the shine went off the ball, Tom Porter struck a superb career-best 175 which enabled St Margarets to post a huge 296–4 off their 50 overs.
>
> He put on a century stand with skipper Roger White, who made 68, before a late flurry of fours and sixes took him past the 150 mark.
>
> St Margaret's knew wickets would be at a premium in the second innings on such a flat track.
>
> It became evident that Longville were going to make no attempt to chase the total, therefore an attritional three hours was going to follow.
>
> However, five wickets from Raj Patel and three from Sam Elliott took St Margaret's to the brink of victory.
>
> With nine wickets down the last Longville pair battled for seven overs to avoid defeat.
>
> Then, with three balls to go Longville's No.11 top edged a sweep and who should be there but Porter to take a superb one-handed catch to secure victory. Longville ended on 193 all out, giving St Margaret's 25 points.
>
> It ended a superb day for Porter, who struck nine sixes and 20 fours in his knock, the second highest in club history.

It should be obvious who is the focus of this story – Tom Porter. His performance is the main talking point from the game.

The supplied report contains most of the details and is helpful but, being written by a non-professional and with a broader club focus, needs reworking.

Many hard-pressed sports desks will run these reports verbatim or with a bare minimum of editing.

Sadly, it doesn't offer the reader much more than if they clicked on the St Margaret's Cricket Club website, where it was posted before it was even sent to the Times/stmaggies.com sports desk. Neither will appeal much to those outside the club.

As a storyteller you need to add value. A couple of check calls and a chat to Tom Porter are needed to enrich it.

After speaking to him you have some biographical background, some more information about his performance and a few quotes.

You are ready to turn the *match report* into a *sports story*.

The report is written in chronological order, starting at the beginning of the match and ending at the finish. Pick up on the pivotal moments in the sequence of events to turn them into a story.

Our pyramid structure works perfectly here. As with news, we start with an intro honing in on the most exciting and extraordinary moments and build up on that through an expansion.

This should be a story about Tom Porter. Our intro focuses on him:

> Tom Porter clubbed a career-best 175 to set up a victory to keep St Margaret's Cricket Club's title hopes alive.

And we stay with him to tell the story of the game.

> The 20-year-old batsman smashed nine sixes and 20 fours as his side piled up an unassailable 296–4 away at last year's champions Longville.
>
> And Porter, whose innings was the second highest made for the club, was on hand to clinch victory with a sensational one-handed catch as the home side were bowled out for 193 in the last over the game.
>
> Architecture student Porter, who feared he would be dropped after a run of low scores, said: "Funnily enough, it was the catch that meant the most because I've spilt a few lately and we went home with all the points."
>
> The victory moved St. Margaret's up to third place, just two points behind second-placed Longville with a game in hand.

We now have a story of the match and not a report of the match. It has added humanity to broaden its appeal.

We have also reached a natural breather. All the key details are included in the first few pars – so readers could exit now with the story in a nutshell.

To continue, we use our pyramid chronology. First, set the scene:

> *Fourth-placed St Margaret's travelled to high-flying Longville 50 points adrift of the leaders in the Prenderghast Builders Premier Division.*

And then we can walk the reader through the game – the level of detail you require may be down to space or editor's preference.

> *They were surprised to be put in on what looked a very good-looking wicket and No.3 Porter soon hit his stride after the loss of an early wicket.*
>
> *He put on a century stand with skipper Roger White, who made 68, before a late flurry of fours and sixes took him past the 150 mark.*
>
> *"It was a great pitch and the ball was coming on to the bat nicely," said Porter, who has made only one other century for the club. "By the end I was seeing it like a football.*
>
> *"I'd made nought, three and seven in my last three knocks and it just shows that you are one inning away from hitting form."*
>
> *In reply, Longville made little effort to chase down the total and, after five wickets from Raj Patel and three from Sam Elliott, their final pair were digging in for a draw.*
>
> *But, with three balls to go, the Longville No.11 top-edged a sweep and Porter ran 25 yards to take a superb one-handed catch to secure victory.*
>
> *Porter said: "It was up there an absolute age and was swirling a bit in the breeze. I clung on and the rest of the side just mobbed me."*
>
> *Longville ended on 193 all out, giving St Margaret's 25 points. They will have to win all their last three games if they are to mount a serious title challenge.*

Your exit points might be links to earlier match reports or others from the club from their Second and Third XI, a panel on five highest scores for St Margaret's or a league table. A picture of Tom or a gallery of images from the game would also be a welcome addition.

In another scenario you work for oddshapedballs.com, the country's leading website for rugby. You attend a Premier League game towards the end of the season between mid-table Blandish and strugglers Dorkington.

Your instinct should tell you that most interest is in Dorkington, champions a couple of seasons ago but now battling to avoid relegation. Blandish have little to play for other than pride, being safe from the drop and too far behind to compete for the title.

The game, which is covered live on a satellite TV channel, is a drab affair with little by the way of flowing passing movements. Most of the home supporters drift away well before the end.

You have live-blogged coverage of the game, sent out regular tweets, posted a two-paragraph holding piece online and now need to compile a fuller story.

Your notes from the game tell you that Blandish won 17–6, scoring a couple of tries through their dominant forwards. Dorkington were woeful and new winger,

Jack Springer, making his debut after being signed to try to lift them out of the relegation zone, barely touched the ball.

In post-match interviews, Dorkington coach, Steve Wilson, is asked about his side's performance.

He responds: 'Hugely disappointing, I'm very unhappy about it. We were disjointed, we didn't pass well and the forwards were always second best in the scrum and the line-out.'

Asked about how he sees his team getting out of trouble, he responds: 'Well, if we continue to play like this we won't. Simple as that. Everything we learned on the training ground goes out of the window as soon as we cross that white line.

'We have brought in Jack Springer and he weren't cheap. He's a quality international player. But where was he?

'The lads gave him nothing. He touched the ball twice and I think he dropped it on one occasion and got tackled on the other.

'It's not good enough. The team needs to bring him into the game and Jack needs to get himself more involved, too.

'They need to step it up, Jack needs to impose himself more and then we have a chance. Next week's game is massive. I have faith in the boys but they gotta give me more.'

It is a surprisingly forthright and candid response. Again, your instinct for a story should tell you that, after an unforgettable match, it is the most interesting thing which has happened at the ground that day.

The post-match quotes should be the focus of our story.

Hence:

> Dorkington head coach Steve Wilson told star signing Jack Springer to step up as he tore into his players after another dismal performance.

Now, having set our approach, we stick with it during our next few pars of expansion. We don't need much of the pitch action, just an early reference to remind anyone who may have missed the score:

> The always outspoken Wilson made his discontent plain following a 17–6 defeat to Blandish at a windswept Froggatt Lane.
>
> He said his side was forgetting what it had learned on the training ground and he wanted to see more from Springer, signed last week on a club record £200,000-a-year deal.
>
> Wilson railed: "It's not good enough. The team needs to bring him into the game and Jack needs to get himself more involved, too.
>
> "They need to step it up, Jack needs to impose himself more and then we have a chance."

Again, we have **converted a match report into a story**. It has strong characters, conflict and a connection with the readers who want talking points from a game many will have just watched.

To continue, we now need a breather, then a chronology in which we reset the scene and a brief recap of the match action before returning to where we started – the reaction of the coach.

> Dorkington, champions two season ago, were in desperate need of a win to lift them clear of the relegation places.
>
> But they turned in an abject performance as the heavyweight Blandish pack dominated the game, swallowing the ball at every opportunity and strangling the free-flowing Dorkington back line.
>
> They wrapped up the victory with tries from Derek Johnson and Simon Monk with just a couple of Brian van der Westhuizen penalties by way of reply.
>
> Afterwards, Wilson laid into his players after being asked if they could avoid the drop.
>
> He said: "Well, if we continue to play like this we won't. Simple as that. Everything we learned on the training ground goes out of the window as soon as we cross that white line.
>
> "We have brought in Jack Springer and he weren't cheap. He's a quality international player. But where was he?
>
> "The lads give him nothing. He touched the ball twice and I think he dropped it on one occasion and got tackled on the other."
>
> Next week, Dorkington travel to top-of-the-table Runchester and a victory is a must if they are to climb out of trouble.
>
> Wilson added: "Next week's game is massive. I have faith in the boys but they gotta give me more."

Sport as news

Sport, to twist a cliché, isn't a matter of life and death – it's more important than that. Hence, it is no longer confined to sports pages or sports channels.

And why not? Sports is often of far greater concern to readers than politics, crime or business. It is, for many readers, welcome escapism.

Personalities lift sports into the news mix. The vast wealth sports stars can accrue has turned them – and those around them – into celebrities and public figures.

The world's best paid sportsman, Cristiano Ronaldo, and his underpants are familiar to those who have never seen him bend a free kick. David Beckham is still making headlines long after football fans lost interest in his ability to execute a 50-yard pass. The ups and downs of Lewis Hamilton's love life are considerably more interesting than Formula 1.

When sports becomes news, approach it in the same way as you would any other story. Apply the same news value judgments about what and who are important and what and who are not. Build a pyramid, write a superb intro and follow all the golden rules.

Remember that sports is just a **setting** – like a court, a council meeting, a press conference – for a story.

Don't waste time recapping what happened on the field of play or describing a principal character's sporting prowess. A passing reference should be enough.

Sport language

Sports reporting comes with a language all of its own. It's rarely that elegant.

Goals are lashed in from an acute angle following a slick move launched by the mercurial midfielder.

Fielders backpedal furiously to take steepling catches after the opposition danger man tries to hoist one into the stands.

A big-hitter launches another monster drive bang down the middle of the narrow, undulating fairway.

It's a form of written shorthand. Having endured it for years, readers have come to accept it and even incorporate it into their descriptions of a game.

Players use the same tired phrases, too. They have developed stock responses to defeat (looking for the positives), to deflecting praise (it was a team effort, it's down to the backroom staff), to avoiding speculation (I'm really happy playing here). They are wary of being hung out to dry if they say anything interesting.

Like all clichés, they are expressions which were once original and illuminating but lose their impact with overuse and finally become stultifyingly predictable.

Sometimes the creative juices run dry and the tried and trusted phase feels apt or difficult to avoid. But it should never become the default position.

Sport has such rich potential for **great writing**: the intensity of the drama, the spectacle and colour, the characters, the small moments that define the contest. In longer or reflective pieces you are especially free to express yourself. It is a freedom news reporters are rarely afforded.

> *Time slowed, and a divine light shone down, illuminating a man without a club. Old Johan surveyed the scene, smiled, waved his hand and, for some reason, sent down a seed of inspiration. Robson-Kanu paused, and then starkly turned. Three Belgian defenders drifted by, ghosts floating away on some doomed and pointless journey that some say they still pursue to this day. The ball nestled comfortably into the corner of the net. Then time resumed as normal, and the Welsh supporters were sent into glorious raptures.*
>
> *The Roar, July 2016*

There is great poetry and beauty in the movement of a game. It is warfare without bloodshed played by civilised societies. Villages, towns, cities and countries send their modern-day gladiators into a ring – sometimes to earn prizes, often to defend honour, always to assert superiority.

Look for **original turns of phrase**. When you write something predictable, scrub it out and try to find an alternative description of your own making. Use metaphor, eulogy, alliteration and every other literary device to conjure up a picture of events.

Nonetheless, **don't get wordy for the sake of it**. Writing needs to be precise, sharp and punchy. Flow and rhythm are vital. Sentence construction, grammar, spelling, punctuation and so forth have to be spot on. Don't write in ugly jargon – avoid using nouns such as *medals* or *podiums* as verbs. In short, remember our **ABBCs and our golden rules**.

When it's written, take time to **read it through**. The disappearance of sub-editors means you need to be your own biggest critic. Check it – then check it one last time for literals, missing words and errors. If you don't spot the howler, your army of ever alert, dedicated and knowledgeable readers will throw it back in your face.

Funnies

Trying to pin down funny is like trying to catch the wind. One man's hilarious cat-falls-off-table video is another's cue for a weary sigh.

However, humour is vital to the news diet. The world needs a break from death, destruction and Donald Trump.

Strike the right tone

Take your lead over choice of material, tone of voice and attitude from your audience and apply it according to your style book.

The *11 best golf jokes ever* might be fine for a sports channel but becomes *11 jokes you will only get if you play golf* in a more general space and W*hat white, middle-class blokes laugh about on a Friday afternoon* if you are trying to be more cutting.

Online, funny is a crowd-pleaser – after all, in-depth political discourses rarely go viral. But with such a high value on it, the **writing needs to be at its sharpest**. Crisp, punchy and precise sentences are a must.

Your structure will be looser and your **tone will be conversational**. Throw in some social media observations and some appropriate gifs.

You can **inject some comment** – but make playful use of witty asides or a pithy pay-off. Even though your audience is likely to be youthful and, arguably, unsophisticated, steer clear of the crass and crude. Keep cultural references current but not obscure.

Droll up with laughter

Don't **try too hard to be funny**. The story should be funny because, well, it is. It does not need groan-inducing puns, shouty capital letters or tortuous analogies to make it amusing. This intro doesn't have much going for it – an awful pun which is downed by the repetition of the word *axe* and comes with the self-defeating *it's not every day that* phrase:

> *It's not every day that you have axe-tra curricular activities as unique as axe throwing but that is the latest offering from Cundall Manor School.*
>
> *Ripon Gazette, May 2016*

Instead, focus on the absurdity of the events and let the natural silliness work for you. The reader will work out what makes them laugh.

It's a fine line, though. You can kill the humour if you are too straight:

> *Police officers in Dundee were called after reports of a chicken trying to cross the road on Friday morning.*
>
> *STV, October 2016*
>
> *Social media users have described the sight of police chasing an escaped chicken through the streets of Dundee as "the funniest thing ever".*
>
> *The Courier, Dundee*

Think of writing funny stories as **akin to telling a joke.** Much as a comedian doesn't dive in with the punchline, your story needs a build-up.

Often, as in the previous examples, a straight intro doesn't work. It's probably because there is not much of a news event and usually it's more of an anecdote, a throwaway line or just an amusing slice of life.

Give yourself a paragraph or so to **walk the reader into a story.** This might have been a more enticing way to dress up the chicken story:

> *It is the opening line to countless silly jokes. But police appear to be taking it rather seriously with a public appeal asking: "Why did the chicken cross the road?"*
>
> *Officers in Dundee were pondering exactly that after being dispatched to deal with a lost chicken which was weaving in and out of traffic on a busy road.*

Don't be a plonker

Don't just plonk an observational remark on your story without making sure it connects to the paragraph that follows. **It must flow logically**.

This leads the reader in well before revealing in the third sentence that one fan from Essex collects Starbucks mugs from around the world:

> *There are plenty of Starbucks devotees out there who plan their year around when they can get their hands on a pumpkin spice latte or a peppermint mocha. But one fan is more committed to the coffee chain than most.*
>
> *Metro.co.uk October 2016*

Remember not to ramble, though, and don't make 'em wait too long for the punchline. This starts promisingly:

> *I think it's safe to say we've reached peak engagement photoshoot.*
>
> *Metro.co.uk, May 2016*

But it is four waffly pars and 104 words later before we discover that it's a story about a photoshoot in a Costco.

Leave 'em laughin'

All good jokes **need a punchline**. The round-off quote, the more understated the better, is the ideal way to finish. Otherwise, look for a pay-off which hints at more to come or ties up a loose end which may have been left unanswered earlier in the story. You can, of course, leave the reader with a wry comment of your own.

After we learn the avid Starbucks mug collector's fed-up wife is on the point of throwing him out, this rounds off the story neatly:

> *As there are only about six spaces left, he might want to start house-hunting*
>
> *Metro.co.uk, October 2016*

On this story about a man in Thailand who snapped his penis during sex, the finishing line nods towards the question which has been left hanging through the previous 224 words. Shame about the spelling error:

> *It has not been confirmed what sexual position the man was attempting when the 'crack' occured.*
>
> *indy100, October 2016*

And this is a well-delivered pay-off on a story of a traveller who photographed himself in risky situations with a sign saying 'Mom, I'm fine'.

> *Well, 28,000 followers and 24 amazing pictures later – we think she may have received the message.*
>
> *indy100, June 2015*

One-liners

Newspapers love the **one-paragraph funny**. Only a sentence or so long, about 20 words or less, they take great skill to craft as they probably have been cut down from hundreds of words. Few deliver these better than *The Sun*, where it is often the headline which makes them.

> *Mash and grab*
>   *A hapless raider who tried to hold up two stores with a large potato was nicked by cops in Rhode Island, US.*
>
> *The Sun, October 2015*
>
> *Gone too spoon*
>   *Illusionist Uri Geller's 7ft statue of a bent spoon in Sonning, Berks, has vanished after a week.*
>
> *The Sun, October 2015*

Note how the focus is on **delivering the joke**, without any clutter. They amount to little more than an intro, although geography – and, in others, ages – are included for a sense of reportage and completeness.

Heard it before?

Some funny stories **tend to resurface** as they get noticed online and start a new social media conversation. A cuttings check would have prevented outraged comments such as this:

> *Wow, reporting that Poundland started selling vibrators. . . . TWO YEARS AGO. And that Poundland selling vibrators was spotted by people on Twitter. . . . TWO YEARS AGO. Real finger on the pulse stuff this (and that's putting aside the fact you'd have to be about 12 years old to be amused by a vibrator FFS)*
> *Huffington Post, October 2016*

Grim grins

Journalists love **black humour** – it's a guilty secret but nothing seems to make them laugh more than someone being killed or maimed – see the previous broken penis story – in a really stupid way. Every year, for example, we have a good chuckle at the world's dumbest deaths as recorded through the Darwin awards, so named because those who have died are deemed to be helping the process of evolution.

However, readers might be more sympathetic. After all, we are writing about real people doing real harm to themselves and leaving behind loved ones who have to deal with the aftermath.

If a story like this is run, then play it straight. Don't force the humour, use bad puns or make unkind comments. If the reader, like us, takes guilty pleasure in others' misfortunes then they don't need us to help them find it funny.

Listicles

The online world is awash with listicles. BuzzFeed was built on listicles; every blogger on the planet, it seems, writes listicles; respected and serious news publishers use listicles.

They're just lists pretending to be articles. Right?

Yes, but there's more to a good listicle than meets the eye.

A welcome break

They are perfect for breaking down unappealing screeds of text into digestible, indexed and skimmable chunks.

In a conventional news environment, a listicle will serve as a different way to present background information. Whereas once a major story would have run alongside wordy break-out boxes, analytical assessments and maybe panels of quotes, now they come with listicles.

So, a major public figure dies or resigns or is otherwise thrust into the limelight and we will see *13 things you didn't know about . . .* , *his/her 11 greatest moments*, *23 of his/her most inspiring/witty/ridiculous quotes*, *19 ways he/she changed the world*, *7 others who . . .* and so on.

Here . . .

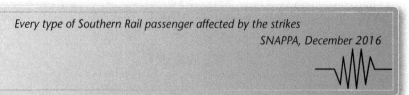

Every type of Southern Rail passenger affected by the strikes
SNAPPA, December 2016

. . . cleverly breaks down what might have been predictable passenger reaction via Twitter into a highly readable list, categorising the types as *utterly infuriated, the sarcastic, the conspiracy theorists, darkly humorous, the smug* and so on.

When to use them

Listicles are a staple of standalone news content. It's usually **lighter and youthful in tone**, aimed squarely at the tech literate, smartphone- and tablet-obsessed generation.

In this environment, they are perfect for presenting personal experience (for example, a travel piece as *9 things I found out about India*), advice (*11 hacks that will help you through a bad day at the office*), opinion (*1,497 reasons to hate Formula One*), observation (*the 13 worst kinds of office letch*), entertainment (*7 adorably cute animals with less than a full allocation of limbs*) and humour (*the 17 stupidest burglars ever caught on camera*).

But there is no reason why they cannot be applied more inventively to harder or newsier material. *Five things we know so far about (a breaking story), 11 ways corruption affects us all, 13 rip-offs that energy companies use, 9 photographs that prove climate change is real.*

Be original

Whatever you decide to tackle, try to come up with an **original idea**. It's increasingly difficult, as any kind of list you can think of has probably been written somewhere at some time.

If it has been done before but you want to cover it again – perhaps because it is topical or trending – make it *the best list, the most definitive list* or the *only list you'll ever need.*

Make it controversial – try something that goes against the established narrative. It's more likely to pick up clicks if it appears **preposterous, outrageous** or **challenging**.

Sort the structure

Approaches include a simple list of single sentences or a list of sub-heads with a paragraph or more of explanation. Also decide if you will use pictures with all of the items or just some, if it will be a slideshow with captions or if each one will display on a separate page.

Spend some time thinking about the **running order**. Think like a story-teller. You want to make a strong start, which shows you have something engaging and original to offer. Make it a controversial or challenging introduction by placing something widely admired as the first among a list of the worst or vice versa. Try to keep the momentum – if, when you read your listicle back, one of the items seems out of place or flabby or slows it down, then cut it out or replace it.

Finish on a high, too. There is an adage comedians use for their stand-up routines. Begin with your second-best joke and end with your funniest. In other words, get them going straightaway and always leave them laughing.

Remember to **number your items**. It might be worth **ranking them** if you are presenting the top, best or worst. If so, decide whether to display them in ascending or descending order. A countdown ending with the best or biggest is the logical approach, as it keeps the reader going through the list to find 'the winner'.

Research suggests you should **use odd numbers** of items rather than even ones. For reasons that aren't entirely clear, **prime numbers** (numbers, such as 11, 13, 17 etc., which can't be divided by any other) seem to be most effective. One study appeared to show that the ideal number was 29.

Round numbers, such as 10 or 20, seem less popular, perhaps because they just look too convenient or polished.

Come up with **more ideas for your list than you need**. Then you can be ruthless and hack away those that don't meet the standard required or stretch the criteria for inclusion.

The right tone

Humour is critical. Write with a knowing wit, as subtlety always wins over puns, unnecessary crudity or juvenile jokes. Insert offbeat pictures or embed GIFs to enhance the copy.

A **conversational style**, using everyday language, is usually appropriate. However, it should still be a piece of journalistic writing, so make sure it is clear, punchy and tight. Sentence construction and grammar still count, too.

Don't be lazy

Some listicles betray the writer's laziness. They are what would once have been sneered at as 'cuts jobs' – a rehash of old material dressed up to make it look new. Search for a popular idea for a list and you will see how often the lists contain the same predictable examples time and time again.

Cutting and pasting after a bit of Googling is rarely a recipe for creating an informative and entertaining mix. Instead, **apply journalistic standards** to your information gathering. Scouring books, reports or other written material which is not available online can turn up gems which are not routinely recycled. Best of all, get some original material through phone calls and interviews.

Wherever you get your information from, **remember to credit** and hyperlinking to other sites you have used as a source is a must.

News in brief

Which are the best-read news stories in a newspaper? The front-page exclusive exposing wrongdoing in high office? A brilliant 3,000-word backgrounder? Maybe . . .

But most likely it will be the news in briefs, otherwise known as *nibs*, *shorts* or *quicks*.

They win because they are succinct, often amusing and take a few seconds to read. They do not look intimidating on the page.

Online, a reader doesn't know how long a story is going to be until he or she clicks on it. But they are unlikely to want to trawl through 1,000 words. Although you have unlimited space, brevity, again, is to be valued.

A familiar technique

Constructing short stories is **the gold standard** for writers. It tests the ability to compress a lot of information into a limited space by picking the right material to include and picking which to leave out.

The good news, however, if you have been following this book, is that **you already know how to do it**. A short is little more than the intro or expansion used to build a longer story. Sometimes it is just the 15 or so words of an intro.

If you want to master news writing, **then write every story as if it was a four- or five-par nib**. It will drive home the importance of focusing on one angle – your story – and building on it, without clutter or diversion.

Just an intro-expansion

If you look at some of the examples of intros and expansion used so far in this book, you will see how they could be used as standalone stories. Everything that lies beyond the breather is of secondary importance.

All that is needed is to thread in details which you would ordinarily save for the chronology so the story is complete.

On our survey story, for example, we would need to tweak it thus:

> A NIGHTMARISH future in which hyper-intelligent robots will rise up and destroy the human race is looming, millions of us believe.
>
> The dystopian scenario, plucked from the realms of Terminator movie fantasy, haunts four in ten of us, new **research** shows.
>
> **A third** of us fear a world in which artificial intelligence begins to evolve beyond our understanding and takes over society, the survey of 2,000 people suggests.

> Robotics experts Professor Noel Sharkey, who was a consultant on the study **for Sky Atalntic**, said: 'It'll all happen very gradually over the next 20 to 30 years until we don't even notice they're among us.'

The tactic of using a **round-off quote** at the end of an expansion always works well in a short.

In court stories told as nibs, it is still critical to include **legal niceties** such as plea, location of courts and so on if it is to be fair and safe. Hence, our story from earlier might read:

> A conman who likened himself to gentleman thief Raffles tricked wealthy widows out of hundreds of thousands of pounds of jewellery, a court heard.
>
> Well-spoken Reginald Young was said to have befriended lonely women online before wooing them with expensive meals, gifts and weekends away.
>
> The 48-year-old convinced them he was a high-class jeweller **but vanished after taking** their most expensive pieces to value them for insurance purposes, **Anytown Crown Court** heard.
>
> When police finally caught up with him, Young, a twice-divorced mechanic from Bognor Regis, was said to have joked with officers: 'Indeed, I'm like Raffles, you know. A gentleman thief.'
>
> **He denies six charges of fraud and the case continues.**

Stick with the **tell first, explain later** mantra. Leave any background to the end and give the news first.

> The brother of Helen Bailey, the missing children's author, has pleaded with her to make contact with her family.
>
> The Times, May 2016
>
>

This, which expands the intro and is the latest development, should have been the second sentence:

> John Bailey said: "Helen, if you see or read this appeal, please let someone know you are OK."

But it was the fourth paragraph after the writer cautiously recapped with two sentences of background about her disappearance.

> Be realistic about the amount of detail you can go into. Sometimes, you may need to compress a detailed story – maybe a complex court story, a major health report or a piece of scientific research – into a few pars. You simply will not be able to include every caveat and side angle. It may feel important but trying to cram it all in is impossible, so **be ruthless**.
>
> *St*y*le*point

Resist the urge to cram just because space is tight. This makes sense but it is hard going with three clauses in a row which could have been spread out.

> *Kimberley Upcott (pictured), 65, a 'trusted' accounts clerk at Loosemores Solicitors in Cardiff for 36 years, confessed on her final day at work. She admitted fraud and forfeited her £6,050 redundancy pay to 'put right her wrong', Cardiff crown court heard.*
>
> *Metro, September 2016*

The cramming would have been solved by starting the second sentence *The 65-year-old (pictured)* rather than *She*.

Data journalism

Data journalism is where geek meets newshound.

At its best, it is an **exciting, innovative form of storytelling**, where research based on computer-processed statistics and other releases of information produces engaging, insightful and informative news, presented in original formats.

While it has a role to play in print, it **flourishes online** where the full potential of mixing reportage, images, animation and interactivity can be exploited.

If done well, it can turn the abstract into real, explain complex situations to readers, make big stories personally relevant and give readers the tools to hold the powers that be to account.

It helps to **re-establish trust from readers** scarred by successive media scandals and a perceived slump in standards. It can **engage new readers** or re-energise old ones who crave the raw information to see where news is made and to judge its value for themselves.

Data can be used to **test the claims** of organisations and individuals with an agenda. If you suspect they are exaggerating or hiding something you can challenge it with the authority of data.

Moreover, it may be **more effective than using just words**. Tests show that information learned using pictures and text is recalled more easily and more frequently than information learned through words alone.

At its most ordinary, however, data journalism becomes all about the data, with too little emphasis on the journalism. The result is masses of pretty figures, charts and graphs thrown out with inadequate context and without much of a point to make. It is a sign the geeks are running the asylum.

Getting, processing and presenting data is not the object of the exercise. Guess what? It is **all about the story** that the data reveals. And, remember, it is not a story about the numbers – abstract, difficult to visualise, impossible to empathise with. Instead, it is about the people who make up the numbers.

Not so new for old

Data journalism appears to be emerging fast . . . but it's nothing new.

News writers have long had to grapple with statistics and wade through tables of figures. Government officials, businesses, charities and countless other organisations, official and less than official, release rafts of them, covering just about any subject you can think of.

The best reporters can **quickly identify the notable statistics**, those which present different angles and those which may challenge the official line but which have been conveniently buried.

Bad – or lazy – reporters are daunted by figures, don't spot the inconsistencies and tend to take the official word for what matters.

Tackling data in tables and graphs is a **basic skill** every journalist needs to acquire. Numeracy is not an optional extra. Neither, now, is **data fluency**.

Data journalism has blossomed because we are in an era when powerful computers make processing massive amounts of data relatively straightforward.

It has coincided with the arrival of countless bits of **free or low-cost software** which simplify both the number-crunching and the processing into easy-to-understand and attractive formats, such as maps, games, tables and graphs.

At the same time, there has been a burgeoning community of public-spirited hackers and data enthusiasts who simply love the sport and challenge of crunching numbers and creating pretty things from them.

Also, government has tended to become **more open**, with organisations committed to releasing the data they hold for others to scrutinise or use for social research. Some push their information into data banks where it sits waiting for analysis. **The Freedom of Information Act** gives journalists another lever for gaining access to the data they want from public organisations.

Data journalism was also given a significant push by high-profile examples such as the Wikileaks caches of military logs and diplomatic cables, along with the MPs' expenses scandal.

The impetus moved a journalistic backwater smack-bang into **the front line**.

On trend

Most editors love data journalism, too. In the digital world where everyone is chasing clicks but largely reliant on the same narrow pool of material, it can offer something unique, **a point of difference** in the morass of so-so information which gets published on every news site from here to Hobart.

It cannot be picked up by rivals and rehashed easily. It is too complex.

The most useful data journalism also has a long shelf life, as it acts as a **reference point** to which users can return. It retains its usefulness if it can be updated when new data arrives.

Advocates also see it as a **much-needed antidote** to the traditional reporter's bias towards public relations officials, anecdotal evidence and spin. They also see it as replacing the oft-claimed but rarely observed notion of impartiality with a new watchword – transparency.

Get it right and a data journalism exclusive can set the news agenda. There is extra kudos attached as the field is seen as groundbreaking – trendy, even.

Furthermore, bigger data journalism projects need not be time-sensitive, so they can be **prepared in down time** without deadline pressure. Ideas can be allowed to blossom and then to be finessed. They can be published when the editor sees fit as a measured, informed reaction to immediate events.

The process

The traditional journalism tends to come at the beginning and the end, while dealing with the data is the filling in the sandwich.

It is also a **collaborative process**, whereby newsdesks and reporters team up with graphic artists, data processors and app developers to come up with ideas. It needs the skills of the traditional newshound with a nose for news, a talent for digging and a way with words alongside the number-crunching and coding skills needed for data handling.

Editors struggle to find such disparate talents within one individual. Numeracy, computing skills and artistic flair are not common bedfellows with news sense and literacy. Even for those who want to stick with words, it is incumbent to gain at least some understanding of the processes involved.

It can be a **time-consuming process**, lasting months on the biggest projects.

Others from outside the newsroom, such as the amateur hackers and coders, might be drafted in to help. Some of the information may even be crowdsourced from readers. Teaming up with researchers, campaign groups or even investigative journalism organisations is sometimes needed.

For the purposes of this book, it is assumed you are a writer by instinct rather than a data expert, number cruncher, coder or graphic artist. This is how you might work as part of a team to catch the data slipstream.

Step 1: The idea

Many projects begin with **a hunch**. That's how it's always been. A reporter sees, notices or hears something and goes off to investigate. Instead of seeking anecdotal or witness accounts to compile a story, the hunt begins for data to shed light on it.

It is how scientists work. They see a problem or notice something about the world and draw up a theory to deal with it or explain it. They then devise experiments to test the idea. If their hypothesis is wrong, it's not a disaster; they still seek to publish their findings to show that things are not always as they might appear.

Using data should let journalists adopt a similar attitude – in the past they have tended to look for evidence to back a point of view and abandoned it when it didn't. This meant they were looking only to reinforce their readers' prejudices, giving them what they wanted to hear.

However, when the data does not back the hunch, a journalist may have discovered something more interesting because it is unexpected or does not match the stereotype or anecdotal evidence.

There will still be times when there is no story; it is just a mass of ho-hum data with no nuggets to be mined. You reach a dead end and the story hits the spike.

Once you have an idea, ask yourself if it is **something that people will really care about** or that directly affects them. Apply a brake if it is no more than producing data for data's sake. If it makes a statistician or data processor coo it is unlikely to excite the readers.

Observe the same principle that drives every kind of journalism – it has to inform and entertain. It has to be **a story**.

Don't forget to **have fun**. Data stories don't have to be serious and worthy. They can cover show business, the arts, celebrities or the plain silly in just the same way as traditional words and pictures. Data can make 'em laugh, too.

Step 2: The hunt

There is a heap of data out there. It is waving a flag at news writers, saying come and get me. Much of it is a few clicks away. That's all.

If it isn't out there already, there is plenty of other information lying ready to be mined with a bit more digging. It might take phone calls, a bit of pestering, even a Freedom of Information request but it is there to be used.

Almost all public organisations – government departments, councils, schools, colleges and universities, health trusts, hospitals and doctors' surgeries, publicly owned companies, publicly funded museums and the police – are **obliged to supply data**.

Being publicly run or funded, they keep lots of records, often in incredible detail. Start by asking nicely. Use an FoI as a backup.

Some of it may already have been mined for another project. Check the government's online records of FoI requests to see if it has previously been fulfilled.

Ethics apply with data, too. Stealing other people's data is a big no-no, so make sure you have permission to use it. If it has been officially published or given to you, either on request or following an FoI, there are no issues.

If the data is already in the public domain, **check there are no restrictions** on its use. Many in the data community and those working with it are passionate about ensuring material is open and freely available; they will signify this by releasing it under a Creative Commons licence, which is an invitation to make use of it. There is an **obligation to reciprocate**.

Other socially aware organisations – such as charities, pressure groups and even businesses – also need data to propagate their messages. Generally, they are willing to share.

Explore **data portals** and stores online. They are not going to contain something on everything but persistence will probably turn up a result or a lead to someone or somewhere with what you need.

Other data can be unearthed with a bit of clever Googling, perhaps by using its filtered search functions. Looking for specific file types, or in-site directories may produce what you need.

Social media is increasingly useful as a source to be mined. Beyond the newsroom, for example, health researchers have shown particular interest in tracking viruses and other illnesses through references on Twitter or elsewhere, enabling them to plot the way a disease spreads.

In a similar way, a trending hashtag can produce tens of thousands of fragments of usable data from across the globe to show how information spreads geographically or over time. It could be used to plot reaction to a protest movement, a humanitarian crisis, an election or just to map what people think about a sporting event or the Oscars.

Occasionally, you can create your own set of data by **getting readers to input it** for you. It has to be a subject which is getting attention and people care about, otherwise you won't get much feedback. It might take time to collect enough to be useful and beware, the results will be skewed because those that respond are likely to be those already engaged and with beefs to raise.

Finally, **use your contacts**. Polite phone calls and eager emails are very often the easiest and most effective approaches. In particular, use those in the data mining and hacker communities, many of whom are eager to help find and process information.

Step 3: The clean-up

We are now entering the technical phase of the process. Much of this lies well beyond the scope of this book. It would take several hundred pages and then some to walk through the manipulation involved in making use of the streams of zeroes and ones you have at your fingertips.

You have collected your data and are ready to set the team on to it. It's rarely as simple as that – data is nearly always messy and someone needs to clean it up. That can be a frustrating and long-winded process.

First, the data needs to be in **a format easily readable by a computer**, otherwise you are scuppered before you start. Statistical data for tables is generally published in spreadsheets using familiar software such as Excel. On the other hand, PDFs are notoriously hard to process. If there is no technical solution, then you will need to find it or ask for it again in a friendlier format.

Next, there may be just **too much data**. Some spreadsheets contain tens of thousands of lines with dozens of columns. Ask yourself which ones matter, or, more specifically, which ones really matter to your readers. Are gender differences important, or is it the geography or the age range? Just as you try to be with words – be concise and be precise. Using only what you need saves time and energy and, if you want your more dedicated readers to have access to every bit of information, you can always publish the raw data.

At the other end of the scale, **the data may be incomplete** with years missing or perhaps some rows and columns only partly completed. If you can't dig up the missing elements, you may have to make a judgment call on how you get round the gaps. It may mean leaving out a specific year or category altogether. At worst, it could invalidate the entire exercise. More searching, more digging, more calls and emails might plug the gap.

There will probably be **errors in the data**. Humans have created it and they are prone to make mistakes. While you cannot be responsible for others' fat finger typing or lack of attention to detail, it needs resolving. If every entry in a category is between one and three, then alarm bells should ring if the odd one appears as an unlikely 103. Again, it may be more calls and digging to try to correct. If the unlikely is correct, then you need an explanation. It could be that it is the sign of an extraordinary story or just a quirk of the statistics.

When looking for true averages, statisticians and scientists tend to exclude the atypical and extreme. You may need to do the same if you are looking for a fairer picture of a situation.

Entries are **rarely consistent**. Those pesky human inputters will have different styles and codes for the same piece of information. A code 3X in one inputter's entry means it's a parking ticket, another may call them 3Y and 3Z, depending on the size of the fine, while a third may call a parking ticket a 'parking ticket'. For cross-border samples, there may be different spellings in different countries or even a different unit of measurement.

All these variations need some scrutiny to resolve. There is usually an index on a dataset, indicating what different entries mean, which could help. Otherwise more research may be needed.

It must remain **accurate**. You can clean it but don't disturb it or twist it out of proportion.

Sensible rounding up and down is often logical, neater and acceptable. Obsessing over every detail is not always healthy.

It is commendable practice to **publish the raw data** so readers can see the figures you are working from. Apart from being transparent, it opens the resource to further comments and improvements, as well as ideas for additional research. It also builds the pool of information available to journalists, researchers and the data community – a healthy you-scratch-my-back-I'll-scratch-yours state of affairs.

Step 4: Analyse it

You have a beautiful set of statistics, all cleaned up and shiny. The next critical question is what does it mean? And, most importantly, does it tell a story?

As with any story you are searching for the **unusual and the unexpected**. To produce firm evidence, the trends and differences need to be notable and enduring. Hunt for the thing that makes you go, 'Gee whiz!'

Start looking for **patterns**. Typically, you may well be trying to determine if something is happening more or less frequently to a specific group of people or in a specific place or time.

Is the pattern strong or just vaguely detectable? Perhaps it is incomplete. Yes, nurses appear to be struck off more often than doctors but only in the north-east, Wales and Cornwall. You have a pattern of sorts but it raises more questions than answers.

You may be able to detect significant **changes over time**. Growth or decline creates dynamic curves and angles on maps and graphs, whereas straight lines are rarely as interesting.

You will also be looking for **comparisons**. Why is one set of figures significantly higher or lower than another? For example, why does one neighbourhood, city or country have many thousands with health, social or other issues, while another has very few?

Look also for what statisticians like to refer to as **outliers**. These are the bits of data that, as the name suggests, lie well outside the norm. Do they suggest something extraordinary is happening, or is it a statistical quirk? Is it a sign of a worrying or welcome trend, or just a one-off? For example, why do such large numbers of people appear to be dying in a particular postcode? Is it a sign of something malevolent at play, or is it just that there are several old people's homes in the neighbourhood?

All data needs to be placed in **context**. This is particularly the case with absolute numbers. Your research may reveal that 500 people have died of a certain disease in one city this year. Is it a story? And if so, what kind of story is it?

If 500 deaths is roughly the same as in any other year, the answer is probably no.

It may have risen significantly over the past 30 years but it could simply be that the population of the city has grown substantially in that time. Or maybe it is a disease which mainly affects older people at the end of their lives, so it could just be a sign that people are living longer.

If 500 deaths is significantly more or less than in other cities then there may be something going on. You will need to scratch a little deeper; clearly, you will need to compare like with like. The total of 500 deaths might equate to one in every 1,000 people in the city. If the rate is one in 750 in other cities then the context suggests something is amiss.

Finally, perhaps the figures are **unremarkable**. Maybe they are too small to be significant or they are too untrustworthy or inconsistent to be reliable. You have ploughed through a database of emails and they detail nothing more than arrangements for a series of meetings and courtesy notes.

It's time for a judgment call. Should you put aside the work you have done and admit you have hit a dead end, try a different approach or plough on in the belief that something is better than nothing? Time available, resources and an editor's willingness (or desperation) may decide that.

Step 5: Visualise it

The cleaned-up and polished data is nothing more than a series of numbers, words or other oddments in a spreadsheet saved on a hard disk. It's little use to the readers.

It is time to add the technical magic that turns it into something both practical and pretty.

If you are a writer and not a data technician, then you may not have much of a hands-on part to play here. It is where graphic artists and designers who are highly proficient in using spreadsheet software such as Excel or data visualisation tools or design software such as Adobe Illustrator step up.

Another set of skills and software again is needed to turn the raw information into a database and a web app.

We are trying to create **something the reader can see**, understand and use. Charts, graphs or maps are the most commonly used and simplest devices. It might be another static form of diagram, such as a timeline or word cloud. But it could be a video clip, a rolling set of slides or an animation. Data can even be worked into a simple video game or presented in a comic book style. If the data is extensive and lends itself to interactivity, it could become a standalone website or app in the hope it becomes a durable tool for readers to return to.

Visualisations can stand alone, with few words beyond a headline and perhaps a few explanatory paragraphs. They are devices to tell a story in their own right.

Take a look at the website Information is Beautiful, where there are some stunning examples of data presentations. They are lovingly created and informative but more encyclopedic than news inspired. Nonetheless, the best tell you a story while illustrating a point about the world we live in.

In a newsroom environment, the finished visualisation is often used to illustrate or expand a point, running alongside a story to contextualise it. You know crime is rising; here are the figures to show it. You know a politician is the most media friendly; here is the statistical evidence. You know trains are always overcrowded; we have another visual representation.

It can be, first and foremost, an **elegant way to take the technical and dry out of prose** and present it to the reader in a more digestible and appealing form.

The richest visualisations, however, offer more than just a two-dimensional illustration.

One joy of working online can be the dialogue with readers. Interactivity in a visualisation makes it involving. Allow readers to change, fiddle, play with, input or respond through it to make it more engaging.

If they can click or roll over something to reveal new information, it becomes **more playful**. You are hoping they stay longer, look at more information and are more enlightened as a result. The more layers of interactivity the better.

Work to exploit the extra functions that **mobile devices** have. For example, geolocation means the device can pinpoint where on a data map the user is standing when they load it. Could the tilt function be used to navigate through or amend a visualisation? Can it use the in-built camera?

Best of all, **personalise it**. If a reader can use it or input something which gives them information relevant to their lives, they will find the data infinitely more engaging. It might be drilling down to information relevant to their street, a school or college they want to attend or a business they want to use, or it may be helping them assess the effects of tax rule changes on their finances – or it might be just something fun, such as using their details to create an amusing meme.

If possible, make a visualisation **adjustable**. It will increase engagement if users can vary the parameters of the information. At its simplest it might allow them to change a running order, such as putting the biggest first or changing the colours. But it might be that by inputting a variation they can see a range of scenarios – for example, how much their bills will go up dependent on, say, a range of changes in interest rates or the effect of a political decision.

The best visualisations are **durable**, so they provide more than a single hit and a brief spike in visitor numbers. A web app may be time-consuming to produce, involving extensive data and more elaborate coding but if it's easy to update when new figures are produced then it can become a valuable resource for readers. School exam results or league tables are a hardy annual.

Crucially, the visualisation should have a point – or, in other words, **tell a story.** Its focus should be to highlight the extraordinary. That could be a worrying (or pleasing) trend, an obvious pattern of behaviours or very high or alarmingly low levels of something.

Keep it straightforward, sharply focused and **clutter-free**. Lots of confusing lines, a morass of colours and dots or converging shapes are troublesome to the eye. A light, elegant touch so it is clean and direct – like the best news prose – wins out.

It should be **obvious** what you are trying to say. It is the impression you create, rather than the in-depth or detailed, that sticks in the mind. For example, a spike or drop in figures should look like a spike or drop, so don't make the scale so large that variations are lost. Use colours and hues that match the message – red is a warning, blue is cool, green is associated with healthiness. Use darker hues for the more interesting zones against lighter for the less so. If it's fun, use cheerful fonts; if it's sombre, stick to traditional ones.

Lastly, after analysing the data and weighing up the possibilities, you may have to ask whether it needs visualisation. Consider what value it adds above a traditional approach with a headline and text. It is possible that the key figures or details – the ones that scream story – are a minor element of a large dataset. The rest is just padding around it – in that case, is it necessary to spend hours preparing a chart or illustration which will not engage the reader or shed any different kind of light on the story you are trying for?

Just because you can make something out of it doesn't always mean you have to.

Step 6: Report on it

Data is a tool, not the story you are trying to create.

It is there to **raise questions**; it rarely gives you the complete answer. As you can see from the analytical process in Step 4, data is a frustrating interviewee. While it tells you what appears to be happening, it won't explain why. It often lacks the most important piece of information – who.

It will indicate trends and point to patterns. For instance, a map of the poorest parts of the country set against highest use of sexual health services may suggest a link between the two. But why? Are poorer people more promiscuous or careless about their sexual health or deprived of good sex education? Do wealthy people with sexual health problems travel to poorer areas for treatment so their neighbours don't see them? Is this newsworthy? Maybe.

There is no meat on the bones. But at least you have sound figures, which may or not confirm the hunch with which you started, as a basis on which to begin asking questions. It is now down to the journalist in you – rather than the data expert – to start digging.

First, **do you need more data?** Figures on sexual health services spending? Information on numbers of sexual health advisers? Do you need to start drilling down deeper into the geography by finding precise locations of clinics? The answer may start joining some dots.

But the real work starts with **asking people about the data**. There will be experts, doctors and health analysts aplenty to ask. There will be charities, health campaigners and even politicians with a view.

Above all, **get into the communities** where the pattern appears to be the most significant. Can you speak to the nurse who administers the jabs or dresses the sores? Can you speak to the sexual health adviser who tries to educate in schools? Can you talk to those who have been treated or, more intriguingly, struggled to find treatment?

Then, and only then, do we have humanity: real people facing real issues that readers can identify with, not just statistics on a chart. Your job is to tell their stories.

Step 7: Write about it

After the shoe leather is worn out, the final step is to write the words.

Those words might support a data visualisation, serving as little more than a covering note or introduction. For this, a commentary style of writing might be the most appropriate. At other times the story is the focus and the visualisation a small element. Most of the time they will have to work together.

One objective when tackling a story based on data journalism is to make sure it **looks nothing like a data journalism piece**.

Why should it scream data journalism? Readers have come looking for a story, told in as compelling a fashion as possible. It may have statistical foundations but it remains of secondary importance to them where the information came from.

Remember the ABBC basics. Keep it legally sound and offer a right of reply.

Abide by the same rules as any other piece of writing. Give it an intriguing intro based on the most extraordinary or revelatory piece of information your data has provided. Having decided that is your story, focus and build on that point alone through the expansion. Then continue through a more methodical, chronological retelling, starting with the hunch and coming back to your findings. Our **pyramid** works here, too.

Try to avoid just creating a few anecdotes or loosely connected quotes to illustrate your figures. It should be a story that stands on its own, with a start, a middle and an end.

Revisit golden rule 8 (Chapter 7), **make it add up**, to see how to tackle stories with numbers in them. Remember in particular not to swamp the text with figures. If your story runs alongside a data visualisation with the figures in it, then leave them out of the text. Those who want to scour the figures in great depth are best served by publishing a link to the raw data.

Don't repeat the information in the visualisation in the text; enrich it instead. The visualisation exists to take the boring bits out of the prose and make them exciting, so any more than a passing reference to them in the prose defeats the purpose.

Take, for example, the simplest of graphics, a table or list of the top 10 or 20 or 100. There, in front of the reader, is the list for them to scan. They can see at a glance what came 7th or 43rd or 88th.

So in an accompanying story, don't just give a run-down of what is in what place in the table. It adds nothing. Instead, focus on why they are in those places or the reaction to the placings.

Take time to **proofread** the visualisation. Check it for clarity, as well as spellings and use of English. If it has been produced by a graphic artist, it is unlikely they are as skilled with words as they are with images and presentation.

In particular, **check for inconsistencies** between the visualisation and the story. If one indicates the rise is 10 per cent and the other says 20 per cent, one or the other is wrong. Check, too, that the spellings of names of people and places, abbreviations and other style points are consistent throughout.

Finally, don't get carried away with **the myth that data journalism is empirical**. It may be based on authoritative-sounding figures or official-sounding information processed by a computer but it has human fingerprints all over it.

It is just as open to manipulation and selectivity as any other form of journalism. Humans collect and record the data – they make a conscious decision about which data to record and which they don't. They may not have access to complete information, or their information may be from unreliable sources. Further, they come with their own frailties, agendas and prejudices which can serve to inflate, diminish or obscure for their own ends. Just because it is from an official or outwardly impartial source does not make it infallible.

Data is fluid, too. Consider a vast database such as population statistics. At best they will provide a fuzzy snapshot – long before the figures have all been collected, processed and published, the world has moved on and the information is out of date.

If the data is, by its very nature, flawed, then it can only tell half the story. Your research and your writing must tell the rest.

Useful software

If you are reading this book, you are probably an aspiring writer first and a technician a very distant second.

But if you work in an environment where data journalism is taking a grip – and many, many more of us are or will be – you will need to have a basic appreciation of some of the tools of the trade.

There are many types of software and every one will have its advocates. Those detailed debates lie well beyond the scope of this chapter. As a starting point, focus on getting a basic understanding of the principles behind these:

Excel: This is the most commonly used software for spreadsheets. It's beloved of accountants and office managers the world over and has thousands of uses beyond journalism. In short, it is a means of organising information in rows and columns, which can be added up, highlighted and manipulated in myriad ingenious ways. There are free and equally useful clones, such as Open Office Calculator, which work in much the same way

Google: For knocking up a quick pie chart or table, this is an excellent place to begin. A simple charts function is found within the spreadsheet utility in Google Drive. It's free, intuitive and customisable, as well as being part of a bigger suite of Google tools, including data journalism stalwarts such as Google Maps. Google Fusion Tables, also free and relatively straightforward, will allow you to become more creative still

HTML: Hypertext Mark-Up Language is the formatting language used for building websites. Invented by web pioneer Tim Berners-Lee in the early 1990s, it uses pairs of tags to define how the text will look on a page or to embed pictures and other elements. It's worth exploring just to build an understanding of how simple sites are compiled and how browsers read them. Its successor, HTML5, allows for more sophisticated use of graphics and videos in web pages

Adobe software: Adobe produces a suite of industry-standard software largely aimed at those working in the media or graphic arts. A working knowledge of Photoshop and Illustrator is a handy starting point for manipulating pictures and creating graphics. InDesign is more widely used by page designers on newspapers and magazines. In their later incarnations they are exceedingly powerful – and expensive – tools which can create visually stunning work. For the super ambitious Adobe Animate CC, which has replaced Flash, and After Effects are standards for animation. If you are on a budget, you can download older, official and still extremely useful versions for free

Glossary of terms

Stand near a group of techies and you will quickly encounter a host of terms, mostly acronyms, which can make it appear as if they are speaking in a different language. Here are a few translations to help you nod wisely at the right moments:

API: Application Programming Interface, the way computer programs talk to and share information with each other

Atom: A format used to distribute updates or new stories on a website to readers via feed readers or through email. Now largely supplanted by RSS

Bar graph: A simple chart using coloured or shaded bars to illustrate different values

CMS: Content Management System. Software which organises all the stories, pictures, graphics and other material to be used on a website (or newspaper). It's what news writers work on every day

Cookie: A small file downloaded to your computer when you visit a website. It remembers your details, such as login information, to save time when you next visit

CSS: Cascading style sheets are files which determine the look of web pages by defining the style for the whole site

CSV: Comma-Separated Values is the simplest of all data formats with information written in text format, separated, as the name suggests, by commas

Data dump: When an organisation publishes a significant cache of data online. For data journalists it is the cue to dive in and start mining for gold

Data scraping: The process of extracting data from a version which can be read by humans into one which can be read by computers so it can be re-used. As the names suggests, **screen scraping** involves extracting the data you might see on a screen, while **web scraping** is extracting the background data used for a web page but usually buried within its HTML code

Data visualisation: Sometimes just shortened to **data viz**. It refers to graphics, charts, maps or any image-led method for displaying information

Data wrangler: A loose term for those who extract and process data

Fever chart: A simple graph in which a dotted line (**fever line**) shows a trend over time, much like a temperature chart for a patient

FoI: Refers to Freedom of Information. Requests for data can be made, usually without cost, to almost all publicly funded bodies under the 2000 Freedom of Information Act

Flash: A plug-in for a web browser for displaying videos and other interactive content

FTP: File Transfer Protocol. A system for moving files, usually from your computer to a web server

GIF: Graphics Interchange Format: A type of picture file

Hacker: A commonly misused term to describe coding experts who break into computer systems to commit acts of sabotage or criminality. In fact, hackers are more likely to be public-spirited coders who enjoy exploring and improving software and systems. Hence, the distinction between **black hat** (bad) and **white hat** (good) hackers. **Cracker** is a better term for those who do bad stuff

Hackathon: An event where coders, hackers, data wranglers and data journalists might come together for an all-day (and all-night) session to work on a joint project or to exchange ideas and techniques

Heat map: A map with colours of varying intensity to show the geographical spread of data

Iframe: Nothing to do with Apple, but an HTML tag which displays one web page, such as a Google Map page, within another

JavaScript: A scripting language used to make whizzier web sites

JPEG: Joint Photographic Expert Group. The most widely used picture file format

Mash-up: A combination of data from multiple sources

Metadata: A simple index embedded in a file containing information such as who created it, when it was created and maybe keywords. It can then be used to sort and source files from within databases

MPEG: Moving Pictures Experts Group. A file format for video

MySQL: My, for the name of the inventor's daughter, Structured Query Language. It is a popular, open-source system for managing databases

Open-source software: Software where the source is published freely for others to modify or improve

PDF: Portable Document Format. A format for publishing, storing and transferring documents. There is plenty of free software – Adobe Reader is the most popular – to enable users to read documents in PDF form

Perl: Scripting language used to sort and standardise information data pulled from websites

PHP: PHP: Hypertext Preprocessor, although it used to be short for the more prosaic Personal Home Page. A scripting language to generate web pages

Pie chart: A diagram in which data is displayed by dividing a circle into coloured or shaded segments

Plug-in: A programme which can be added to a content system or internet browser to perform a specific function

Python: Named after Monty Python, it is a popular computer language used for internet applications

RSS: Really or Real Simple Syndication. A format used to distribute updates or new stories from a website to readers

Ruby: Open-source programming language used to create websites.

Ruby on Rails is a framework, based on Ruby, which has pre-prepared common tasks to make them quicker and easier. Django is its best-known rival

SEO: Search Engine Optimisation. Techniques for improving website ranking on search engines, usually Google, or promoting stories in aggregators such as

Google News. Important for writers to understand if they want their stories to be easily found and read

Sparkline: A small fever line used within a bigger chart to illustrate a specific trend

SQL: Structured Query Language, a programming language for working with databases

UGC: User-generated content. Material such as comments, photos, graphics or videos submitted to publications by readers

UI: User Interface. The bit of a software application or website which users see and interact with

URL: Uniform Resource Locator, posh name for a web address

UX: User Experience. A term for how easy or hard it is for your readers to use, or navigate through, a website. Too many intrusive ads and badly written stories makes for a poor UX

Widget: Small application on a desktop, website or social network which might bring news updates and allow readers to share them easily

Features

It's wrong to impose rules on feature writing. Features, be they light and frothy or serious and newsy, should be individual and shot through with the writer's unique approach and turn of phrase. Some of the most engaging are deeply personal. Structure, language, judgments and tone belong to you, the writer. Let them live or die by that.

Apply self-restraint

Nonetheless, while feature writing should not be constrained, **the best is highly disciplined**. You might have several thousand words to play with. That is a considerable investment in time you are asking of the reader. Without some self-restraint you may struggle to hold their attention.

You still need to get **the basics right**. It is still **storytelling**, albeit at a more leisurely pace and perhaps months or years after an event. Features are also reportage, so the details – from spellings to dates to descriptions – have to be accurate. A relaxed style does not justify journalistic sloppiness.

Features give freedom to explore a topic in depth. However, be conscious of just **how interesting the subject really is**. Step back and think like a reader.

Ask yourself how many words and how much detail will your readers really want. A 2,000-word thesis on the six best mobile phones will enthral the readers of mobilewetdream.com but bore the pants off a more general audience. Don't just write 2,000 words because you can; it's better to write 800 well-chosen ones.

Structure it

When building a feature, you still need to **apply some structure**. There are countless ways to do this and, as features are more personal, even sometimes written in the first person, you should find your own style.

But it might be helpful to borrow a few ideas from writing harder news.

You need a **powerful hook** – the first sentence should be intriguing, a lead into an opening passage that invites further reading. It sounds a lot like an intro, expansion and chronology from our pyramid.

> *A jumble of wires. They seemed to be connected in the wrong order. To the wrong ends of the detonator. It was a deadly confusion.*
>
> *As Sgt Pete Simpson, lying belly down on a dusty Iraqi road, tried to decipher it, the doubts crept in. Years of training which had turned him into the Army's go-to man for clearing improvised explosive devices were screaming at him: Cut the blue wire.*
>
> *It was hot, too, under the desert sun. He hesitated, sweat building inside his protective suit. His throat was dry.*
>
> *Lives were at stake. His life, too. He leaned forward. And cut the red wire. And lived.*

Much like a great movie or novel, this (imagined) feature on Army bomb disposal crews **dives into the heart of the action**. There is limited backstory or explanation, just a moment in time, a scene-setter to get the feature going.

Just like news, it could easily be followed by a quieter moment.

> *Simpson chuckles as he recounts the story. Ruggedly handsome, tattooed, with a gap-toothed smile and a thick Scottish accent, he knows his job is deadly serious but making light of it seems to ease the stress.*

The strength of your opening, of course, will depend on how well you interview your subjects or how willing they are to let you into their world.

But by this stage your challenge is to have the reader wanting more. If you achieve that, don't lose the momentum.

Features need flow

Features are a long read and you need to lead the reader by the hand on that journey with you. No sudden lurches in one direction or another, each paragraph logically connected to the previous one.

Every sentence must count, must add a layer to the storytelling. If it doesn't, then it is padding, so cut it out.

Once you have reviewed sentences, **scrutinise every word**, too. There may be room for more descriptive passages. Sparse or newsy prose can be grinding in a long read but, just as brevity is a necessity in news writing, there is no benefit to flabbiness in features.

Check that you are not **repeating yourself**. If you are – especially if quotes are starting to cover the same ground – then it's time to explore a different facet to the story or end it all together.

Adding depth

Use the extra space a feature gives you to **explore layers of colour and detail**. You can paint between the lines in a way a news story does not always allow. A personality piece benefits from observations about their demeanour and appearance; a travel feature needs a patchwork of tempting morsels to create a portrait of a country a reader may yet have to visit; a news feature can use them to explain all the circumstances under which events have taken place.

Polish your vocabulary to make sure you can write elegantly. It doesn't mean learning lots of long words to sound posh or clever but to make sure you don't fall back on journalese or brusque news writing staples. Employ literary devices you might be denied in straight news writing, such as fragmented sentences or a flurry of questions. Personal observation works, too. Strive for rhythm and grace.

> If you are writing for a specific publication, make sure you **stay in style**. If it's for a younger audience, it might be earthy and aggressive; middle of the road still needs to be honest and punchy; a high-brow publication demands a literary approach; an arty audience may be esoteric.
>
> *Style*point

Round it off

A feature needs a pay-off paragraph – the best are sharply observed lines which summarise or suggest more to come. Try drawing the reader back to the opening salvo. We might, in our imagined example, say:

> *Simpson has to leave for another call-out. He grins again. This time, he's hoping the wiring is a bit more straightforward.*

Most news writers, whose day to day work might require them to shovel a book's worth of information into 400 well-honed words, welcome the relative freedom of writing features. You are off the creative leash, so enjoy it.

Blogs

Remember our noisy news party with millions of voices clamouring to be heard amid the cacophony?

Much of the racket in today's crowded media landscape comes from bloggers. Every one of them thinks they have something important to say. Most of them believe they are saying it with style. Many of them, however, are just creating white noise.

A blog is the perfect tool for a news writer to blow off steam. There is freedom to tackle a subject you care about, throw your personality at your writing and make an impression – a chance to be the most entertaining guest at the party.

A blog might be an opinion, analytical or colour piece to run alongside news reportage. There may also be a standalone channel for comment to which news writers are expected – and should want – to contribute.

And your point is . . . ?

The starting point is to **have a point**. A shrewd one. On a subject your readers care about. Set out with a clear idea of what you want to say and say it loud. Don't shirk, don't be mealy-mouthed or um and ahh. **Boldness** is, after all, one of our ABBCs.

Say **something different**. If you are one of ten thousand voices saying exactly the same thing, no matter how eloquently you write, who will notice? Challenge conventional wisdoms and dare to go against the accepted narrative. Why not argue why cancer is a good thing, why North Korea should be allowed nuclear missiles, why Victoria Wood wasn't very funny.

If you are part of the consensus, try coming at the subject in an **original way** – maybe by sharing something deeply personal, suggesting a bad thing for a greater good or focusing on a small but critical point which you feel has been overlooked.

More than a rant

Have some **facts, figures and evidence** to support your point. Without them it's just a rant.

Try offering some **original research**. Use your newsgathering skills to drum up quotes or to unearth a previously unseen document or a set of fresh statistics. Letting others do the journalistic graft and then spouting off about it is freeloading.

Honesty also counts for a lot. If you care about your subject it will shine through, while it's easy to spot a writer going through the motions or reeling off a few hundred words just because the editor has demanded an opinion piece. Being controversial is part and parcel of opinion writing but being controversial – or even offensive – just to gather a few clicks is a hollow victory.

Add style

Use **humour**. If it's a serious subject, humour can be disarming before delivering the sucker punch. If it's a light-hearted subject, then humour adds to the readability.

Quirky can work but it takes great flair to pull it off consistently and being quirky for the sake of being quirky quickly becomes tiresome. Wry wit always out-classes sledgehammer jokes and don't use a blog just to show how side-splittingly funny you are. You probably aren't.

Hit them with a **good opening line**. Just like an intro on a great news story, you need a hook that intrigues the reader. Steal from the news pyramid by hitting hard for a few paragraphs, then taking a breather. Rewind and begin adding context and explanation.

Polish the words. Make it precise and punchy but flex your literary muscles while crafting each sentence carefully. Follow the ABBC and remember the basics of sentence construction and grammar. Cut out every extraneous word.

There is more to a blog than just the words. Once it's written, you need to sell it. Craft a clickable **headline**, think what **pictures** will help and use **social media** to promote it.

Don't outstay your welcome. Make your point, make it well, then cut and run. You may have plenty to say but only continue writing if each sentence adds another layer.

Reviews

Getting sent to review a concert, a play, a film, an art show or even a new restaurant is often part of a news writer's lot.

On smaller publications, perhaps without specialists and where everyone has to pitch in, it should provide a creative break from the routine of hard news.

For underpaid reporters it's also a free ticket to a night out – even if you wouldn't choose to see the Anytown Amateur Operatic Society's toe-curling version of Calamity Jane.

Informed opinion

First and foremost, remember that **a review is not reportage**; it's an opinion piece. Hence, the first step before writing is to form an opinion. That means saying what you thought of a performance and not regurgitating the plot. For a restaurant review it should not be about what food was on the menu but what it tasted like and how well it was served.

Its purpose is to **advise people** whether this is something worth paying for or to provide feedback and a focus for discussion for those who already have.

You will need to **know your stuff**. While you can't bone up on the history of rock music to judge a pub band, you can listen to some of their material, read their biographies and find out something of their approach and what they are trying to achieve.

Sometimes you may be sent to review something of which you have little experience. Bluffing is not an option, so make a merit of it – be honest with readers by explaining you prefer opera to death thrash metal or it is your first time seeing Beckett performed in French.

Theme it

Once you have a view, **shape it into your theme**. The performer has lost his edge, the artist uses too much blue, the film sacrifices character development for battle scenes, the plate was chipped but the filet mignon was to die for.

Your critique **needs this focus**, as much as a news story needs an angle. Stick with it as you would for writing news because it will help to reinforce quickly the impression you are trying to create.

You can **borrow from the news pyramid**, with a catchy opening salvo, a few pars of expansion on that point and then a chronology, perhaps beginning with a brief recap of plot, what you saw or ate or how a computer game worked, before expanding again on your earlier theme.

Try ending a review by referencing your opening paragraph. Bringing it back to the beginning will **round it off neatly** and create a sense of wholeness.

Fair and honest

Be **honest** when you write. If it is an opinion honestly held then you are free to express it and generally safe from legal comebacks. If you hate something, then fine, say so but don't pretend to dislike something you secretly enjoyed just because it makes sharper copy.

Be **fair**, too. Don't judge an amateur show by West End standards or a children's show against what you would expect from adults. You cannot realistically expect a £10-a-head eat-as-much-as-you-like buffet to match a Michelin-starred restaurant. There are very few experiences which are uniformly bad and most have good and bad points. It's grossly unfair to focus exclusively on the bad and, besides, unremitting negativity can be wearing even if it seems fun to pour scorn.

Avoid personal remarks. It's fair to comment on someone's singing ability – even an enthusiastic amateur – but why cast aspersions on their physical appearance? Remember, it's extreme – and untrue – to say someone can't sing or act; they can but they maybe don't do it very well.

Just because something is wildly popular doesn't mean it is without merit. **Don't be snobby**. It's incumbent on you as a reviewer to understand the commercial appeal of something that may lack what you see as artistic integrity. By the same token, you need to understand why, say, a silent Latvian art house film shot entirely in black and white with only two characters who spend most of their time staring out to sea attracts an audience of three.

There is **no shame in positivity**. It's easy to sneer but it can make for very unattractive writing. Much of what you will be asked to review is probably going to be ho–hum – neither great nor terrible. Start with what you found enjoyable, then pick at the weak points later. Criticism should be constructive – then, even the most sensitive of performers should embrace it.

The subject is irrelevant – it's the story that counts
Learn to love covering any subject – it's the people that count
Apply the **same level of skill to all subjects** – it's the writing that counts

*Key*points

10

WRITING FOR BROADCAST

In a book dedicated to words, we now need to learn not to use them. Or, more precisely, only to use them when they are absolutely necessary.

Broadcast journalists are something of a breed apart from those who work online or in print. They should possess the same core skills – our ABBC – and use them to tell fascinating stories about real people and events.

But they tell their stories in a very different way – with pictures and sound, not with words.

A half-hour TV news programme might contain a couple of thousand words – about the same as a busy page of a broadsheet newspaper. In broadcast news, words enhance; they do not tell.

Types of reports

Traditionally, there are two kinds of broadcast reports.

The first, only two or three sentences long, are short stories designed to be read over a short film clip or still images, known as a ULAY (from *underlay*). In radio, an audio clip might be dropped in to enhance them.

A fuller report consists of a three- or four-sentence lead, also known as a link or cue in radio and much like the intro and expansion of our pyramid. It is read in the studio and followed by a recorded report, known as a package.

However, radio and TV broadcasters are making increasing use of live two-ways (also known as *one-to-ones* or *live links*) with reporters, who are interviewed from the studio by the anchor, while making use of sound bites or other clips to be dropped in at the reporter's prompting. Two-ways are felt to be more dynamic and immediate than a scripted segment.

Writing for TV: pictures first

In a filmed TV report, the script has to complement the pictures. It is **pointless simply describing what the viewer can see** for themselves. Instead, the words spoken by the reporter add detail.

For example, if you have footage of a crashed train, there is no point in telling the viewer there are some crashed train carriages, they were badly damaged and the track was buckled. Instead, add information they cannot see – that the crash happened at rush hour, that there was standing room only, that the train on the left is a soon-to-be discontinued 50-year-old model and that the one on the right had only been in service for three weeks.

Meanwhile, **guide the reader around the pictures** – you might tell them the wooden box in the distance is the signal box where something went wrong or the man being led away bleeding is one of the drivers, who has 30 years' experience with the railway company.

Think of a script like a sports commentary. Why tell the viewer that Jones has passed the ball to Smith – they can see that. A good commentator might, however, tell the viewer that it was the 13th pass Jones has made or that he is usually substituted by this point in the match. Indeed, the best sports commentary is when less is said rather than more – a particular challenge when the excitement is high. The greatest commentators know exactly the time to say nothing.

Make sure the **pictures and words are consistent.** If your script talks of white-collar workers over footage of men in boiler suits emerging from a factory, then it will look ridiculous. Viewers will pick up on the slightest technical error – it can be sport for some to spot anything, from footage of the wrong person or location to a mislabelled model of car.

You need to tell the viewer what is happening in the pictures only when it is off camera or is not easy to see, for example, on poor quality phone or CCTV footage.

> **Adverbs and adjectives are unnecessary** – if you can hear or see a fierce, noisy, lengthy gun battle, then you do not need to say that *A fierce, noisy, lengthy gun battle raged.* Perhaps, just add *The shooting went on for five hours.*
> **Abandon journalese** – it's a language invented for newspapers and people don't speak that way.
>
> *Style*point

Making the most of pictures

Reporters need to be brave with their scripts. If the pictures are truly dramatic, then leave them to run without commentary. Perhaps **use the sound** on the film itself – the roar of traffic, the chatter of a crowd, the crack of gunshots.

Abstract and wordy stories based on MPs' reports or findings of committees may be worthy and illuminating but without worthwhile footage to elevate them they are unlikely to make good television. Broadcasters must be bold with their choices – while major stories have to be covered even if the pictures are weak, others may have to be ignored.

The challenge is to find pictures that make the abstract story work as TV. Shots of an armed police raid as they bash down a door and swoop on an unexpected suspect before emerging with evidence of drug dealing make for great footage. It is a visually exciting way to illustrate a story based on a dry report from a committee of MPs on rising numbers of drug crimes. The stats and the comments of the suits in parliament are the launch-pad and must be included but leave them until much later in the package.

It makes sense to **write the script only after seeing the pictures** – if something is obvious from the footage, you don't need to say it and, likewise, you will recognise what details you do need to add.

However, the process starts before the camera is turned on. Reporter and cameraman – on the increasingly rare occasions they are separate people – need to work together, planning opening sequences and other shots they know will pin the package together. Ideas for the script can be formed as they go along.

Striking the right tone

Good scripts **lead the viewer by the hand** through the story. Imagine you are talking to a single person rather than to an audience of millions, the adage goes. Think as though you are telling the story to your favourite auntie over the garden fence.

Your style should be personable and open. **You are on the side of the viewer**; you are one of them, nudging them along. They are not *the public* or *the audience*. To reflect this, **make your language inclusive** – *we* is a much better word than *you* or *I*. Avoid in-house phrases – why should a viewer know what a package or a lead is?

Be prepared to put a little of yourself into it – not opinion but to provide personality and a feeling of familiarity. If you are working in regional television, there's something to be said for dropping in the odd dialect word, just to remind viewers you are one of them.

Keep the story flowing

Much as the best writing flows from one paragraph to the next, it is an imperative in broadcast that a script has a **logical and clear progression**, using **smooth transitions** to change the subject of sentences.

Remember that viewers are unlikely to pause and rewind a news item to go over what you have just said. It needs to be **crystal clear at the first time of telling**. Ugly jumps of subject and switchbacks only serve to confuse.

It is best to **focus tightly** on one facet of a story. While print and online writing has space to sprawl, covering every angle, you can't cram everything in. It will become too wordy.

Write as you speak

Words in broadcast are written to be spoken, not read. Good English is important but sentences need to be **structured how you would say them**.

For example, a news writer should strive to keep the active, interesting part of a sentence at the beginning, burying the source or attribution at the end. Hence, we might write, *A blogger who repeatedly abused the royal family was out to destroy the fabric of society, a court was told today.* While it reads better that way, it doesn't sound natural when we say it. We don't talk like that.

For broadcast, putting the keywords at the end of the sentence gives the viewer a moment of adjustment time and allows a build-up of emphasis. Hence:

> *A court heard today how a blogger repeatedly insulted the royal family.*
> *The jury was told Graham Sergeant wanted to destroy the fabric of society.*

Always **attribute clearly**, taking special care with anything wildly controversial. It's easy for words to slip by unnoticed, so avoid this style of script:

> *All Muslims should be banned from America until the threat of terrorism is seen off.*
> *They should be locked up in jail and given basic rations until they can prove they are good citizens.*
> *So says Donald Trump . . .*

Better to tell it straight:

> *Donald Trump thinks all Muslims should be locked up.*
> *He thinks they should be given basic rations until they prove they are good citizens.*
> *It's the latest in a string of inflammatory remarks . . .*

*Style*point

Use simple sentences

Language must be **simple** but not patronising. Active, precise sentences using single- or two-syllable words and shorn of jargon are a must. They should be capable of being read in one breath. That means a limit of about 16 to 18 words. Vary sentence lengths to make it more interesting.

Break down long sentences so each has a single idea – someone does something . . . , they did it because . . . , they are going to carry on.

Negatives become hard to understand when spoken, so keep the script full of positive notions and actions. If you must use a negative, it is good practice to cap up NOT to make sure it is NOT missed.

Alliteration, especially if it becomes a tongue-twister and especially with lots of soft 's' sounds, should be avoided. It is, by design, hard to say.

> Whenever possible, **use the present tense** to suggest immediacy. Scrub the word yesterday from your vocabulary – it makes the report sound dated. If you use a flashback to the previous day's events, bury it within the filmed segment as far as possible. On international news channels, it is better to say what day something happened because a broadcast could be on different days in different countries.
>
> *Style*point

Sidestep the rules of grammar in favour of what sounds right. For example, while *the family is* would be correct for writing, *the family are* is better for broadcast. Contractions such as *it's, can't* or *should've* are preferred.

Sentences of just three or four words can be effective but use them sparingly as they can make reports sound aggressively staccato.

Even **sentences without verbs** can work, although not all editors like this approach:

> *Another day at the diamond fields. Back breaking work in the thirty-five degree heat. Limbs aching. Sweat glistening on their brows.*

Strip out clauses wherever possible, as they can be confusing to follow when spoken. Hence . . .

> *Brett Williams, who narrowly avoided death when he was hit by a car while out on his bike last year, is taking his fight for cycle safety to the High Court today.*

. . . is too wordy for broadcast and needs breaking down:

> *Cyclist Brett Williams narrowly avoided death when he was hit by a car last year. Now, he is taking his fight for cycle safety to the High Court.*

Use **punctuation sparingly** and only when it helps the script be read fluently and with clarity of meaning.

Sidestepping technicalities

Avoid bombarding the viewer with **technical or statistics-heavy information**. If there are figures to include, graphics and animation can make them more palatable but always keep them to a minimum and stick to the headline-grabbing numbers.

Give viewers an **easily understandable sense of scale**. If you are filming an enormous bridge or tree, show someone standing next to it. If you are showing something microscopic, show them a human hair or a pin head next to it.

Unless it is the only visual you have when a story breaks, don't keep **images, graphics or maps** on screen too long – a few seconds at most. It's dull TV. Explain them while they are on screen, not later.

Making use of interviewees

Packages will include interviews with people featuring in the story. Generally, **a pithy sentence** or two is enough to let them get their views across.

Occasionally, the interview can be so compelling it's worth letting it run longer. If subjects are emotional yet remain coherent and concise, consider allowing them more time to tell their stories in their own words. Their faces and emotions will often say a lot more than their words.

Introduce your interviewees cleverly and seamlessly. **Don't just repeat the on-screen caption** (known as a *name super*). Instead add a detail. For example, on a story about family doctors, switch to a clip of a campaigning MP by saying, *It's a problem only too familiar to MP Rosie Walsh, herself a former GP*. Don't repeat what the speaker says before or after the clip.

Try, too, to find interesting ways to segue into the filmed segment from the lead. Don't just say *Here's our reporter Joe Roseberry*: try something suggesting involvement and a sense of 'being there', such as *Joe Roseberry visited the last mine in Wales to find out . . .*

Don't let **your ego** get in the way of the storytelling. The reporter should never be on screen more than the people he or she is interviewing. There is a fine line, too, between reportage and opinion. An inflection or raised eyebrow might be interpreted as comment, rather than the neutral stance reporters are expected to take. The viewer probably doesn't care much what you think of an issue you are covering, so why waste energy telling them?

The power of suggestion

Research suggests that viewers understand as little as five per cent of what is broadcast at them. They may be easily distracted or even have the TV (or radio) on only as background noise. Today, people are often looking at more than one device at a time – one survey found six in ten of us 'dual screen'.

However, if you can hook a viewer, they **tend to stick through an entire news report**. Once they begin to invest effort into watching, they like to see how it turns out.

It means you can afford to **be suggestive**, creating an impression but leaving questions unanswered. The viewer may not entirely grasp the plot all the way through but they will, like someone watching a detective mystery, wait for a reveal.

How to wrap up

A news report needs **a good pay-off**. Wrap it up by projecting the story forward with an indication of what is to come, such as:

> *Next week, Sir Frederick will have his chance to out the record straight when he appears before the committee.*

Always find something more imaginative than the clichéd *It remains to be seen . . .*

Another tactic is to return to the characters you introduced at the beginning to close the loop.

> *Doctors believe they are close to a major breakthrough in treating this debilitating disease. Until they do, people such as Tom Fisher will have to continue their gruelling daily routine of pills and therapy.*

Script setting

TV scripts are usually set out something like this. The page is split into two, with pictures on the left and words on the right (see Table 10.1, page 252)

Numbers are spelt out as they would be read, rather than as figures. A double hyphen, double slash or ellipsis is used to mark any pause in the script. Use *one hundred/million/billion* rather than *a hundred/million/billion* in case it is misheard as *eight hundred/million/billion.*

Some old-school correspondents write phonetically to prevent pronunciation stumbles. Others like to cap up any words which might be mispronounced or misheard and to underline or italicise any words which need to be emphasised.

The words need to be read at a measured speed, not too fast to become garbled and not too ponderous to become soporific. **Three words a second** – or 180 words a minute – is a rule of thumb for measuring the length of a script.

Read a story or script out loud before committing it to tape to ensure it makes sense, flows and has rhythm. It may be the only chance you get to hear the script before it is aired.

Handling two-ways

TV news programmes are making growing use of two-ways – and it can be a nerve-jangling experience for the broadcasting rookie.

TABLE 10.1 Example of TV script layout

CAMBODIA Khmer Rouge trial Prono: Khmer Rouge Kuh-mer rooj Phnom Penh Puh-nom Pen	Suggested intro: In Cambodia, the two surviving leaders of the Khmer Rouge have been found guilty of mass murder and genocide in their war crimes trial in Phnom Penh. It's estimated around 1.7 million people died during the Maoist regime between 1975 and 1979. Claire Stone reports
Courtroom scenes NC and KS as verdict read out Reaction in court Prono: Nuon Chea Noon Chee-ah Khieu Samphan Cue Sam-pan	(upsound verdict) (We find both men guilty) Barely a flicker of emotion as the verdicts are read out. So-called Brother Number Two Nuon Chea, and the de facto president of the Khmer Rouge, Khieu Samphan, now face spending the rest of their lives in jail. Guilty of the deaths of perhaps a quarter of Cambodia's population during their rule in the late 1970s.
Black and white file fields, prison camp	Many died of overwork and starvation working in the fields. Others were put to death in the notorious Killing Fields, or here at the S21 torture centre in the capital Phnom Penh.
Reax outside court Caption: CHUM MEY, Khmer Rouge survivor Prono: Chum May	Chum Mey survived his time at S21. He was jubilant at the guilty verdicts This is fantastic, I've waited for this day for 35 years.
Caption: CLAIRE STONE, Phnom Penh, Cambodia	PTC This verdict is only the start of the court process. Claire Stone, Phnom Penh, Cambodia

For these, the correspondent will have to **work off-script** and suggest spontaneity. It's fine if it is a little rough round the edges as it adds humanity.

The key to looking off the cuff, of course, is to be **thoroughly prepared**.

It is a given that the correspondent **knows the story inside out** – if you haven't done all your research, you can't sound authoritative as you pass that information on to the viewer.

Some correspondents prepare questions for the presenter in the studio to ask but care is needed not to look staged. Others prefer to have five or six **bullet points** written down on a notepad as prompts. Leave one or two of them out of any filmed segment so you have something fresh to offer during the two-way.

If you are positioned in front of a scene where something is happening behind you, **guide the viewer** through what they can see – a car arriving, diggers turning up, the crowds gathering. It can give the viewer a sense they are watching events unfold.

> Sometimes you may want to drop a pre-recorded clip into the two-way. Use a **pre-arranged cue**, such as *Here is what the minister had to say earlier* so it slides in seamlessly.
>
> *Style*point

If you do a series of two-ways, **try not to repeat what you have said previously**. Always have an update at hand – the latest from the scene – and focus on that. It's not always realistic if a story is moving slowly and it is unlikely the same audience is watching each time.

Working off script comes with legal and other risks, too. Don't speculate too far and push what you know to the point of distortion. BBC reporter Andrew Gilligan's infamous 2003 Today programme two-way on the Iraqi war dossier had far-reaching implications because he strayed too far from certainty.

Writing for radio

Radio is a more **intimate version of broadcasting** than TV. It is a soothing sound in the corner of the room. Sometimes the listener is distracted, may even leave the room for a while or may have the radio on only as an accompaniment to more important tasks. But, commonly, it is just one voice, like a **friend dropping by for a chat over a cup of tea**.

There are far fewer people involved in radio production than there are in TV. It might be just one presenter and a producer. As a radio reporter it is vital to grasp the notion that you are talking not to an audience of thousands or even millions but to **an audience of one**. It was the quality that earned broadcasters such as Terry Wogan great admiration – he was speaking to millions of people but connecting with each and every one of them individually.

> Learn to wince every time you say *you* or *I* – it should always be we.
>
> *Style*point

Keep it simple (again)

News writing for radio follows most of the rules as for TV. Reporting requires a mix of short items for half-hourly or hourly bulletins and longer reports formed of leads read in a studio followed by a taped package. Similarly, live two-ways are widely used for a sense of greater immediacy.

The approach, style and language need to be **down to earth**. Keep sentences simple, clear and logical – just as with TV, there is no rewind button for news on the radio and listeners get one shot at understanding your report. Use the present tense and active sentences and strip out formality.

Fill in the blanks

The lack of images only adds to the intimacy of radio. Your voice carries the news, becoming the **calm and authoritative source** without pictures to enhance – or distract.

Your reports need to fill in the blanks. If they need to understand what something looks like, you will need to **describe it**. Hence:

> *It's a cavernous space, three times the size of the O2 arena. . .*
> *This shattered shell of a building, the last one standing in a sea of rubble. . .*
> *It is an impressive show of support. Thousands of marchers, dressed in brightly coloured clothing, dancing and singing as the procession snakes through the broad city streets . . .*

The spoken word is more evocative than pictures. If we see something, we do not have to imagine it. When we have to conjure them up, the images persevere far longer because we have created them. To create those images you will need an **observer's eye** and a **rich but unpretentious vocabulary**.

Make use of sound

Radio, however, has one powerful extra weapon – sound. Use it in your reports to create a theatre of the mind. **Incorporate sounds** that tell or enhance the story. The clunk of keys on a locked door, the sound of carriage wheels on a cobbled street, the screams from a noisy classroom. They set up the scene and give the listener context.

Mix these sounds with the natural words of those you interview. Don't prepare or rehearse questions for your interviewee, instead just chat to relax the interviewee before turning on the microphone. In radio it is critical that the **conversation sounds natural**, a two-way exchange with hesitations and words spoken instinctively. Studio recordings sound cleaner but if you are interviewing a campaigner on road safety have the noise of traffic in the background; a bishop should be heard in the echoing vastness of a cathedral, a factory boss against the backdrop of clanging machines.

Story structure

Borrow from our **pyramid model** to structure your story. Put the most interesting element at the top as an intro, flow neatly into a second and third par as you expand. Remember to tell; don't explain. That will give you 60 or so words – about 20 seconds of broadcasting time – for a news item as part of a bulletin or the lead into a recorded report.

Radio news **becomes stale more quickly** than TV. The goal is to capture the situation now, not as it was several hours ago. Stories need refreshing by adding a new angle or update with every bulletin. Perhaps drop a different clip into a bulletin or at least tweak the wording to breathe new life into it. No item on the evening news should be a repeat of one aired at breakfast time. If nothing has moved for a few hours, then it is probably best to drop it altogether.

TV is driven by images – your script need only say what the viewer can't already see

Radio is driven by sound – your script needs to fill in because the listener can't see

Broadcast to an audience of one – adopt a conversational tone

Remember storytelling basics – our ABBC, a good structure, a flourish to finish

*Key*points

Broadcast glossary

Actuality: Material recorded on location

Anchor: The main programme presenter, usually based in the studio, although sometimes sent to the scene of major stories

Atmos: Sound recorded on location to provide, as the name suggests, atmosphere

Blue screen: A technique for filming a presenter in front of a blank screen to superimpose their image on other images. Also a **green screen** and used to be known as **chroma-key**

Clip: A segment of recorded interview dropped into a radio (or live-link TV) report. Also known as an **insert**

Close-up (CU): Shot of the face so it dominates the frame and little or no background can be seen. A tighter frame for a **big close-up (BCU)**, or tighter still for an **extreme close-up (ECU)**. A **medium close-up (MCU)** shows the head and shoulders

Cover: A sequence of pictures run while interviewing a guest who is off screen. Also a **float**

Cue: A signal in a script or gesture to begin or to stop

Cutaway: A brief shot to hide an edit or to break up a lengthy piece of footage of one subject

Dead air: Silence during a radio broadcast. A sign something has gone wrong

Delay: A system for delaying a live transmission by a few seconds in case inappropriate material needs to be stopped from going out

Disco: A round-table discussion in the studio

Dissolve: Fading out of one picture to move to another

Donut: A term that seems to vary in meaning. Some use it to refer to a reporter introducing and rounding off his or her own filmed report live from the scene. Alternatively, it may be where the studio hands over to the reporter who does an interview on location before handing back to the studio

Establishing shot: A long shot at the beginning of a report to establish place or location. Also a **set-up shot** or **cover shot**

Fade in (FI): A shot that begins in darkness or is underlit before becoming fully lit

Fade out (FO): A shot that begins fully lit before fading to darkness

FX: Sound effects

General view (GV): As the name suggests, general shots of the scene

Lead: The segment of a report read by the newsreader before going to the filmed or taped portion. Also the **intro** or **cue**. **Lead** can also refer to the top story

Long shot: Frames shot from afar to take in the background

Medium shot (MS): Shows someone from head to hips. A **medium long shot (MLS)** goes from head to knees

Montage: A collage of brief shots or still images stitched together to form a segment of a report

Name super: A caption on screen. Also known as an **aston**

Noddy: A brief cutaway shot of a reporter or interviewer nodding his or her head while listening to the person speaking. Usually shot after the interview for use as a cutaway

Overrun: An item, such as a studio interview, which goes on beyond the time allotted

Package: The recorded segment of a news report

Panning: Moving the camera horizontally across a scene

Point of view (POV): Footage filmed as if through the eyes of the person taking part

Run down: The schedule of items to appear in a bulletin. Also **running order**

Rushes: Unedited footage, also known as **raw footage**

Sound bite: Very short clip of someone speaking, taken from a longer interview

Stand-up: Part of a package when a reporter speaks directly to the camera. Also called a **piece to camera** or **PTC**

Sting: A musical clip to introduce a major subject within the bulletin, such as election coverage

Stock footage: Archived footage used to illustrate a story for which there is no live material

Teaser: A trail for an item later in the programme

Ticker: A line of type moving across the top or bottom of screen, often containing the main headlines or an item of breaking news. Also known as a **crawl**

Tilt: Moving a camera vertically, ie top to bottom or bottom to top, in a scene

Titles: Opening and closing sequences

Tracking shot: Footage taken while the camera is moving

Two-way: Where a reporter is interviewed live from the scene from a presenter in the studio. Also called a **one-to-one** or **remote**

TX: Transmission

Underlay: Footage which plays while the presenter talks over it or interviews someone who is not on camera. Often abbreviated to **ulay.** The BBC calls it an **OOV** for **out of vision**

Video tape (VT): Recorded footage, although mostly in digital format these days

Voice over (VO): When a presenter talks over footage

Voicer: A recorded report by a radio journalist often used to provide a change of speaker from the newsreader during a bulletin. May not include clips, also known as a **voice report**

Zoom in: To go from a distant shot to a close-up or vice versa (**zoom out**)

11

THE NON-RULES OF GRAMMAR

News storytelling calls for exceptional writing.

A rich vocabulary and smart turn of phrase are fundamental. A love of words must shine through.

But news writing is not about grand literary flourishes. It is about the under-stated elegance of expressing ideas simply, concisely and precisely.

The first step is to understand the 'rules' and when it is wisest to ignore them.

Grammar v style

Everyone agrees that news writing needs to follow the rules of grammar.

The problem is no one can agree what the rules are.

There is no governing authority, no court of grammar, to stipulate what is right and wrong. There are no penalties for anyone who breaks the rules.

It leaves news writers stuck between the rock of convention and the hard place of the pretty-much-anything-goes reformists.

At one extreme stand those who might call themselves purists, the traditionalists, the sticklers who believe writing should be properly regulated. The label 'grammar Nazi' is a badge of honour.

Their approach is based on the principle that English evolved from Greek and Latin and that we should structure our writing in the shadow this casts. They hon-our the 'original' meanings of words and phrases, are horrified by split infinitives and would never end a sentence in a preposition. They are devoted to the differ-ence between restrictive and non-restrictive clauses and they chuckle knowingly at dangling modifiers.

They have a point. Apart from enforcing consistency, strict rules rarely leave clarity to chance and, for news writers, that is a prize worth pursuing.

Trying to outwit the sticklers are those who believe language is a breathing, evolving thing which should be written to reflect the way we use it. They embrace nouns being turned into verbs, cuddle up to colloquialisms and dismiss the pedantry of the purists as a poisonous plot to hold back relevance and creativity.

They also have a point. News writers are communicators and, if they tell their stories in language that sounds remote, forced or archaic, they will lose their audiences.

The march of the digital age, with its haphazard, conversational style, may be turning the argument in their favour.

The best news writers **have a foot planted in each camp**. They need to move with the times, embracing changes in language so they stay in touch with their readers.

It is pointless, for instance, trying to force formality on to viral content, which is, by definition, a conversation.

Yet writers must know the traditionalists' rules, too. If they break them, they should be aware they are doing so and have a legitimate and logical explanation for doing so.

The lazy, catch-all 'Yeah, but language evolves' refrain is often trotted out as an excuse for sloppy writing and is no substitute for a reasoned appraisal of both sides of a grammatical argument. You cannot justify yourself if your base point is ignorance.

The wisest approach is to start by learning the traditionalists' rules. Understand why the sticklers are so disturbed when they are broken.

Then, make ready to ride a coach and horses through them.

Challenge the sticklers

So, when is it safe to challenge the sticklers?

▪ When it makes my writing briefer or punchier

There are occasions when 'proper' use of English sounds stilted. This sentence has been cast to avoid the faux pas of ending on a preposition.

> *Mr Corbyn has faced claims that he has tolerated anti-Semitism in those with whom he associates.*
>
> *MailOnline, March 2016*

But it would have been shorter and no less elegant had it been:

> *Mr Corbyn has faced claims that he has tolerated anti-Semitism in those he associates with.*

Or better still:

> *Mr Corbyn is said to have tolerated anti-Semitism in his associates.*

▪ When it sounds more natural

Sometimes a rule forces writers into an ugly place. It may be 'correct' but it sounds unnatural or awkward when we read it.

This Australian website takes the sticklers' approach to plural nouns and is 'correct' when it reports:

> *Spinner Nathan Lyon claims Australia is ahead after the opening day of the second Test played on a soporific pitch.*
>
> *Sydney Daily Telegraph, February 2014*

But, in Britain, this sounds strange. We would say and write *Australia are ahead*.

The need to sound natural is crucial for TV and radio writing, where the style must be conversational – far better to break a 'rule' for familiarity than to stifle a story with stuffy English.

▪ When I'm looking for stylistic effect

A proper sentence needs a subject, a verb and an object. Right? Not so. Just like these.

There are occasions when you are looking for impact. Playing with words is fun and should be part of your writing. It can bring the reader up short and improve readability and engagement.

But what about starting a sentence with a conjunction? In news writing it's rarely frowned upon. It is an acceptable device to help the reader switch between contrasting ideas. And it breaks up lengthy sentences.

▪ When it adds to the richness of the language

Great writers have long sought to manipulate language to add to the power of expression.

Frequent offender Shakespeare, who came up with *This was the most unkindest cut of all*, Jane Austen with her double negatives and Charles Dickens with his rambling sentences all forged decent careers despite their supposed shortcomings.

That's not to say you should come over all James Joyce or e. e. cummings in news writing. As long as the meaning is clear, then inventiveness has its place.

▪ When I'm writing in a conversational style

These headlines from the homepage of one viral news website would make a stickler choke.

> *You have been reheating takeaway curries wrong your whole life, doctor warns*
> *Sheffield sinkhole: Massive 20ft hole opens up in road*
> *This Science Museum appears to have gotten much more expensive*
> *Those tiny buttons on your jeans are actually really important*
> *Woman totally freaks out playing virtual reality monster game*
> *Don't panic, but soon robots will have actual human vision*
>
> *Metro.co.uk, April 2016*

They're not elegant but they're not meant to be; they are conversational tempters.

▪ When I'm following a style guide

Your style guide is unimpeachable. If it has a grammatical approach you don't agree with, tough. You have to ride with it.

> *NO-ONE: with a hyphen.*
>
> *PA style guide*
>
> **No one** *not no-one*
>
> *The Guardian style guide*
>
> *"Noone is talking any more about $30 a barrel oil."*
>
> *Bloomberg, December 2016*

Which is right? They all are.

Style sins

What makes for bad news writing? Anything that stands in the way of clear, precise, elegant prose.

Tautology

Tautology – saying something twice in the same expression – is the kitchen sink approach to news writing: Throw everything at a sentence in the hope of making a bigger impact. Invariably, it is a swing and a miss.

It is a symptom of a growth in the conversational style of writing but it rarely adds the desired emphasis, just **unnecessary words**.

Common examples include *added bonus, sworn affidavit, opening gambit, gathered together, free gift, safe haven, fellow countrymen, old adage, exact replica, stop completely* and *yell loudly*, but the litany is endless.

To spot tautology, simply take away one word and see if the meaning has been changed. If not, you can leave it out.

Try it with these examples by omitting the word in bold. It should be *patently obvious* (oops):

---

*A new treatment for breast cancer has **completely** eradicated tumours in just 11 days.*

MailOnline, March 2016

*However, the **common** consensus that zebra stripes are used as camouflage to protect them from predators has been refuted in a new study.*

Independent, January 2016

*The council is **currently** carrying out a public consultation on its budget plans for 2016–17.*

Nottingham Post, January 2016

---

*The revelation comes just 24 hours after pro-EU Home Secretary Theresa May said she was against an **ever wider** expansion of the Union.*

The Sun, April 2016

*It will **broadly** outline changes he wants on migration, border control and welfare.*

The Sun on Sunday, November 2015

Watch for phrases beginning with *re-* and ending with *again* or *back*. Re- means again and as such makes nonsense of phrases such as *revert back, return back* and *refer back*.

Similarly, you can usually lose the *pre-* in phrases such as *pre-conditions, pre-booked, pre-owned* and *pre-arranged*.

Past, future and *advanced* all seem to set writers up for a fall. *Past history, past records* and *past experience* all creep in alongside *advanced booking, advanced warning* and *advance notice*, as well as *future plans* and *future prospects*.

Conditionals such as *could possibly, might potentially* and *potential risk* all cry out for the delete button.

Completely, absolutely, entirely and *totally* add nothing to the values of the words they precede – they can be removed from phrases such as *completely exhausted, entirely different, absolutely spotless* and *totally drunk*.

Take the word *time* away from *at this moment in time, in three weeks' time* or *in a few hours' time* and it is clear it serves little purpose.

Acronyms – *ATM machine, PIN number, OPEC countries, BAFTA awards* and *HIV virus*, for example – can be another stumbling block.

Take care with foreign phrases. For example, *eid (eisteddfod*, too) means festival, hence Eid al-Fitr, which marks the end of Ramadam, does not need to be called *Eid al-Fitr festival*. Likewise, the *wat* in Angkor *Wat* means temple, so don't refer to the *Angkor Wat temple*.

Descriptions such as *shorter in length, green in colour* and *round in shape* are clear cases where one word can do the job of three.

Journalese

It seems a curious thing to do . . . develop your own language when you have a perfectly fine one at your disposal.

Journalists love to lapse into journalese.

Let's not get all pompous here. It's been a useful tabloid language, often injecting welcome energy and urgency into plodding copy.

The meaning is usually clear and it can be a godsend for headline writers looking for the shortest form of words to convey a complex idea.

But it's time to get out of the habit.

Consider the story of a misbehaving politician caught with his trousers down while playing happy families. It is unlikely that anyone looking for the story online will put *love-nest, stunner* and *distraught wife* into a search engine.

A planning application for a new supermarket in your hometown? Would anyone look for the terms *thumbs-up* or *given the green light* before they tap in *approved*?

We no longer need journalese to sell the story.

This story illustrates how journalese has become incorporated into writing without thinking whether it makes sense or brings anything to the story:

> *British drivers heading for Calais faced misery today as traffic was brought to a halt in a protest calling for the destruction of the Jungle migrant camp.*
>
> *Evening Standard, September 2016*

The reader might get the gist but how exactly does a driver face a concept such as misery? It's journalese, oddly used as shorthand for the fact that the drivers may face *serious delays* or *disruption* and that the experience may be *miserable*.

The story continues with the second par telling us that protesters were *launching a human chain* across the A16 motorway.

The journalese *launching* is an overused catch-all phrase to suggest something is being initiated.

The odd construction suggests the protesters hurled a line of people holding hands across the road. *Setting up* or *organising* would have done the trick.

The third par tells of banners being *hung on the demonstrating vehicles*. The vehicles are lumps of inanimate machinery, have no feelings on the issue of migrants and are incapable of demonstrating. The desire to breathe journalistic urgency into the prose meant the correct word – *demonstrators* – was overlooked.

All those involved in Operation Snail are *furious*, the fourth par tells us. The reader has an image of red-faced, swearing, spitting, out-of-control protesters.

It may be the case there was anger, irritation and frustration – but the demonstrations were well planned and peaceful.

Breathlessness

A kissing cousin of tautology and journalese, this disturbing affliction is caused by an irresistible urge to make copy seem more colourful, compelling writers to insert unnecessary adjectives and adverbs into copy.

This is a common symptom:

> *Man forced women to perform 'sex show' then brutally stabbed them.*
> *Metro.co.uk, June 2016*
>
> *A mother-of-two has revealed how her former partner brutally raped her before threatening to kill her and even made her write her own suicide note.*
> *MailOnline, November 2016*

All killings, rapes and other violent attacks are brutal.

Similarly, journalists always think *suburbs* are *leafy* (hello, Croydon?), *apologies* involve *grovelling*, *damaged ships* always *limp into port* and *ranks* have to be *serried*.

Talks are always *last-ditch* or *eleventh hour* and, if they go on for a while, they are *epic* or *marathon*. Speed is always *breakneck*, which means any *pursuit* is *hot*. An *inferno* is hot . . . so why do we call it *blazing* or *raging*?

Likewise, brain surgery is always *delicate* . . . and is invariably carried out by a *trained* doctor (thankfully).

The list of such tired phrases is endless. This is a *timely reminder*, a *stark warning* of the *dire consequences* if you use them.

Muddled tenses

Make sure the story is written in one tense – for print, it is usually the past tense, while websites (and broadcasting) may be better suited to the present tense to give a sense of immediacy. The present tense is often more appropriate in lighter lifestyle or survey stories. Whichever is chosen, try to be consistent.

Make it an unimpeachable rule not to mix tenses in a single sentence or you risk mangling the language.

> *Migrants were currently identified by authorities as economic migrants, who are typically not allowed to stay, or as refugees from wars and persecution, who are offered protection.*
>
> The Times, May 2016

> *He moved to Sky Sports in 1999 and fronted Jimmy Hill's Sunday Supplement, a panel show on which journalists discuss the football topics of the day.*
>
> MailOnline, December 2015

When describing a current situation it is better to keep the sentence all in the present. Like this:

> *Mentally ill people in Croydon face waiting lists that are too long, are not listened to, and are too often being prescribed medication instead of other therapies, a new report says.*
>
> Croydon Advertiser, August 2016

But when it is historical, change the verb in the sentence to past tense. Here, the *said* and the *were* match correctly . . .

> *The report said patients were being sent home alone, afraid and unable to cope and in some cases without their relatives or carers being told.*
>
> *Daily Telegraph, May 2016*

. . . but the next sentence jumps two time frames from the pluperfect to the present:

> *Too often, patients had been (pluperfect) discharged from hospital before they are (were) fit to leave or without making sure they can (could) cope on their return home.*

The most common trap is in reported speech. The phrase *he/she/the report said* casts the sentence in the past tense so the rest must follow:

> *The Terrence Higgins Trust said (past tense) government guidance on school sex and relationship education is (present) out of date and is (present) older than the majority of the pupils learning about the subject.*
>
> *ITV, July 2016*
>
> *Last year, the World Health Organisation and Unicef warned (past) that a lack of progress on sanitation threatens (present) to undermine child survival. . .*
>
> *The Guardian, November 2016*

Similarly, avoid using *he said* (past) he will/can/shall (future) . . . it should be *he said he would/could/should*.

Verbifying

There is a long history in English of turning nouns into verbs. Most add a layer to the language, are natural and readily absorbed – *to pepper, to contact, to question* and so on.

But verbifying – known as denominalisation by linguists – has become a contagion. Noun-verbs that appear to have been invented simply for the sake of it are springing up like weeds on a neglected lawn. They look unsightly, they are hard to dig out once established and some of them are poisonous.

We expect it from public officials and politicians who probably think it makes them sound clever. After all, we now have a *Department for* **Exiting** *the European Union.*

Their assaults on innocent nouns are merciless.

> **❝** Mr Corbyn appointed me and **press released** this without my knowledge or consent whilst I was in the middle of cancer treatment.
> *Labour MP Thangam Debbonaire, July 2016*
>
> We were elected to take the tough decisions and to deliver the infrastructure that allows the whole country to thrive – **greenlighting** Heathrow ticks all the boxes.
> *Stephen Crabb, September 2016* **❞**

New technology spawns new verbs (*trend, email, text*) but some sound odd: (especially with the double *who*):

> Ed Vazey said anyone who who screenshotted a Snapchat message and shared it with others could be sued by its original sender – and face a prison sentence.
> *Independent, March 2016*
>

If a noun-verb doesn't add anything to the language, then stick with simpler alternatives. We don't speak in noun-verbs, so why use them when we write or broadcast?

Take the word *impact*, which dutifully served for centuries as a noun meaning a forceful collision. It's ugly and stark, onomatopoeic. Now, it has all but replaced the soft and elegant *affect* or the simple and more precise *harm* as a verb. This is a teeth-grindingly awful example:

> She believed between 80 and 100, of the approximate 130-plus strong flock died, impacting the local population for some time as many of the victims were young adults who were yet to breed.
> *Northern Echo, December 2015*
>

Let's stop the practice being stretched to extremes:

> *Martin Crowe farewelled (**funeral held**) in Auckland*
>
> Cricinfo.com, March 2016
>
> *The carpet company, which is headquartered (**based**) in the town's Worcester Road. . .*
>
> Worcester News, December 2016
>
> *Chelsea boss Antonio Conte has hinted that John Terry is already transitioning (**switching**) to a coaching career with the Blues.*
>
> Metro.co.uk, December 2016

Americanisms

George Bernard Shaw claimed Britain and America were two countries divided by a common language. Many readers see Americanisms as irritations, as unwelcome invaders sullying their beloved language.

However, the world has shrunk and writing for an online audience means writing for a global audience for whom many Americanisms are the norm, not a linguistic abomination.

Many have slipped across the Atlantic with little pain: for example, *lay off* is shorter and sharper than *make redundant*.

Few of these new arrivals are hard to understand but even if we know what is meant by an American phrase or word, there is usually a perfectly good British alternative. British sites, even if appealing to a global audience, should have a British character.

The list of words – from *automobile* to *zip code* – that need translating is lengthy, even if many of them are now familiar to British audiences.

Americans are champions of turning perfectly good nouns into verbs (see previous section on verbifying); they also love to add unnecessary prepositions, as in *deliver on, head up, check out, free up, consult with, check up on, divide up, outside of* and the all-pervasive *meet with*.

Then there are occasions when they drop prepositions which are needed. For example, they *protest decisions* rather than *protest against decisions* and they hold a *meeting Sunday* rather than *on Sunday*.

They have different spellings – they drop the *u* in *armor, flavor, color*, the *-ue* from *catalog* or *prolog*, use *-ce* in verbs such as *licence* and *practice* and use se instead of ce in nouns, as in *offense* and *defense*. They also dislike double vowels and so prefer *estrogen, anesthetic* and *fetus*.

Although it was a style that went out of fashion over here well before it became the practice over there, the Americans end words in *-ize*, rather than the English *-ise*. Similarly, they prefer the *-or* ending rather than *-er*, as in *protestor* or *advisor*.

> For those working with copy from American wires and other sources, it is worth noting they take a guarded approach, sometimes rendering the copy stilted, overly formal and pedestrian. They will attribute every fact. This means you end up with sentences such as *Seventeen people were shot dead when a gunman went on the rampage at a school, police and hospital officials said yesterday.* Learn to take ownership; see Chapter 7.
>
> *Style*point

Apostrophes

Of all the punctuation errors that news writers make, misuse of the apostrophe winds up readers more than anything.

The rules are so simple – apostrophes denote possession or an omission – that it screams amateurism when it goes wrong:

> *Plan to replace six Oxfordshire council's with one published*
>
> BBC, January 2017
>
> *The 22-year-old, who's mum is Demi Moore, has been photographed stripped down to nothing but a pair of white pants . . .*
>
> The Sun, October 2016

Confusing *it's* and *its* is one that particularly galls readers:

> *'Five-Star' and 'Luxury Hotel' is bandied around so often that it can lose much of it's meaning – but Cap Estel has impact, that is for sure. Perched on the end of it's own peninsula near Eze . . .*
>
> Country Life, August 2016

Inanimate objects

There is a fine line between the figurative and literal. But beware giving **inanimate objects** human qualities – a tic known as personification.

Companies and political or other organisations which *make* statements and venues and stadia which *see* events taking place won't disturb too many readers.

But you can create bizarre scenarios:

> *A driver has apologised to a petrol station after he sparked a large blaze when trying to kill a spider with his lighter as he filled up.*
>
> *Sky News, September 2015*
>
> *The CGT said that 16 of France's 19 nuclear stations had now voted to join the strike, raising the prospect of the country being plunged into darkness.*
>
> *Mirror Online, May 2016*
>
> *TV archive discovers couple who beat Kirk and Uhura to first interracial kiss.*
>
> *The Guardian, November 2015*

Remember that research, studies and surveys are processes, not capable of doing or saying anything, while a report is the written iteration of the conclusions. A report may *say* something, or a study may *find* or *suggest* something but no more:

> *The report made the calculations by dividing average house prices across towns and London boroughs by average property sizes, excluding outside space.*
>
> *PA, May 2016*

> *Polar bear numbers could drop by a third in 40 years, research says*
>
> *Sky News, December 2016*

Beware, too, applying **too much sentimentality to animals**. It is doubtful they have the human capabilities some writers ascribe to them as they try to get the tears rolling (and tenses muddled).

Mrs James said she believes the black and white sheepdog must have somehow persuaded good Samaritans to feed him on his way home, as he didn't appear to be malnourished.

Metro.co.uk, April 2016

Homophones

English is full of homophones – words which sound the same but are spelled differently and have different meanings. Mixing them up has embarrassing results:

The group met at Barkingside Station to canvas support with Wes Streeting – MP for Ilford North – before stopping for lunch.

Ilford Recorder, March 2016

Manilow had vocal chord surgery on Monday but after playing a sold-out show in Memphis on Thursday, was rushed to hospital.

Metro.co.uk, February 2016

"It was probably to put a gloss on it as the real reason was, we couldn't stand the site of each other!" he said.

Exeter Express and Echo, January 2016

Scientists made the discovery after testing volunteers with large helpings of chicken korma curry and Eton mess desert.

PA, October 2016

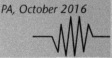

Avoiding writing as we speak may help to prevent them:

The cast has remained relatively tight-lipped over spoilers, with journalists previously having very little of substance to actually ask the cast accept 'is Jon Snow really dead?'

indy100, March 2016

Misuses

News writers are guilty of many assaults on the English language. There are count-less traps into which the unwary will tumble.

Their vocabulary lets them down . . .

> *In a clip uploaded to the 16-year-old's Instagram, the dad-of-four is seen laying perfectly still on some steps*
>
> *Huffington Post, February 2016*

. . . they misunderstand the meanings of words – more than one in this case:

> *Workers awoke on Sunday to discover the railway, which was built in 1908, was partially submerged by debris, while a public toilet block at the foot of the cliffs was destroyed.*
>
> *The Guardian, April 2016*

. . . they misconstrue the meaning of sayings:

> *Like the proverbial curate's egg, Rachel Treweek's appointment to the House of Lords on Monday as the first female bishop to sit in the Upper Chamber can be seen as good in parts.*
>
> *FT.com, October 2015*

Some go unnoticed by all but the most stickly of sticklers. Their meaning may be understood and, in the looser style of writing now used online, it may not matter much.

But, if words are your tools, a skilled writer should know as much about them as possible. Understanding their origins gives command over them and opens surprising levels of nuance and precision.

And, besides, it will stop aggravating, sorry, irritating your readers.

And finally . . .

In news writing, it is known as Muphry's law – and this book is probably a prime example of it.

The law – also known as McKean's Law or the Law of Prescriptivist Retaliation – says if you write a story highlighting other people's linguistic failings, then your copy will contain at least one dumb mistake.

> *Because of the spelling error hashtag soon was flooded with people saying this is why the country needs more grammar schools.*
>
> *MailOnline, September 2016*
>
> *In every instance, the readers rated the writer of an email containing grammatical errors less desirable than those who sent a mistake free message.*
>
> *May 2016, Metro.co.uk*
>
> *Many off the drivers spoke very little English and who would often have to ask bus passengers for directions, she said.*
>
> *MailOnline, August 2016*

And, it seems, the same law strikes even when recruiting those responsible for training the next generation of journalists:

> *Professor in Journalism*
> *Cardiff (Caerdydd) Dependant on Experience CARDIFF UNIVERSITY*
> *The School of Journalism, Media and Cultural Studies is looking to recruit a Professor of Journalism.*
>
> *Online ad, July 2016*

> **There are no rules of grammar**, just conventions
>
> **Become a stickler** – so you know when not to be one
>
> **Break conventions for effect** – but remember **clarity is king**
>
> **Don't copy the way we speak** – you are a writer now
>
> ***Style*point**

FURTHER READING

Before you even think about how you are going to write news, you need to master the skills that will enable you to gather news.

There are too many excellent *How to be a journalist* guides to select one or two. So I am going to cheat and say just read as many as possible – even the weaker ones will contain titbits of advice that will stay with you for life.

If you want to learn about the law, you cannot be without *McNae's Essential Law for Journalists* (ISBN 9780198748359), although *Online Law* by Cleland Thom (ISBN 9781530848454) may be even more handy for those working online.

If you are particularly keen on data journalism, go for the *Data Journalism Handbook*, which is available free at http://datajournalismhandbook.org/

On things digital, Paul Bradshaw from Birmingham City University has established himself as one of the most prolific authors. A list of his books can be found at https://onlinejournalismblog.com/

For a guide through the maze of the English language, have a squint through *Bryson's Dictionary: for Writers and Editors* (ISBN 9780385610445). It's not that it's markedly more informed than others but it lacks the pomposity of those who tell us what is right and wrong and think the best way to learn English usage is to be thrashed daily by the Latin master for failing to conjugate properly.

Alternatively, read – yes, seriously, read – a great big, thick dictionary, such as the *Oxford Dictionary of English*.

Most importantly, become a nerd and start studying publishers' style books.

The best is not publicly available – it is *The Sun*'s in-house style guide, which says quite simply: "We should communicate great content as simply, as accurately and as compellingly as possible." Make it a test of your journalistic initiative to get hold of a copy.

Failing that, *The Guardian*, *The Daily Telegraph*, *The Times*, the BBC and *The Economist* are among those who do publish their guides online for free or in book form. They are written by journalists working at the highest level and who have seen it and done it. Worth scouring for style gems such as *Meat Loaf: sings; meatloaf: doesn't sing.*

INDEX

Taylor & Francis eBooks

Helping you to choose the right eBooks for your Library

Add Routledge titles to your library's digital collection today. Taylor and Francis ebooks contains over 50,000 titles in the Humanities, Social Sciences, Behavioural Sciences, Built Environment and Law.

Choose from a range of subject packages or create your own!

Benefits for you

>> Free MARC records
>> COUNTER-compliant usage statistics
>> Flexible purchase and pricing options
>> All titles DRM-free.

REQUEST YOUR FREE INSTITUTIONAL TRIAL TODAY

Free Trials Available
We offer free trials to qualifying academic, corporate and government customers.

Benefits for your user

>> Off-site, anytime access via Athens or referring URL
>> Print or copy pages or chapters
>> Full content search
>> Bookmark, highlight and annotate text
>> Access to thousands of pages of quality research at the click of a button.

eCollections – Choose from over 30 subject eCollections, including:

Archaeology	Language Learning
Architecture	Law
Asian Studies	Literature
Business & Management	Media & Communication
Classical Studies	Middle East Studies
Construction	Music
Creative & Media Arts	Philosophy
Criminology & Criminal Justice	Planning
Economics	Politics
Education	Psychology & Mental Health
Energy	Religion
Engineering	Security
English Language & Linguistics	Social Work
Environment & Sustainability	Sociology
Geography	Sport
Health Studies	Theatre & Performance
History	Tourism, Hospitality & Events

For more information, pricing enquiries or to order a free trial, please contact your local sales team:
www.tandfebooks.com/page/sales

 Routledge
Taylor & Francis Group

The home of
Routledge books

www.tandfebooks.com